Life with My Idiot Family

A True Story of Survival, Courage and Justice over Childhood Sexual Abuse

Life with My Idiot Family

A True Story of Survival, Courage and
Justice over Childhood Sexual Abuse

Kathy and Gary Picard

Lake Town Publishing, LLC

"Kathy Picard tells a haunting story that will be sadly familiar for all too many people. She faces her childhood experiences of egregious sexual abuse with extraordinary courage, honesty, and good cheer. But more than that, she shows how she transformed her personal wounds into sources of great personal power, and made a real difference through advocacy for thousands of other survivors. This book will both comfort and inspire all readers."

William N. Brownsberger State Senator,
Second Suffolk and Middlesex District, MA

"Kathy Picard's book, Life with My Idiot Family, *is a must read for anyone who doubts the ability of the human spirit to overcome extreme obstacles. Ms. Picard not only overcomes, but uses her childhood pain as fuel for a life of activism, with astonishing accomplishments in the service of others."*

Rebecca Street, Author of *You Can Help: A Guide for Family & Friends of Survivors of Sexual Abuse and Assault*

"Kathy has shared her world with us in these pages, giving us an uncensored look into a life marked by childhood sexual abuse. You will shake your head at how something so awful could go on for so long. You will see the patterns of denial and abuse spread through an entire family too, but there is also much that will comfort and inspire. You'll read about how she takes her life back and begins to help as many as she can along the way. This book will educate, inform, and inspire everyone who reads it."

Lisa Foster, Survivor

"Kathy Picard is that special kind of hero who comes full circle to turn her scars into stars for children still in the shadows of abuse. After surviving childhood sexual abuse, she went on to break legislative ground by working with lawmakers to expand the statute of limitations for survivors who need time to come forward. She was also the first in her state to employ this new law to prosecute her predator.

Every survivor's story matters, and in this book, Kathy uses her powerful voice to educate, create awareness, and inspire us all!"

Sara O'Meara & Yvonne Fedderson
Founders of Childhelp

"Survivors of sexual abuse, as well as anyone seeking justice, will want to read this awe-inspiring book. As you read about Kathy's childhood abuse, and the betrayals of her family, your heart will fill with compassion for her, and for all innocent children harmed in this way. Her book tells the story of a broken and shattered childhood, and her fight for justice. Discover the power of Kathy telling her truth, and how this power helped her heal. This is one amazing girl whose story offers hope and courage for victims of any kind of abuse."

Dave O'Regan, Director of Boston-Worcester SNAP (Survivors Network of those Abused by Priests)

"Life with My Idiot Family *provides survivors with a renewed sense of hope that we are not alone. It offers us a sense of belonging, understanding, and the realization that we can transition from being victims to survivors.*"

Mitch, Survivor's Support Group

"*Kathy is fierce! She is a trailblazer on a mission, pushing the boundaries by openly addressing child sexual abuse! Not only is her story frank and vivid, it is a window into the long journey of recovery for survivors. Child sexual abuse does not respect education, socio-economics, color, or gender. It happens, it's real, it can happen to any child, and it's up to us to protect our children.*"

Audrey Murph Brown, MSW, LCSW, Ed.D

"*One of the most rewarding aspects of being Lieutenant Governor was the opportunity to work with passionate child advocates such as Kathy. I have the greatest possible respect for survivors who turn their extraordinarily difficult personal experiences into a mission to safeguard children everywhere. Kathy's strength and determination in sharing her experience, and her tireless work on behalf of sexual assault victims, demonstrates exceptional resolve and resilience. Her advocacy is commendable and her story important.*"

Kerry Healey, Former Massachusetts
Lieutenant Governor

"*Be prepared to have your heart opened and your spirit inspired on a topic few want to look at but everyone needs to understand. Kathy takes her readers through the harrowing experience of being sexually abused as a child. The heartbreak continues as you learn of the awful and all too typical truth that she was rejected and not believed by most of her family. But don't let this bad news turn you away, for this is a hero's journey.*

Kathy's quest to find justice was long and hard, but a winning one. What this woman has is grit – the combined qualities of passion and perseverance. Do you want to know if the world can be changed for the better? Do you want to know how? Then read this book and learn."

Donna Jenson, Sister Survivor, Founder of
TimeToTell.org, Author of *What She Knows: One Woman's Way Through Incest to Joy*

"*Kathy Picard is a fighter and an inspiring beacon for children and adults. Her tenacity in advocating and educating for child safety is not only her own mechanism of self-care, but has inspired many people and communities to implement safe practices. She empowers children to be leaders in their own right, and works to provide both children and adults with the know-how of taking care of self and others.*

The story of Kathy's journey is compelling, her strength and perseverance a true testimony of survivorship. I want to be like her when I grow up!"

Tamara R. Thompson, MSW, LCSW
Sexual Assault Response Coordinator

"Kathy's journey is a source of inspiration for all of us."

Deval L. Patrick, Former Governor
Commonwealth of Massachusetts

"Kathy is an absolute inspiration to all victims of abuse. Her book reveals the story of how she survived her own childhood of sexual abuse—complete with its own evil twists – loss of innocence, loss of trust, and loss of family. She is a determined advocate for survivors, and has given a voice to so many people through her work, and this book."

Maureen Ingram, RN, Survivor

"When you read Kathy's book, you learn about the horrible situation she battled and survived to become someone determined to make a difference – not just for herself, but for others who struggle with how to stand up for themselves. This is her story of determination, of overcoming long odds, of collaboration, and ultimately the victory of the human spirit.

We are our brother's (and sister's) keepers, and we can't be afraid of getting involved when we see something "isn't right." This is what makes this book a "must read" for anyone with kids, or who deals with kids."

Kevin Brassard, Chief Information Officer,
Nichols College
Debora Brassard, Data Coordinator, Town
of Oxford School Department

"Unlike the church that shunned her, the author is a true life patriot... beyond the womb. A great read!"

Reverend James Scahill
Pastor Emeritus, St. Michael's Parish
East Longmeadow, MA.

"At a time when most little girls are carefree and enjoying life, Kathy faced child sexual abuse. Her journey is a testament to the strength of the human spirit, and to the healing power of speaking out to protect all children. No more shame. No more blame. No more fear."

Donna Palomba, President and
Founder, Jane Doe No More

"Kathy shines light on one of society's darkest secrets, and her story has given me strength and inspiration to face my abuser and promote healing. A must read for ALL parents, teachers, and victim support counselors."

Michael J. Stevens, Survivor

"With grit, integrity, perseverance, and the support of others, victims are able to become survivors. Kathy Picard's life is one such journey. Read it and learn."

Kevin Cullen, member of The Boston Globe
investigative team that exposed the cover-up
of sexual abuse by priests in the Archdiocese
of Boston.

"It was an honor to serve as Kathy Picard's Senator and to nominate her for the Commonwealth's "Unsung Heroine" Award. This book chronicles her journey from child sex abuse victim to child advocate, and is a tribute to her indomitable spirit. She is unbowed by the horrific betrayals of people she trusted, and she remains determined to do all she can to help prevent the victimization of children, and show other victims a path to justice. She is one of the most courageous people I have ever met."

Senator Gale Candaras, Massachusetts

"Back in the day, when child sexual assault was not openly talked about, getting help was next to impossible. Even today, the cycle of abuse tends to keep going until one person decides that enough is enough and stands up. Kathy Picard is one of those people, and her story single-handedly proves that one person can change the world. Very well written, and a must read!"

Caroline de Chavigny
Author of *Letter to a Monster*

"Kathy's story about what she endured as a child is horrifying, but to see how she's persevered through life by helping others is encouraging for victims/survivors of child abuse. Not only does this book provide hope and strength for people trying to deal with their own abuse, it also speaks to people struggling to survive any type of tragedy."

Detective Barbara Fenn

"Kathy Picard's childhood journey from being a victim of sexual abuse to a thriving survivor is a true profile in courage and resilience. She gives hope and inspiration to all victims and survivors of child sexual abuse to come out of the darkness and tell their stories. This is a must read for any person who has experienced child sexual abuse, and all people who want to tear down the wall of silence surrounding this hidden epidemic."

David E. Sullivan
Northwestern District Attorney

"Kathy Picard isn't just a victim of childhood sexual abuse. As an adult, she advocated for legislation to extend the civil statute of limitations so that she, and other survivors, could finally obtain justice by suing their abusers. Kathy has dedicated much of her adult life to advocating for protecting our children through education and by raising awareness. I'm proud to know Kathy, and it is my privilege to recommend this book."

Susan Burgess, Survivor of Childhood
Sexual Abuse

About the Names in This Book ...

There are many names in this book. In a few cases, we used an initial instead of a first name. With politicians and public figures, there was no problem with using real names. Most of the names belong to people I've interacted with over the years, or are the names of close family and friends. In both of these cases, their names appear with the person's permission.

All the names of the immediate family I grew up in have been changed – with the exception of the two who are part of the public record as a result of the court case. But just to be clear, these names weren't changed to protect anyone's innocence. They were changed because it's not my place to expose them, or put them on trial for what they did or didn't do when they had the chance.

Lake Town Publishing, LLC
P.O. Box 411
Ludlow MA 01056

Edited by Valerie Utton
Cover design and graphics by Valerie Utton
Back cover photograph by Jordan Chmura

Library of Congress Control Number: 2017903613

ISBN 10: 0998474002
ISBN 13: 978-0998474007

Dedication

To the memory of my Aunt Judi, whose love and
guidance inspired me to be the best person I could be.

To my fellow sexual abuse survivors,
I wrote this with you in mind.

x

Foreword

There is nothing glamorous about being the victim of a crime, particularly when that crime involves sexual assault and rape. Victims feel confusion, embarrassment, and shame. Add in the fact that the victim is often a child, and the fact that the perpetrator is likely to be a family member, and not only are those feelings magnified, they can also become entangled with love, fear, and guilt.

Sexual assaults involving family members are all too common, and perhaps, one of the most under reported crimes because the victims of these crimes are most often children who are easily manipulated and intimidated into silence.

With over 35 years in law enforcement, I have seen firsthand the short-term and long-term effects that crimes of this nature can have on the victims. Many develop very low self-esteem. Some become suicidal. Some become substance abuse users, or exhibit other forms of escape-oriented behaviors. Without some kind of intervention, guidance about what's right and wrong, or someone to help them make sense out of what happened to them, some might even become sexual predators themselves.

A common factor among many victims is silence. It's very common for victims not to come forward until they reach mid-life – if ever. And in too many cases, by the time someone is ready to pursue criminal prosecution or civil litigation, it's too late due to the statute of limitations.

One victim of childhood sexual abuse, Kathy Picard, did speak out. Since then, she has dedicated her life to advocating for the safety of all children. She testified before the Massachusetts State Legislature in support of extending the criminal statute of limitations for crimes of this nature, and became involved in the process of getting a law extending the right of victims to sue their perpetrators in civil court passed. She speaks to whoever will listen, talks with anyone needing help, and advocates for providing prevention programs in schools.

Kathy was once asked at a speaking engagement, "Why do you do this?" Her answer was simple. "He told me never to say a word to anyone. If I don't speak out, he will have won."

She will not let him, or others like him, "win." This is her story.

Louis M. Barry
Chief of Police, Granby, MA (ret.)

<u>Still</u>

They might ignore your story,
but still
whisper your smallest peep.

Never stop telling
or yelling
even if still
it means you won't look so sweet.

Screaming from rooftops
may still
fall on deaf ears
for years.

But still,
someday, some way,
someone will hear.

Still, don't sit still.
Keep telling and yelling.

They finally heard me
after telling and yelling
as decades passed by.

Still,
I struggle with tranquility.

But still,
I never stopped telling.

- Anonymous

Part One

Early Times

I was born on a late summer night in Springfield, Massachusetts. My mom was only sixteen years old when she had me. No one even knew she was pregnant until her water broke while she was standing at the kitchen sink washing dishes.

It seems almost impossible that someone so young could be nine months pregnant without anyone knowing, but maybe she wore a girdle to hold her stomach in, or wore really baggy clothes. Maybe the family was preoccupied because her own mother was pregnant with her third child at the same time. However my mom did it, she kept her pregnancy well hidden from her family.

How she managed to go unnoticed outside her home is just as hard to believe because people always noticed my mom. Most kids think their moms are attractive in one way or another, but my mom was truly beautiful. Heads would turn when she was around. So much in fact, that her father became very possessive of his prettiest daughter, and kept a watchful eye on her — at least as much as he could.

I've been told that my mom was a wild child who snuck out of the house late at night, sometimes with, sometimes without, her older sister, to hang out or go looking for boys. Because she was so pretty, my mom never had any trouble finding boys who were interested in her.

Most of the time the girls were able to sneak back into the house without incident, but on a few occasions, their father was waiting for them with his black leather belt. It might have been their laughter and giggling that woke him from a sound sleep. Or maybe he'd gotten up for some reason and noticed his daughters weren't in their rooms. Whatever the case, not even the possibility of getting a whipping ever stopped my mom from sneaking out to have a good time.

After I was born, my mom and I lived with her parents, Grammy and

Poppie. This was my first home and I have a lot of happy memories of my grandparents in that big old house. When it was nap time, I was put in

Grammy's bed. The round clock on her nightstand with its steady ticking would drown out the traffic noise coming through the bedroom window and soothe me to sleep.

Grammy used to have tag sales on the front porch. All kinds of clothes were hung on white corded rope, and people were always chatting as they made their way up the sidewalk to our house. It was a lot of fun, and even though I was told to stay out of the way, I stayed close enough to listen to my Grammy talk with all the people who stopped by.

The one place in the house I wasn't allowed to go into by myself was the basement. It had a dirt floor and Poppie had his workshop down there. He was a skilled woodworker and his workbench was covered with tools. Poppie was quiet, didn't talk much, and was always tinkering with something. He once made a wooden boat all by himself in his workshop, but must have measured wrong because he built it too big to fit through the doorway.

With meals to prepare, and dishes to hand-wash and dry, I remember our big white kitchen was always full of activity. To the right of the kitchen sink was the pantry where Grammy stored her food and dishes. On one wall there were two windows that were so tall, they reached almost all the way from floor to ceiling. Between the windows sat our kitchen table.

Every time I think of Poppie, I picture him the way I saw him the most, sitting at the kitchen table with a cigarette in his mouth and a beer in his hand. He liked to keep a pack of cigarettes in his shirt pocket so that no matter where he went, he could always have a smoke. Poppie would just sit there, staring out the kitchen window, drinking and smoking. He always seemed content to be by himself.

I remember my time in that house as happy, and I have lots of memories of Grammy and Poppie while I was living there. What I don't have are any memories whatsoever of my mom or dad during this time.

When my mom and dad got married, we moved out of Grammy and Poppie's house and into a duplex. It was a friendly neighborhood and it was fun to play in the front yard because when someone walked by with a dog, they would stop and talk to me while I pet their dog.

About a year after moving into the duplex, the twins, Keri and Sheri, were born. The following year, my youngest sister Meri was born, and even though our family had grown by three, I don't remember my mom being pregnant. She never sat me down to explain that I was going to have a baby brother or sister to play with either. All I recall is that our apartment was cramped and full of stuff, and there wasn't a lot of room to move around.

I've often wondered why I don't remember sharing that small apartment with three younger sisters, but haven't ever come up with an answer. I just recall more of my early life while living with my grandparents than I do of living with my parents and my three sisters.

While we were living in the duplex, I began first grade. Comments made by my teachers on my first report card were that I was "pleasant and well behaved" but that I had "poor work habits" and that "much effort needed to be applied to Kathy's (my) number work."

Well, no wonder. I don't recall either my mom or dad playing with me, reading to me, singing to me, or helping me with my homework. But I clearly remember being plopped down in front of the TV for long periods of time. It was a shock when I recently re-read my first grade report card and found out that I went to speech therapy twice a week.

My report card also said I was "content and participated in all activities." The last paragraph said, "Although she has made progress this term, she is still working below grade level. We feel another year in first grade will be beneficial to Kathy."

Right after I finished first grade that year, my parents bought a house and we moved. Our new home was a five room ranch in a working-class neighborhood. We had our own back yard to play in, and a basement with a real cement floor. The twins shared one of the bedrooms, and I shared a bedroom with my youngest sister. She was born sickly, and as the oldest, it was up to me to look after her. My parents took the biggest bedroom.

School started a few weeks after we moved into our new home, and it was a nice surprise to realize that so many of my classmates lived in our new neighborhood. I did repeat first grade, but it was at a new school, so I didn't realize I was being held back. To me, it was just a new school.

Unfortunately, my mom and dad's style of parenting didn't improve with the move.

Life with My Idiot Family

Confusing Times

Not long after we moved in, I started hearing conversations between my mom and dad about my youngest sister Meri. The conversations became more frequent, and one day they sat me down and told me that Meri was really sick and needed an operation. I was scared because I thought that meant she was going to die.

My parents found us a babysitter so they could make the long trips to and from Boston together. Before they left for each trip, my dad would always say to me and my sisters, "Behave. Do as you're told. Be good girls."

After many trips to and from the doctors, a date was selected for Meri's operation. My parents decided my mom would stay in Boston before and after the surgery, and my dad would stay at home with me and the twins.

While my mother and sister were in Boston, my dad would let me stay up late with him. We sat together on the couch, and he would tell me how much he loved me and what a special girl I was. I had never been treated this way before so this was all new to me. He made me feel special by holding me, touching my hair, and kissing me on the cheek. He told me this was our special secret and I couldn't tell anyone. So I didn't.

I didn't understand what he was doing. I just thought I did something really good and my dad was really happy with me. And why not? After years of being ignored by the grownups around me, my dad was saying nice things and paying attention to me. I was happy. Confused, but happy.

After a few weeks, my mom and my sister finally came home from the hospital. I was told to keep an eye on Meri, and I took that responsibility seriously. Our bedroom had a trundle bed, and because I was the oldest, I got to sleep in the big part of the bed while Meri slept on the roll-away. But when she came home from the hospital, I let her have the big bed and I slept on the trundle. That made her happy.

With four girls to raise and a new house to pay for, both my parents needed to work. Grammy and Poppie couldn't babysit us because they both needed to work too. We were too young to be left alone, so my mom and dad settled on working opposite shifts, and for as long as I can remember, my dad worked days at the post office while my mom worked nights at a grocery store.

On the nights my mom worked, my dad would often quietly enter my bedroom and tap me on the shoulder. He never put the light on because he didn't want to wake up my sister. The twins slept across the hall, but never seemed to hear him sneaking about. It didn't matter to him if I was really sleeping or pretending to be asleep either. If I didn't respond, he would just shake my shoulder a little harder until I woke up.

◆　◆　◆　◆　◆

Soon after we moved into our house, our basement was converted into a large family room. This was where my dad would take me on those nights. The thick cement walls of the basement muffled any sound I might make, and we were far enough away from my sisters that they wouldn't be able to hear us either.

My dad had a new "game" to go along with the new family room. He would sit me on his brown recliner, or lay me on the couch next to him.

Taking my hand, he would rub his crotch while telling me what a good girl I was, and what a good job I was doing. As always, he would tell me this was our secret, and I was his special girl.

In the spring of 1971, I made my first communion and completed second grade. My report card from that year said, "Kathy has progressed in reading and arithmetic. She uses her spare time wisely and is eager to please."

Right after school got out for the summer, I started taking swimming lessons and on August 6th, I received an I.D. card from the American Red Cross certifying me as a *Beginner in Swimming*. A few weeks later I turned nine years old.

My dad was also beginning to pester me with more frequent nighttime trips down to the basement.

◆　◆　◆　◆　◆

That same summer, my mom and dad had a pool installed in our backyard. My dad built a large deck around it and my three sisters and I swam in our new pool just about every day. Once in a while my dad would join us, but my mother never did.

One day, just after my sisters had gotten out of the pool, my dad swam up to me and put his hand down inside my bathing suit to fondle me. It happened so quickly, and then he winked at me. I didn't know what that wink meant.

That was also the summer when my dad kissed me on the mouth. Not like a father kisses his daughter, but more like the way I saw him kiss my mom. He kept telling me it was alright, but I was confused. I didn't like it, but we were taught both at home, and in school, to listen and obey our parents.

Although I didn't know what to call it then, the stress of what was happening was beginning to build up inside of me and I tried to say something.

◆　◆　◆　◆　◆

None of my grandparents were the typical retired Grandma and Grandpa type. They all worked and came from the "kids were meant to be seen and not heard" school of parenting, so they had very little time for us kids. Still, I loved my Grammy because she was quiet and kind, and would talk to me from time to time.

One afternoon, Grammy and I were sitting on the pool deck and I said, "Grammy, sometimes at night when my mom is at work, my dad wakes me up and takes me down into the basement. He touches me in my private parts and makes me do the same thing to him."

"Shhh… don't talk about it Kathy," was her response.

So naturally, I thought it really was a secret, and I really wasn't supposed to talk about it. Unfortunately, her response reinforced what my father was telling me all along. From her reaction, I just believed she knew about such things. That meant that what was happening to me was just part of growing up, a part every young girl goes through but isn't supposed to talk about. She was the first person I told — my own grandmother, my mother's mother.

Life with My Idiot Family

Bad Times

Around the time I was ten years old, my dad woke me one night with something different in mind. Down to the basement we went.

"Here Kathy, I want you to try this."

"What is it Daddy?"

"Just be a big girl and try it."

Then my dad forced me to take a few sips of his beer. I could smell it on his breath too.

"But I don't like it."

"That's okay, just a little bit more."

Once he figured I'd had enough, he rubbed petroleum jelly on his finger and inserted it inside my vagina.

"Daddy it hurts."

"Shhh. It's okay. I'm so proud of my good girl."

As time went on, my dad became more creative. He introduced me to oral sex by describing his penis like a lollipop.

◆　◆　◆　◆　◆

If there was one room in our house where I felt safe, it was the bathroom, because there was a lock on the door. Soaking in a hot bubble bath was relaxing and peaceful for me.

One night while enjoying my bath, scratching noises got my attention. As I turned towards the bathroom door, I could see the handle turning. The door opened and my dad came in. He put the screwdriver he used to break in down on the sink and came over to the tub.

Right away I grabbed the wash cloth and tried to cover myself. My dad smiled down at me while stroking my shoulder. He was talking in a soothing tone, but I was scared. This was supposed to be my safe place and I had no idea what he was going to do.

I didn't know you could just walk through a locked door and when I thought about it, I was even more scared. There was nowhere else I could go. No safe place left. He had taken that away from me, and wanted me to know there was no place left to hide. He didn't do anything else to me, and after a few minutes he left. I was relieved, but still scared.

The next time he broke into the bathroom he was naked and got into the tub with me. Both times we were alone in the house.

◆　◆　◆　◆　◆

In order to fully appreciate my home life, let me describe my family as I remember them. There was nothing complex about my mother. She was simply a blade of steel with a tongue to match. At will, she could be kind and sweet, like when I had friends over to our house. But if it was just us kids at home, she swore at us, belittled us, or outright ignored us. If we did something to upset her, she would say things like "go to your room asshole" or "look what you idiots did." It's a wonder any of us ever learned our real names!

As an example, for years she volunteered as a chaperone for school field trips. My girlfriends would comment on how young and pretty she was, and how lucky I was to have her for a mom. But when we were back in our own car after the trip, she'd yank on my ponytails and call me fat until I cried. Then she'd tease me by calling me a cry baby. When we'd get home, she'd cut off all my fingernails. I was always confused by her behavior. Confused and scared.

When I started my period, she tossed a box of Kotex at me and said, "Here, figure out what you need to do." That was typical. My mom wasn't a person who wasted any time or effort on sentimentality.

The only music ever allowed in our house was the loud static drone of the TV. Any conversation between our family while we were watching TV usually ended up in a yelling match. I couldn't stand my parents screaming at each other so when they did, I retreated to my room and snuggled with my dog Poochie, a small black mutt. He was the family's dog, but spent more time with me, and slept in my bed at night.

With four girls to do the housework, my mom was free to watch TV, or visit her girlfriend next door. My mom was a lousy cook, and we ate too many cheap fish sticks, greasy fries, and hot dogs. My mom had no patience, especially with me. When I was around fifteen years old, she became frustrated while teaching me how to crochet and smacked me in the face. The ring on her finger chipped my front tooth.

My mom was never easy to talk to, and she gave me the impression I was bothering her whenever I went to her for something. I realized that my friends were much closer to their parents, and that they were able to talk to them too. I admired that, so one day I got up the courage to ask my mom, "How come you never tell us you love us?"

"Because my mother never said it to me," was her reply. Then she got up and left the room.

There were no goodbye kisses in the morning when I left for school, and no stories or hugs at bedtime. In the beginning I didn't feel sorry for myself because that was all I knew. That was my life, and I just assumed everyone else's life was the same. It wasn't until years later that I realized my childhood was not normal. I tried to think of something good and positive to say about my mom while writing this, but the only thing I came up with was that she always drove me to and from swim practice, and to and from all the activities of all the other clubs I joined over the years.

◆　◆　◆　◆　◆

My dad was a "good" provider. He worked for the post office, was handy with remodeling projects, and kept the house in good repair. For a short time, he was an auxiliary police officer. He played softball, and once in a while his teammates would come over for picnics, or to watch sports and drink beer. There was always plenty of beer in our house.

He was a loud bossy Italian who swore too much and beat his four daughters with a leather belt. It seemed like we were always being threatened with that belt. Because I was his "special girl," I didn't get smacked as hard as my sisters — or so he told me. But the belt wasn't the only thing we were afraid of. My dad got drunk one night and chased Sheri around the car, threatening her with his gun. Like my mom, my dad was two-faced, and his public face was quite a bit different from his private one.

My dad's father died young, so I never knew him or heard anything about him.

My dad's mother, Noni, was an old woman who never talked much, at least not to me. She was cold and distant but doted on my three sisters. I never received birthday or Christmas presents from her, or any acknowledgement of any kind. Not even a lousy card. Ever.

When I was younger, I asked my parents why she forgot me. They said that she was old and must have forgotten. Then they would buy me a present to make up for it. Eventually I stopped asking why she kept forgetting about me, but never forgot my sisters. This was not a secret—the entire family was aware of how she treated me.

Noni's sister was my godmother, although I rarely ever saw her. Like her sister, there was no warmth, no love, and no acknowledgement of me of any kind. Ironically, I was raised in an Italian family and never knew who my godfather was! I grew up surrounded by these horrible people for years, but please don't think that I'm telling you this looking for sympathy, or a pat on the back, or so you'll think "oh you poor thing." This was my life—my reality—as seen through the eyes of a child.

Grammy and Poppie were my mother's parents. They were the ones I lived with after I was born. I loved Grammy dearly. She was soft spoken, wasn't afraid to spend time with me, and just wanted everybody to get along. She knew my dad had a temper, and she would do anything to avoid a confrontation—which might help explain the bad advice by the pool. And even though Grammy worked full time, her house was always neat and clean. She wasn't too bad of a cook either. As close as Grammy and I were though, she never actually told me she loved me. My mom was right about that. There was no showing of emotions in this family.

Grammy and Poppie were married for many years and Grammy took very good care of Poppie. So good in fact, he was totally helpless without her. Poppie would never admit it, but it was true. He couldn't cook for himself, shop alone, or even make a long distance phone call without her help. One would think Poppie would have treated Grammy like a queen with all she did for him, but that wasn't the case.

Poppie picked on Grammy and bossed her around. He spent his days at a bar while she was on her feet all day, working in the meat room at a grocery store. He was her ride home from work, but he didn't leave the bar when her shift was over. He left when he decided he was ready.

My grandparents never had much money, and in their later years, they lost their house and ended up living in their car. Sometimes they parked either in front of our house, or my aunt's house. Occasionally, they shared a meal with us and used our bathroom, but they never lived with us. I don't know why. Eventually they got a job working together at a motel where they were given a free room to live in. When I was younger and living with them, I was happy. But looking back, I realize that theirs was not a happy marriage.

That's how I remember my family during those early years. And yet, through all of it, I still have some happy memories too. I had a lot of good times with my cousins and with friends who came over to swim in our pool. I also started participating in activities both in and out of school.

One of my girlfriends asked me to join the Brownies with her, so I did. I quickly realized it was a fun way to spend time with my friends while spending less time at home with my dad. We sold Girl Scout cookies, experimented with arts and crafts, and worked on earning as many merit badges as we could. I had a lot of fun as a Brownie.

I asked for feet pajamas for Christmas, hoping they would keep my father away. It didn't work.

By the end of third grade, I was getting the hang of school and doing fairly well. I won a composition contest, and the composition I wrote was featured in our school newspaper. My last report card for that year was all "satisfactory" and stated that I was "a good worker and a very conscientious student."

◆ ◆ ◆ ◆ ◆

Nothing else seemed to change in my life. Most Friday nights my parents got together with my Aunt Judi and Uncle Moe to play cards. My father and my Uncle Moe were brothers, and my mother and Aunt Judi were sisters. They'd all known each other since they were kids, although I doubt any of them knew my father as well as they thought they did.

Sometimes they came over to our house. Other times we went over to theirs. I liked it when they came to our house. Neither my aunt nor my uncle drank, smoked, or swore. Unfortunately, as much as I had hoped, none of their behavior rubbed off on my parents.

They had four boys, and their ages were almost mirror images of me and my three sisters' ages. Looking back, it's almost like they had some kind of family competition to see who could get pregnant more often. While our parents played cards and laughed about their week over coffee or beer at the kitchen table, all of us kids watched TV and played games.

15

Those were some of the happiest memories of my childhood.

◆　◆　◆　◆　◆

In fourth grade, I had trouble with arithmetic. My teacher wanted me to do arithmetic drills at home, which would have been great if my parents had been the kind of parents who helped their children with their homework—they weren't. But somehow, without any support or

 encouragement from my parents, I managed to pull it together enough to finish the school year. My report card read: "Kathy is having difficulty regrouping in arithmetic. Her reading will improve if she pays greater attention to the content and meaning of the stories. Improvement in self-control would help also." Happily, I was promoted to fifth grade.

Moving up from being a Brownie to a Girl Scout was great because it helped me stay busy and gave me reasons not to be at home. I heard about a club where you could learn about animals and nature called 4-H. It sounded like fun, so I joined. I liked it. I also liked the fact that the meetings were held after school. It was one more thing I could do so I wouldn't have to go home right after school.

I continued taking swimming lessons for the next several years. Three nights of the week I swam at the local junior high pool. Having a pool in our backyard was a big help too. I earned swimming letters in both seventh and eighth grade.

I was now old enough to realize my life was split into two parts. Outside my house, I had school and all my other activities to look forward to. Life on the inside of my house was completely different. As soon as I walked through that front door, it was like a curtain closed behind me, cutting me off from the outside part of my life. Once I was inside the house, I tried to stay busy and out of the way. I was never sure how the night would go, but I knew I could look forward to the next morning when I could walk out the front door and leave this world behind.

Outwardly, I tried to look like and be like every other kid. Inside, I hoped that participating in so many activities might help me feel more normal. What did I know? I was just a kid.

Worse Times

To this day, I hate the color brown, but there is no brown quite like the brown I remember as a young girl. The recliner where my dad began touching me was brown, and it was on that same brown recliner that my dad raped me for the first time. I was twelve years old.

He tried to make me believe it was a game. He rubbed petroleum jelly on his penis and then on my vagina.

"Come here Kathy and sit down on me and see if you can sit all the way down."

I was afraid and didn't know what this new thing was. But I did what I was told.

"Don't worry," he coaxed. "You can do it. See what a big girl you are."

"Daddy, it hurts."

Everything he did to me hurt.

"Now Kathy, this is our special secret and you can't tell anyone. Do you know what would happen if someone found out about this?"

"No."

"Well, to start with, they won't believe you. They'll call you a liar, and liars get punished, don't they?"

My body was shivering, my stomach hurt, and my mom was at work. I nodded.

"That's right. But just suppose for a minute someone did believe you. Do you know what would happen then? Your mom and I would have to get a divorce and that means the whole family would split up, and all of us would have to live somewhere else. Now, if that happened, who would look after your sisters, and who would take care of Poochie? What would all your friends think? You wouldn't want to be responsible for all that, would you? You know how much your sisters look up to you."

◆　◆　◆　◆　◆

Over the years, I heard that speech so many times. Of course he used a different version when I was younger, but the theme was always the same. If I said anything, I would bring shame upon my family and never see my sisters again. Now, as an adult, I know he was brainwashing me. From the age of seven, he slowly, methodically, secretly, and steadily groomed me, and my thoughts, to the point where I believed him and everything he told me.

Many people will say one of the first steps in healing and putting yourself back together is to forgive… to leave it to a higher power… to not carry the hate. Well I'm not one of those people. I hate him for what he did to me. I have not, and will not, forgive him. He ruthlessly abused me sexually, psychologically, and emotionally to the point where he had total control over me. And during all that time, my mother was nowhere to be found.

People think they can't move on if they don't forgive, and that they'll somehow be stuck, just treading water until they do. Not true. I can't forget what my dad did to me, and I haven't forgiven him, but by God, I was still able to move on and make something of my life! Just remember, it's not where you come from that matters. What matters is how you spend the rest of your life once you get past all the crap. Do not allow the bad people to win. Hate is a powerful motivator. If it's the only thing you have, use it.

When my dad started to molest me, he spoke with loving and soothing tones. As I got older, I began to see his temper and how he treated others. But when it was just the two of us, once again, he was loving and comforting, as if I were a small child. For him it was a game, a game he worked to perfect over the years.

For me it was weird and hard to understand. There was my dad sneaking around quietly, telling me everything was alright, but he didn't want me to say anything to anybody. If everything was okay, why did he want me to keep it a secret? This confused me, but I loved my dad, and I did what I was told. I kept my mouth shut.

"Normal" Times

Fifth and sixth grades were almost identical. My grades were mostly C's, a trend that followed me throughout my school career. I did enjoy school, but I decided I was no genius. I was very quiet in fifth grade as the D on my report card for "Participates in discussion" proved. Guess I didn't have much to say that year.

At the end of sixth grade, I received a certificate for *Outstanding Citizen in Room 116*. Although I don't remember what I did to earn it, my grades and attendance for that semester were good, and I was happy to be recognized.

I was still having a great time being a Girl Scout too. They taught me how to cook, sew, and how to babysit. Babysitting helped me earn extra money, and gave me another way to get out of the house.

I found out that if I sold enough Girl Scout cookies, it would help defray the cost of going to Girl Scout summer camp. I knew I was going to have to come up with most of the money myself, but when I told my parents I wanted to go to camp, they still sat me down and told me they didn't have enough money to send me. I thought it was odd because there always seemed to be enough money for them to buy beer and cigarettes, not to mention all the clothes my mother was constantly buying for herself.

In a rare show of support though, my parents did take my cookie order forms to work with them while I went door to door on my own, and with their help, I sold enough cookies to qualify for one week of Girl Scout camp. The following year, I sold enough cookies to qualify for two weeks.

I'd never been camping before, but I couldn't wait to go. With the exception of a few sleepovers at a girlfriend's house, this was going to be the first time I went someplace without my parents, and the first time I'd be sleeping someplace other than home. I was really looking forward to that.

I had a purple footlocker that I packed and repacked in the weeks before camp, wanting to make sure I had enough clothes and supplies to last the whole week. Each time I thought of something else I wanted to bring, I repacked the trunk to make sure everything still fit. Besides, it was fun thinking about this new adventure.

At camp, we went swimming and boating on the lake. We sang songs, hiked the nature trails, and everybody pitched in to get all the chores done. It was a good opportunity to meet other girls, and there was a bond of togetherness we all felt. When it got dark, we sat around a bonfire singing, playing games, and roasting marshmallows. It was perfect.

Sleeping outdoors in a tent in the middle of the woods was worlds away from my house. It was also the first time since my dad had started sexually molesting me that I slept peacefully. Here, away from him, I was just another happy kid at camp.

◆　◆　◆　◆　◆

My three younger sisters and I had your basic sibling relationship. Sometimes we got along well—other times not so much. As the oldest, one of my jobs was to babysit my sisters when my parents went out. Another one of my jobs was to make sure they did their weekly chores. The reason I was given this responsibility was because the twins were slobs, and my mother was tired of constantly nagging them to clean up their messy room. Her solution was to put a list of chores on the refrigerator door and put me in charge of making sure they were done and checked off.

No matter how hard I worked to make sure everything on the list was checked off, there always seemed to be one more disgusting "chore" I had to do for my dad. Many times I could hear my sisters playing outside while I was trapped inside with him. Only after he was through with me and I cleaned myself up, could I go outside and play.

I loved my neighborhood though. There were so many different people there. Hairdressers lived alongside school teachers, insurance salesmen, and adults going to night school. The houses were all ranch style homes built so close together that it was easy to hear your neighbors talking, or yelling at one another. If it was a warm summer evening when every window in the neighborhood was open, you could easily learn what was going on in other families.

In the summer, fathers spent their weekends cutting the grass and grilling hot dogs and hamburgers. As kids, we rode our bikes in the street and walked to all our friend's houses. In the winter, there were hills for sledding at the school down the street. As I got older, I started babysitting for many of our neighbors too. Unfortunately, I still had to go home every night.

◆　◆　◆　◆　◆

With my parents working opposite shifts so that one of them would always be home with us, they barely saw each other during the week. When they finally got together on the weekends, they did a lot of yelling and fighting, and sooner or later, someone would start throwing something. After a fight, they sometimes gave each other the silent treatment. I was secretly grateful for those quiet times.

My parents were obviously too selfish and immature to ever be a happy couple. If they were drinking and my mom wanted to be particularly nasty, she would tease my dad about his first marriage—a short-lived affair that ended badly. During those fights I heard the words "impotent" and "violence" thrown around by my mom over and over again. I was too young to understand what they meant, and I was never able to piece together the whole story, but I do remember those two words: impotent and violence.

◆　◆　◆　◆　◆

I know now that there are children who fall right asleep at night and don't hear what's going on in their houses. I didn't even know what it meant to sleep peacefully through the night until I went to Girl Scout camp. Right after my dad raped me for the first time, I started having trouble sleeping. I'd be in bed literally trembling, afraid that when I fell asleep, my dad would slip in and wake me up. So I had to wait to fall asleep.

First, I had to wait until my sisters fell asleep. I had to wait for a short time after that to make sure they were sleeping. I had to wait to see if this night would be one of "those" nights. And while I lay there waiting, I kept hearing the replay of my dad's voice telling me what would happen if I told, and of my Grammy saying "Shhh Kathy.... We don't talk about this."

I would lay there knowing there was nothing I could do. I'd remind myself that if he did come in, there was no way to get out of it. Then I'd try to convince myself that if he did come in, it would be over quickly, and he would leave me alone so I could get some sleep. But my sleep was always a restless sleep. As I got older, on the nights when he did come to my room, he was usually already half drunk.

It was so different in the 70's. There were no school programs in place to educate children against monsters like my dad. Sexual abuse wasn't discussed on TV, and it certainly wasn't covered in the Girl Scout handbook. Inwardly I was isolated and miserable. The first and only adult I confided in was my Grammy, and she basically told me to shut up about it.

I was too afraid of my mom to talk to her about anything, let alone about the fact that her husband was raping me on a regular basis. The silence that resulted made me the perfect victim for a predatory man. If there had been a program at school, I'd like to think that I would have spoken up to someone, but I don't know how. Because of all the brainwashing, I was too afraid to do or say anything. Afraid of losing my sisters. Afraid that people would find out. Afraid of so many things.

As I mentioned, nights were terrible for me. I felt so vulnerable. Half the time I didn't even realize I was doing it, but I began pulling out my eyelashes and eyebrows. It quickly became a nervous habit and I couldn't stop. After about six months, my mom finally took me to a dermatologist. On the first visit, I was diagnosed with blepharitis and given tubes of ointment to dab on my eyelids.

Even back then, I knew they were wrong. It was stress and fear manifesting itself into destructive behavior. Not wanting them to find out the real reason my eyelashes and eyebrows were missing, I forced myself not to do it as often so it would look like the ointment was working. I endured dabbing that stuff on my eyelids for a few years. Eventually I stopped doing that to myself, but only because I realized it made me look different from everyone else. That was the last thing I wanted.

Meanwhile, my body began to develop and I made a conscious decision to start wearing baggy clothes to try and hide myself. I was still wearing feet pajamas.

Out of the blue, one of my girlfriends asked if she could sleep over at my house. It sounded like fun, but I wasn't sure how my mom would react to the idea. Surprisingly, she said yes. We had such a good time. We played games, talked about boys, swam in our pool, and chatted all night long. The next week she invited me to sleep over at her house. We swapped sleepovers like this for years, and I figured out that whenever I had someone sleep over, both my parents were well-behaved, and my dad stayed away from me.

A few years before I began writing this book, I bumped into this friend's mother and we struck up a conversation. It turns out that my friend's father was molesting her at the same time my father was molesting me. Only my friend was able to tell her mother about it. Her mother quickly divorced him.

She gave me her daughter's phone number and I called her as soon as I could. I wanted to tell her she was not alone in this. There were so many things to talk about and get caught up on, just like we used to. But I never got the chance. Her life had been very difficult, and she didn't want to talk about any of it. It would have meant a lot to me, and possibly her, if we could have re-connected after all those years. We had a lot in common, and mutual support goes a long way in the healing process. Unfortunately some people will just never talk about it. I think about her often though.

As much as I was grateful for all the sleepovers and activities that got me out of the house, I was equally grateful for the friendships I made and the experiences I had. I gave every club and every team I belonged to all that I could. Unfortunately, I was shy and struggled with low self-esteem, so I wasn't able to maintain many of those relationships long term. Maybe that's a part of growing up we all have to learn to deal with, but inside, I always thought that somehow people knew about my secret and because of it, nobody really wanted to be my friend.

Clearly, the abuse I suffered went way beyond just sexual and physical. My dad not only hurt my body, he also had a way of wording things that made it seem like the things he was forcing me to do were alright. Everyone knew he had a temper, and he unleashed it on us kids with his belt. This violence, coupled with his manipulative ways, kept me quiet and submissive for years.

It may be hard to understand how it was for me if you haven't lived it. If you haven't, count your blessings because if you have, then you know you can never forget. I was a prisoner like this until I was seventeen years old.

◆　◆　◆　◆　◆

During seventh, eighth, and ninth grade, a few interesting things happened. I was still plugging away at school, and at the end of eighth grade I received two certificates. One for: "Outstanding Effort and Achievement in Art," and one for: "Outstanding in English." Not major awards, but it proved that I was trying. And something new was beginning to grow inside me. I was proud of my accomplishments! Despite the disadvantages I had, I still went to school every day and gave it the best

effort I could.

Gymnastics looked interesting, so when I was thirteen years old, I joined a dance studio. I learned how to stretch properly, and how to perform cartwheels and back flips. Shortly after my first recital I fell off the balance beam, got scared, and quit.

My parents didn't care if I quit or not. In fact, I don't even remember if they came to my recital. They must have because the only way I could have gotten there is if they brought me. But I don't know for sure if they just gave me a ride to and from, or stayed for the recital. Maybe if we had celebrated afterward, like going out for ice cream or something like that, I would have had a reason to remember.

With swimming and homework and everything else I was trying to cram into my life, my eating habits changed. I was so busy, I was skipping meals. And when I did eat, it was usually junk food. Because I wasn't nourishing my body properly, I began to have fainting spells once or twice a month. They began with a buzzing noise in my ears. Then, after a few seconds, I was out. Didn't matter where I was or what I was doing.

After the first few times I fainted, my mother took me to see my doctor. He ran the standard tests and found nothing unusual. He told me if I started eating better the fainting spells would go away. He also said it was normal. Well if it was so normal, why weren't any of my friends fainting? He was right though. I started eating better and within a few years the fainting spells stopped.

Happy Times

My mother's older sister Judi was my favorite aunt and my guardian angel right here on Earth. Everything I am today I owe to this woman. As an adult, she would tell me I was the daughter she never had, and I would tell her she was the mother I always wanted. For me, my aunt's family became my real family. They were the people I connected with most. They were the family I wished I had been born into.

My aunt's heart and soul was her family. Everything she did, she did for her husband and her four sons. In addition to cooking and cleaning for five guys, she drove her sons to hockey practice, hosted young Canadian hockey players in her home, and cooked huge meals for all their buddies and girlfriends.

Her husband was a good father and a hard worker. For years, he worked two jobs to provide for his family. Despite his busy schedule, my Uncle Moe always made time for his boys, and they always seemed to enjoy each other's company.

All my cousins played sports and their rooms were full of trophies and awards. Their buddies liked to hang out at my aunt's house too, and my aunt and uncle had good relationships with all the guys. Laughter always filled my aunt's home in a way that everyone was drawn to.

The neighborhood they lived in was about twenty minutes away from ours, but it was very much like ours — friendly and inviting. Weekend tag sales sprang up here and there, and it seemed like everyone had a pool. Neighbors came out after dinner to talk and catch up on the latest news while their kids roamed the neighborhood playing.

One Friday night while my aunt and uncle were over at our house playing cards with my parents, my aunt surprised me by asking me if I wanted to spend the weekend at her house. She promised me mint chocolate chip ice cream and long talks. Maybe she needed a break from all the guy stuff and wanted some girl time together, or maybe she felt sorry for me because of the way my mother treated me. Whatever the reason, I didn't care—and she didn't have to ask me twice. I happily accepted.

Luckily, I didn't have any babysitting scheduled for that weekend, so while the adults continued their card game, I packed my gym bag and hung around trying not to make eye contact with my dad. He didn't show it, but I knew he was pissed. I didn't care. I was thrilled over this new adventure and couldn't wait to leave.

That first night at my aunt's house we turned her spare room into my bedroom. She made me feel right at home. After the room was organized and my clothes were unpacked, we had the ice cream she'd promised and talked late into the night. Not about important things, just silly girl stuff really. She asked me how I was doing in school... did I have any boyfriends... things like that. It was refreshing to have an adult friend like her. When we talked, she smiled and looked right at me with her sparkly blue eyes.

What I really wanted to talk about was what my dad was doing to me, but I couldn't. I didn't want to bring that ugliness into her home and spoil our special girl time together. It didn't belong there. Besides, I didn't know how to begin, or what to say. I was so brainwashed by then that I was terrified that if I told her she would call me a liar and never invite me back to her house. So I said nothing.

When my aunt hugged me goodnight that first night, I wanted to hold her and stay there forever. After she said good night and closed the door, I crawled under the cool summer sheets feeling totally safe and at peace. Even her sheets had a fresher scent. I snuggled down and slept great.

◆　◆　◆　◆　◆

For the next several years, I tried to arrange my babysitting schedule so I could spend every other weekend at my aunt's house. I truly treasured spending time with my aunt and her family. With four cousins, there was always something to do and someone to do it with. We played games, swam in their pool, took in a movie, or went roller skating. My cousins made me feel like a sister, and we were always comfortable and relaxed in each other's company. It was like I was part of a real family when I was with them. Spending time with them helped me understand the value of a real family, and how good it must feel to be a part of a real family.

I spent a lot of time with my aunt, especially in her kitchen. She did the cooking and baking, and I helped clean up. The whole time we just chatted away like "a pair of old birds" as she would say. My mom never had the patience to cook, so I really enjoyed this special kitchen time.

At night, we'd sit on the couch next to each other with our bowls of ice cream. We'd watch TV, talk, or just sat there enjoying the quiet. Some nights she had her knitting out and worked on infant-sized hats she donated to the hospital. For the holidays, she made afghans, hats, slippers, and doilies. Did it really matter to me what we did? No. They were still the best weekends ever.

My aunt's home was neat, clean, and beautifully decorated, but it was so much more than that. It had a comfy and welcoming feel, as if the home itself was actually another member of the family. It was filled with warmth and the strength of love, and in that safe environment, her family thrived. My parents owned a house, but my aunt had a home.

My Aunt Judi was kind and sweet and just being around her made me a better person. By example, she showed me the importance of a loving family, and that there were other ways of communicating besides the yelling and fighting I was used to with my parents. Her family made me feel like I was worth something, and for the first time in my life, I was beginning to feel normal.

Sunday nights depressed me because I had to leave my aunt's house and go back to my parents. There, I still had chores to do and homework to finish. Avoiding my dad was altogether another chore. To leave such a loving family only to go home to my idiot family didn't seem fair. But at least I had my aunt, and I clung to that knowledge.

◆　◆　◆　◆　◆

I was getting older now, maturing, and from the strength I drew from my aunt combined with a hidden part of myself that was beginning to surface, I could feel a change starting to take shape within me. I still did the terrible acts my dad made me do, but in my mind I began questioning things. Then I had a thought I'd never had before. Maybe I could say "no" to my dad! And once that thought took hold in my mind, it didn't go away.

My sisters were getting older too, and I decided I wanted some privacy. So, when I was fifteen years old, my parents agreed to build me a bedroom in one corner of our finished basement. Of course, my new bedroom came with a price. Since it was going to be my room, my dad insisted that I help him with the project, and as I held the paneling in place for him to nail, he took every opportunity to brush against me or lean into me. It was annoying and humiliating, but I got my room.

After the room was completed, I realized something else. My new bedroom was directly below my parent's bedroom and I could hear their bed squeak when they were having sex. Hearing it made me sick to my stomach at first, but it didn't take me long to figure out that if they had sex, my dad would leave me alone for a while. As much as I didn't want to know what was going on with them, it was still a relief because I knew I'd be able to sleep uninterrupted—at least for that night.

I always knew when someone was coming down to the basement, because it was dark, and whoever was coming down had to flip the lights on with the switch at the top of the stairs so they could see where they were going. When my bedroom door was closed, I could see the strip of light along the bottom of my door, and then I knew someone was coming down to the basement. My dad was sneaky though, and never turned the light on.

◆　◆　◆　◆　◆

In ninth grade, I decided I wanted to go to a private Catholic high school instead of a public high school. The school I wanted to attend had an outstanding reputation, but my parents refused to pay the tuition, and told me that if I wanted to go, I had to pay for it myself.

So at fifteen years old, I worked with my dad at his part-time office cleaning job on Saturdays. My job was to empty the waste baskets and help him wax the floors. On a good day, there were people working and we weren't alone. A bad day was when it was just the two of us. It didn't always happen, but it did every once in a while. My father would start masturbating, and then force me to perform oral sex.

On one Saturday when we were alone at work, my dad approached me and I backed away. I told him "No" and said that I thought what we were doing wasn't right. As soon as the words were out of my mouth, I tensed up. He was angry. I knew my dad's temper and how he could be if he didn't get his way. Now, it would be worse for me later. I'd pay the price for saying no to him, either verbally or with the belt.

When I was a young child, I had to do what my dad told me to do or else I'd get in trouble. I was still just a kid, but that day, I wasn't the same kid. And that day, for the first time, I said no.

As proud of myself as I was in that moment, I was equally scared. I'd just said "no" to a command I'd been trained to obey from the age of seven. He didn't care, and he forced himself on me anyway.

Still, it felt like I'd scored a victory for myself. I'd finally stood up to my dad. I tried to get out of going to work with him after that, but he didn't allow it, and neither did my mother.

◆　◆　◆　◆　◆

To gain admittance to this particular high school, I had to pass an entrance exam. I took the exam towards the end of ninth grade, and passed. Then all I had to do was come up with the tuition. I saved every penny I made babysitting and combined that with what I earned working for my dad. When that wasn't enough to cover my sophomore year's tuition, my parents grudgingly loaned me the difference, making a big to-do about their "generosity."

I started school that fall as a sixteen-year-old sophomore. A few months later I got a job waitressing at Friendly's restaurant and paid my parents back from my tip money every week. Then I told my father I wouldn't be working with him any longer.

Changing Times

There was a lot going on in my life now that I was in high school and working part time. My aunt's influence was guiding me, and giving me the strength and courage I so desperately needed. I wasn't where I wanted and needed to be with regards to my father yet, but I was on my way. I had a taste of what power and independence could be like when I said no that first time, and I told myself that his bullying days would soon be over.

Being a C student, I didn't think college was in my future, but I was okay with that. I liked school, just not that much. What I wanted from this school was a solid education so I could get a good job, move out of my parent's house, and live in my own apartment. When I wasn't dreaming about that, I was focusing on school, waitressing, babysitting, and spending as much time as I could with my aunt.

◆ ◆ ◆ ◆ ◆

My youngest sister caught my father in a compromising position behind me in the laundry room. For some time now he'd been raping me whenever it pleased him — day or night. It didn't seem to matter to him who was home either. That day, it happened after I got home from school. I can't remember why he was home from work, and I don't know where my mother was. I still had my school uniform on when he took me into the laundry room. As he hoisted my skirt up and forced me over, Meri walked in with an armload of dirty clothes, stopping dead in her tracks when she saw us. She innocently asked what was going on, and my father yelled at her to go back upstairs. Keri came downstairs soon after, but he yelled at her to get back upstairs before she came into the laundry room. Even almost getting caught didn't stop him from raping me though.

Later that night, Meri asked me what happened down in the laundry room. I came up with some lame story about how he was helping me fix my ripped skirt. She never asked me anything else about it.

◆　◆　◆　◆　◆

I met my first boyfriend at the restaurant where I was waitressing. He was a cook, a year older than me, and went to a different high school. He smoked, drank beer, and drove a Mustang. I thought he was so cool; it was practically love at first sight. I looked forward to going to work when he was cooking, and I made extra sure to always look my very best.

He lived a couple of towns away from mine. His family's house was always spotless and very well organized. It looked like a museum. His parents were strict too. We weren't allowed in his room, so we sat on his parent's porch, or hung around outside for privacy. My parents wanted to meet him, but I was nervous about it. True to form though, when they did, they put on their fake faces and were polite. Still, it was a very uncomfortable evening for me.

If we weren't at my boyfriend's house, we'd hang out where most teenagers did in the 70s — the mall, the pizza place, and the park. He also liked to drive us around in his Mustang while we listened to Jimmy Hendrix and The Doors.

While we were dating, I missed two of my periods. He drove me to a clinic and they confirmed that I was pregnant. After discussing it with him, we decided to abort the pregnancy, and a few days later, I walked to the bus stop, he picked me up, and we drove to the clinic. Once they found out how old I was, I had to call my mother for her consent. No paperwork or parent signature was required. All they needed was verbal consent over the phone. She gave it. She didn't ask me anything about it when I got home either.

I never told my boyfriend about my father. We were just two kids in love and I wanted to keep it that way. There was no need to creep him out with the details of what my father was doing to me.

What I couldn't tell anyone, because I didn't even know for sure, was who the father was. It could have been my father's child, but it could have also been my boyfriend's. In the end, not knowing the answer to that question was the deciding factor in my decision to have an abortion. I've cried over that decision many times over the years. If my father had been normal, and I'd been part of a normal family, I might have made a different decision. But when I got pregnant, I was only sixteen years old.

Looking back now, I clearly remember my father leaving me alone for weeks after the abortion so I would have time to heal. I'm not one hundred percent sure, but I think it was around that time that my father also had a vasectomy. No one else ever knew I was pregnant—not even my aunt.

◆　◆　◆　◆　◆

On the first day of school my junior year, I took a seat in a class that was taught by a priest. He began his class by thanking us for paying our tuition. Then he motioned us over to the windows and pointed out his new Cadillac in the parking lot. I was working hard to pay for school, not his car, and I did not appreciate his comment.

Even as a junior in high school, I always respected the curfew my parents set for me. One night though, my boyfriend and I got into a fight. I was still learning about relationships just like most kids my age, but when it came to the whole idea of what a *normal* boyfriend-girlfriend relationship looked like, I didn't know.

By the time he dropped me off at my house, I was more than an hour late on a school night. He offered to go in with me because he knew how my parents were, but I didn't want him to see how bad it could be. He gave me a quick kiss and then headed home as I made my way to the front door. My mother was waiting for me with a cigarette hanging from her mouth.

"You're late," she said as I walked through the door.

"I know. I'm sorry. We had a fight and needed to straighten out a few things."

"Yeah, I bet." She replied sarcastically as I took off my sweater and draped it over a chair.

I could tell by the look on her face that she was upset, but so was I. It had been a long day for me and I was beginning to get a headache, so I sat down on the couch and waited for the lecture to begin. She just paced back and forth in front of me mumbling. I closed my eyes and massaged my temples. This was the first time I'd ever been this late, and I hoped she was struggling because I was always on time and she didn't really have a reason to make a big deal about this one time. Whatever she was going to say, I just wished she'd say it and get it over with. I was tired and I wanted to go to bed. I had school in the morning and wasn't in the mood for a big scene.

After a while, she stopped pacing and stood staring at me with her hands on her hips. Her voice was scratchy and she was shaking. When she spoke, what she told me took me totally by surprise. "You know, I didn't have to have you. Your grandmother wanted me to keep you but I had a different idea. I would have given you away."

I blinked a few times, and tried to make sense of what she'd just said. This was not the lecture I expected. "Mom, what are you talking about?"

"Your father's not your real father Kathy. Your real father died in Vietnam." She blurted it out like it had been bottled up inside her.

Again I had to repeat my question. "What are you talking about? Are you telling me dad's not my real father?"

"Yes," She said.

I sat there with my mouth open, shaking my head not knowing what to say or do. How does anyone make sense out of hearing something like that? I stood up, but when I did, she stormed out of the room and headed for her bedroom.

This was about as sudden and confusing as life can be, and I just stood there, alone in the living room, shocked by what I'd just been told. Then, the man who had been passing himself off as my father for my whole life, walked into the room as if he'd been waiting for his cue, and reached out for me.

"It's okay Kathy," he said. "I'll still be your father. I love you... it's okay."

But it was definitely not okay. I was lied to and deceived by these two adults who claimed to be my parents. I pulled away from his embrace and went downstairs to my room.

Sitting on the edge of my bed, my mind replayed the events of the last few minutes over and over. And that's all it took really, just a few brief minutes to change my life forever. It was difficult for me to process what I had just learned along with all the emotions that were flooding my mind. I was trying to make sense of everything, but all I kept hearing in my mind was, "*Your father's not your real father.*"

Once the buzzing in my head subsided and I was breathing normally, my thoughts became more focused. I understood that I wasn't really his daughter and he wasn't really my father, but what did that mean? Would my life change? And if it did, how would it change? Did anyone else know? I suddenly understood why I didn't look like any of my sisters, and so many things started to make sense. Like if my stepfather's mother, and my godmother knew — which I'm sure they did — that would explain why they never wanted to have anything to do with me. They knew I wasn't his daughter. I was someone else's daughter. That realization alone made me feel better because now I knew that the way they'd treated me didn't have anything to do with me!

◆　◆　◆　◆　◆

I didn't sleep much that night. I kept thinking about how grateful and relieved I was that I wasn't related to a monster who had pretended to be my dad. I thought about all the crap I'd had to put up with over the years, and now that I knew he wasn't my real father, I also knew that I didn't have to listen to him any longer. I was so mad, but I was devastated too. The truth might be able to help me from this point forward, but it could never erase what he had done to me. As I laid there feeling sorry for myself, tears streaming down my face, I made a promise to myself. I promised myself that he would never ever touch me again.

After that night, he thought he would still be able to threaten and manipulate me whenever he pleased, but I was no longer scared or intimidated by him. I was finally able to stand up to him, on my own, and never bend to him again.

He tried his old act a few times, but as soon as he came anywhere near me, I threatened to expose him to everyone. He backed right down, and didn't even put up a fight. And just like that, it stopped. Forever. His power to manipulate and exploit a scared and impressionable girl was gone. All I saw when I looked at him from then on was a pathetic drunk. He knew it too, and slunk away like a defeated bully.

◆　◆　◆　◆　◆

A few days later, I asked my mother who my real father was. Her response was, "You don't need to know."

Her answer didn't surprise me because that was how we were raised. "Don't worry about it" and "You don't need to know" were my parent's responses to most things. They didn't foster independence in us; they said and did things to keep us under their control.

◆　◆　◆　◆　◆

During my senior year, I waitressed to pay off my tuition, my stepfather stayed away from me, and my boyfriend dumped me for a married woman at work he'd been sleeping with. After that, there was a lot less drama in my life.

The end of my high school career was clearly in sight, and since I no longer had a boyfriend, I asked my cousin to accompany me to my senior prom. And finally, on May 29, 1981, at 2:00 p.m., I graduated from high school along with 540 of my fellow classmates.

Part Two

Limbo

I'd been so focused on graduating from Cathedral that I didn't give much thought to what I was going to do with my life after high school. I had studied general business in high school though, and that meant looking for an office job. It was a different world back then too, so getting a good job was still fairly easy.

Mass Mutual's home office was — and still is — in Springfield, MA. I already knew a few people who worked there, so it was one of the first places I applied. After a few weeks and several interviews, I was hired. I was so excited to take this next step in my life. I quit my waitressing job and went clothes shopping.

Mass Mutual was a great place to work. I started out in Group Accounting, filling out lapse policy notices for policyholders in danger of cancellation due to non-payment. It was a low level entry job, but my foot was in the door. I worked in a cubicle with my name on a nameplate attached to the gray fabric cubicle wall. As far as I was concerned, I had made it big time. I didn't have to put on a waitressing uniform six or seven days a week. I got to dress up in a woman's business suit and go to work Monday through Friday.

The building felt like a tiny village. Two large cafeterias served full breakfasts and lunches. There was a dry cleaner on site, as well as a barber shop, video rental kiosk, credit union, fitness center, company store, etc. I was one of around 5000 employees happy to take advantage of all the goods and services a busy executive could ask for. It was all very fast paced, and I did my best to make sure I fit in.

One of the things I wanted to do was to work out. It seemed like everyone was working out back then, but I wasn't comfortable using the coed fitness center at work, so I joined an all women's gym called *Figures and Fitness*. Armed with my stylish body suit and leg warmers, I did aerobics three nights a week. After the class, I'd indulge in a soak in the hot tub, or enjoy the sauna for a while.

◆　◆　◆　◆　◆

I finally felt like I was pointed in the right direction. With my new job, I was beginning to feel like the distance between me and all those exciting and interesting people was starting to shrink. I had a real job in the real world now. Unfortunately, I couldn't afford my own place yet, so that meant continuing to live in my parent's house.

Living in that house was now both awkward and creepy. It was like nothing and everything had changed all at the same time. The yelling and fighting I grew up with was still being played out, but I tried my best to ignore it. My stepfather stayed away from me, but he also walked around like nothing had ever happened. I was fine with that because he was keeping his distance from me, and that was all I really cared about.

Still, I wanted to get out of the house, so I started looking for a roommate to share an apartment with. I couldn't find anyone. Most of my girlfriends were either going away to college or not ready to move out on their own yet. So, for the foreseeable future, I was stuck. Luckily, between going to work and the gym, I didn't see much of the family.

One day I overheard a few of the instructors talking about needing to hire more help. I'd been a member for quite a while by then, so everybody who worked there already knew me, and I knew all of them. I asked for an application, and they hired me as a part-time fitness instructor.

I was trained to sell memberships and give facility tours, but my favorite part of the job was teaching my own aerobics class. Even today, more than 25 years after giving my last aerobics class, people still stop me at the mall or supermarket and tell me how much fun they had in my class. We'll hug and chat for a few minutes, and then go our separate ways. My husband has witnessed this first hand and always gets a kick out of it. He does roll his eyes when they tell me I haven't changed a bit though.

When I wasn't at work or at the gym, I found other ways to stay out of the house. During the summer of 1982, I went to Hampton Beach with a group of friends and acquaintances for the day. One of the people in the group was D, the brother of one of my girlfriends. We'd originally met in high school, but had never really talked to each other until that day at the beach.

D was cute and funny and we started dating right after that. He was my first real adult boyfriend. He still lived at home too. His mom was a hardworking woman who raised five kids by herself. Her husband was out of the picture, and I admired her for all she'd accomplished on her own.

D worked at a gas station and when I wasn't working or at the gym, I'd hang out with him while he worked. When he wasn't working, we usually just sat around and watched TV. It didn't really seem to matter what we did. We just had fun.

At first, I wondered if I should tell D about what my stepfather had done. Weren't people in normal relationships supposed to be honest with each other? But I never came close to telling him. That part of my life was over. It would never ever happen again, and all I really wanted to do was erase it from my memory.

I couldn't change what happened though. I couldn't undo all the ugly and awful things my stepfather had done to me. The older I got, the more I realized how bad it had been. It was an awful kind of knowledge, and even though I might have been beginning to understand that it wasn't my fault, it still left me feeling dirty and embarrassed. I didn't want people to think I was different, or worse, question why I never told anyone.

All I could think of was my Grammy holding a finger to her lips and saying, "Shhh." So I continued to keep the secret and didn't tell anyone… not a soul.

◆　◆　◆　◆　◆

I'd been out of school for a year now. I was working two jobs and finally saving a little bit of money, but I didn't feel like I was getting any closer to the independence I craved. I wasn't sliding backwards, but I wasn't moving forward like I thought I would be by now either. D was a nice boyfriend, and my life was certainly better than it had been, but I wondered if this was what my life was going to be like. Would I always be working two jobs and squeezing my time with D in between jobs while still living at home? I tried to stay positive and not get too overwhelmed, and then, a random piece of mail got me thinking.

A travel school in Kissimmee, Florida called Southeastern Academy was looking for prospective students to enter the travel industry. It certainly looked interesting, but I had never considered anything like this before. For days, I secretly read and re-read that brochure. Then I told D about it and we talked about all the possibilities for weeks. My work life needed a boost and this sounded like a good opportunity.

Finally, I mustered up the courage to give them a call. They scheduled an appointment and a female representative from the school came to the house. She was middle aged, very professional, and answered all my questions. It was a chance to get away and travel. I was always looking for opportunities to get away, so when she presented me with an offer, I jumped at the chance and signed up right then and there.

Southeastern Academy's training was simple, basic, and direct. Six months of home study material followed by three intensive weeks in Florida to complete the course. Despite working both a full time and part time job, I made the time to study and applied myself to every lesson. This was my chance to do something special, and I wanted it badly. After I passed the home study portion, I gave my notice to both Mass Mutual and Figures and Fitness, and headed to Florida to complete my training in the travel industry.

The campus was a lot like I had imagined it would be — small, but nice. There were multiple buildings spread throughout, with the men and women staying in separate dorms. It was way better than high school. The staff was friendly and knowledgeable, and provided me with a good background in what I thought was a promising field.

There were a lot of students like me, people from working-class families looking for adventure. Most of us had flown down to Florida so we didn't have cars. Sightseeing was pretty much impossible, and money was so tight for me that I stayed on campus during the weekends studying and making friends.

In March 1983, my mother and stepfather came to Florida for the graduation ceremony. It was fine having them there because we were all still in "pretend" mode. I introduced them to everybody, and we took pictures just like any other normal family would.

When I got back home (I couldn't believe I still referred to that place as "home") I started mailing out resumes, following each one up with a phone call. I read the classified ads everyday too. Unfortunately, the few opportunities I did find all required experience. The United States was in the midst of a recession at that point in time, and as hard as I tried, I couldn't find a job as a travel agent.

On top of that, I had to deal with my mother. I'd been able to stop my stepfather, but my relationship with my mother hadn't really changed. I should have realized that her support for my new career had a price tag. I shouldn't have been surprised to learn that she expected me to help her fly for free as a result of my new career. The longer it took me to find a job, the more upset she became. Once again, she was being self-centered to her core.

I was so tired of the way she still treated me. I didn't know if she knew what my stepfather had been doing to me, but it was really hard for me to believe she didn't at least have an idea. There was no way I could ask her either. No way I could yell at her, or let her see how mad I was at her for not being there to protect me. I just didn't know how to stand up and fight for myself.

I wasn't raised to be strong and independent, or to speak up, and now it just wasn't in me. I was trained to be passive and to not make waves. Unfortunately, being brought up that way wasn't doing the adult me any favors. If anything, it was crippling me and limiting my chances of making something of myself. Instead of taking charge, I just let things happen around me and dealt with whatever came my way as a result. I was a shy quiet girl the whole time I was growing up. Now I was a shy quiet adult wishing for a normal life.

I continued to try and find a job as a travel agent, but I just couldn't find one and started getting nervous. I needed a job. So I joined a temp agency and ended up back at Mass Mutual. I was able to get my old aerobics instructor job back too. It was a relief, but I was right back where I'd started from — except that now I was making less money.

Out of the blue, D dumped me in the summer of 1984. I knew our relationship hadn't been an earth-shattering romance, but we got along well. The caring part was there. We were there for each other. We had fun together. We didn't really fight, and I thought there was a bond between us. I even thought he was a guy I could marry. He told me he was splitting up with me because he "didn't want to cheat on me." Of course I was upset. In my mind, our relationship had been progressing just fine, but I had been wrong.

Another few months went by, but my life wasn't getting better. If I hadn't quit my job to go to school to become a travel agent, I might be one of those young executives racing through the halls of Mass Mutual by now. Instead, I was just a temp — and a very disillusioned one at that. I was still struggling to make more money, still living at home, and now the sight of my stepfather was making me nauseous.

I was desperate and turned to my Aunt Judi for help. She'd always been like a mother to me, and I didn't know what else to do, so I asked her if I could move in with her. I knew it was a lot to ask. Three of her sons were still living at home, but Judi smiled at me and told me there would always be a room for me in her home. She didn't ask why, or for how long I would be staying. She simply said "Yes." How can you not love a woman like this?

With a profound sense of relief, I moved into her home late summer, 1984. I was finally safe, free, and joyfully rid of my idiot family. After I moved into Judi's house, I never spent another night under my mother's roof. I was thrilled about that part, but after I moved, my sisters and I started to drift apart. They had their own friends and boyfriends now too. I was working two jobs, and it wasn't like we called each other and talked on the phone for hours. That's not how we were raised — that's not who we were. We saw each other at family functions, but I was still avoiding my stepfather as much as was humanly possible, so we didn't talk much on those occasions either.

Better Directions

It didn't take long to get into a routine in Judi's house, and I made sure to help out as much as I could. Judi made me feel loved, and included me in all of the family's activities. I wasn't sure her husband was as happy about it as I was though. It wasn't like he said or did anything deliberately; it was just a feeling I had. But it was a feeling I experienced sometimes anyway... as if people would look at me, could tell there was something wrong with me, and then decide they didn't want me around because of it.

After the move, my commute to Mass Mutual took about an hour. After work, I usually went to the gym. When I finally got home, I'd stay up late hanging out and talking with one or more of my cousins. We all just picked up right where we'd left off when I used to spend weekends with them. It was like I was their sister again. Those were long days, but they were happy comfortable days too. I wouldn't have changed a thing.

I had so much love for Judi and the way she welcomed me into her home and her life. But as close as we were, I couldn't bring myself to tell her what my childhood had really been like. I was beginning to feel like I wanted to tell somebody what had happened, but her family was about as close to perfect as I could ever imagine, and I just couldn't bring that kind of ugliness into her home. I hoped I'd be able to tell her at some point, but I wasn't ready yet.

◆　◆　◆　◆　◆

A year after I moved in with Judi's family, they purchased a three family house in Holyoke. Judi said it was strictly an investment, but what she really meant was, *Now that you and your cousin are older and both working full time, there's no reason for either of you to be making that long commute every day. Living in Holyoke, you'll both be closer to work and you can look out for each other.* Once again, Judi was showing her wings as my guardian angel.

On moving day, I was able to fit most of what I owned into my car. The rest was loaded onto a moving van, along with my cousin's things, and on a late summer day in 1985, we moved into one of the apartments. When we got there, my mother was there to help hang the curtains. My cousin left for a while, and I was left alone with her.

It was always strained when we were together. I secretly hoped she would tell me she was sorry, and if she'd wanted to say something to me, that would have been the perfect opportunity because it was just the two of us. But she didn't say anything. We were back in "pretend" mode, and that was her one and only visit. In the four years I lived there, none of my sisters ever stopped by for a visit either—not on a holiday, a birthday, or even just to see their big sister's first apartment.

After my mother left, my cousin and I started moving boxes from room to room when his girlfriend showed up and informed me she was moving in too. I looked at my cousin, but he just shrugged his shoulders. He hadn't told me, and she just came barging in with the attitude that this was *her* apartment and that I should be grateful to have a place to stay.

I already knew what she was like. She was loud and bossy and turned on her charming southern accent when she wanted to get her way. On moving day, she was in her glory, telling us where everything should go. It wasn't anything like the TV sitcom *Three's Company* though. She just took over, and I felt like a third wheel. The only space I was allowed to make any decisions about was my room. I decided to stay put though, and to make the best of it despite her. It was my own place, and I was still living in "Judi's house." Eventually, the three of us got along fine—probably because I was always working and hardly ever home.

◆　◆　◆　◆

In late October of 1986, one of my cousins married his longtime girlfriend. She looked so pretty, and everyone could tell how happy they were just by looking at them. Needless to say, it got me thinking about getting married. It wasn't like I was looking to get married in the near future. It was more that someday I might want to be married just like every other normal person.

I was still working my two jobs, but I wasn't getting anywhere. I needed to make more money, so I started looking for a job that would pay better and maybe even provide benefits. I found a full time job at a law library doing data entry, filing, and book cataloging, and quit my job at

Mass Mutual.

As soon as I started working at the library, I left my job at the gym and got a second job working in a popular restaurant that was literally right down the street from where I lived. The restaurant was part of an inn, and was considered a fine dining establishment.

As a Christmas gift in 1986, I gave Judi and her husband a weekend package deal to stay there. Judi had told me that she and her husband had never had a real honeymoon, so I figured this would be a nice romantic getaway for the two of them. I had a fresh bouquet of roses along with a bottle of champagne waiting for them in their room, along with a sexy nightgown for Judi.

I made sure to work the weekend of their stay too, and still have the pictures of the three of us — me in my white cap, blue dress, and apron — with the two people I loved most in the world. It's one of my most cherished memories.

The restaurant was also where I met T. He was one of the bartenders, eight years older than me, and very smooth. He drove a Trans-Am, and until he met me, he had been living the ultimate bachelor's life. I was 26 years old now and thought of this as my first serious adult relationship. When I was with him, I felt older and wiser and more mature, but I still wasn't ready to talk about my childhood.

With T, I was treated to things I'd never really thought about before. In the past, I'd always offered and happily chipped in to pay for my share. This was definitely different. T wined and dined me, and gave me expensive gifts. He always knew the right thing to say, and when to say it. He showered me with a lot of attention, and when I spent the night at his place, he made it very romantic with candles and music. I really liked him and wanted the relationship to work.

I thought of this as a mature relationship and believed he was marriage material. The girls I worked with at the restaurant tried to warn me about him, but I was too into the relationship to listen. Things were good for quite a while, but after about two years, he started becoming bossy and rude. Then I got a tip from a co-worker that I listened to, and when I got out of work, I went to his apartment and waited for him. I caught him stumbling up the stairs, drunk and arm in arm with an ex-girlfriend. I took one look at the two of them and that was the end of T. It wasn't easy, and it hurt, but I was relieved that I hadn't told him about my stepfather.

Not too long after T and I broke up, I quit my job at the restaurant. The owner caught me ladling soup the wrong way and yelled at me. I tried to explain to him that the customer had asked for it that way, but he wouldn't listen. So I went downstairs, changed out of my uniform, and walked out. I made good money there, but I'd had enough of people yelling at me. I'd been yelled at when I was a kid at home and had decided that no one was going to treat me that way as an adult. It felt good to stand up for myself. Fortunately, I still had my job at the law library.

While I was working there, I became friends with a co-worker who was attending law school and working part time at the library. She was a shy skinny girl with nerdy glasses who sat across from me, our computers between us. Over time, our friendship grew and we began revealing bits and pieces about ourselves from behind our computers.

It didn't take long for me to realize what a special friend she was. I felt so comfortable talking to her that I just knew I could trust her. It wasn't even like I made a decision to do it, and I didn't just blurt the whole thing out, but one day I started talking about my childhood. Maybe it was easier to tell her because our big clunky monitors were back to back between us, so I couldn't see her face, or her expression, while I was talking. Telling her wasn't exactly easy, but I didn't feel dirty telling her about it. I didn't feel uncomfortable either. It was simply a huge relief to finally tell someone and not have them treat me like I was different afterwards.

After about a week, she'd heard the whole story. I hadn't gone into every detail, but, for the first time, I'd told the story of my abuse to someone outside of my family. We don't live as near to each other as we did back then, but she was — and still is — a very dear and trusted friend.

I was still living in the apartment with my cousin and his girlfriend, but when the older couple living in the first floor apartment moved out, I told Judi I wanted to move into it. She thought it was a good decision, and the deal was done.

I was thrilled. I finally had the independence I was looking for, but now I had to pay all of the rent and utilities on my own. Fortunately, I'd been saving money. Now I just needed to find another waitressing job. Even if I had to work seven days a week, I had my own place, and that meant I was moving along.

Relationships

I was a good waitress, so I quickly found a job at a steak restaurant in West Springfield. It meant I would be working every weekend, all weekend long, but that was okay. Between working there and the law library, I was making enough money to keep my apartment. The only problem with working so much was that it was hard to find time for food shopping, laundry, and house work. I was always busy and on the go... and I thrived on it.

After I'd been working at the restaurant for a while, the restaurant manager, R, invited me out for drinks after work one night. At first I thought he was actually asking me out, but then I found out that a bunch of people from the restaurant would go out together after work on a semi-regular basis. I was happy to say yes because now that I was working all weekend, I didn't have any time to go out and meet new people anyway. Still, it was nice of R to ask, and his invite got me thinking about him.

R was an attractive funny guy with a good personality, and definitely a little bit on the wild side. I don't exactly remember when, but at some point we started dating. I found out that his father had raised his family with a strict hand. He said his sisters were all well-behaved, but I knew that R drank, partied, and went to concerts — all things I'd never done before. Still, I'd always heard that opposites attract, so I gave it a go.

We hit it off so well that after a few months I asked him if he wanted to move in with me. It was a big step for me because I'd never lived with a guy before. But I was ready to see where this relationship could go. He said yes, moved in, and we lived together in my apartment until we decided to rent a house for just the two of us.

Over time, I began to realize that R partied way too much and was probably not good marriage material. I wasn't exactly looking for a husband, but the thought of a long-term relationship was always in the back of my mind. Needless to say, we started drifting apart. We both realized it too, and decided to rekindle the romance with a trip to Jamaica.

I booked the trip through the Liberty Travel office at the Holyoke Mall. While I was making arrangements with them, I found out they had an opening for a travel agent. Once I told them I'd gone to travel school in Florida, they said they wanted to talk to me about the position as soon as I got back from my trip!

What I remember about Jamaica was that it was very humid. I knew R and I were supposed to be having a good time vacationing together, but I was excited to get back home so I could go for my interview. After we got back, I interviewed for the job and was hired. I immediately gave notice at both the law library and the restaurant so I could finally focus on my new career.

It had certainly taken longer than I expected, but it was my dream job! I finally was a travel agent! As part of the training for my new job, I had to spend a month at their training facility in Ramsey, NJ. It was tiring driving back and forth on the weekends, but it was also exciting and I envisioned all kinds of faraway vacation destinations in my future.

After the month-long training, it became clear that my relationship with R was going nowhere. Maybe it was because my past kept getting in the way. I still hadn't told R about my stepfather, and didn't feel like we were ever going to be in a place where I could. Maybe it was because I'd seen him talking with one of the waitresses at the restaurant and it looked like he was flirting with her. I didn't want to be caught by surprise — not again. Maybe I was just a bitch. Whatever. I found a nice efficiency apartment close to the mall and moved into it while he was at work. I called him to tell him our relationship was over and that I'd already moved out. He said he was too busy to talk, but it didn't sound like he cared one way or the other, and that was the end of that.

It might sound like moving out that way was a cowardly thing to do, but I actually felt empowered. In the past, I would have waited until something happened. This time I didn't wait. For the first time, I took a stand and ended a relationship because it was a good thing to do *for me*. I was starting to realize that I had power over my life and could do things *I* wanted to do. It felt good.

◆　◆　◆　◆　◆

I absolutely loved my career as a travel agent. My apartment was so close to the mall that I could have walked to work. Because the office was located in the mall, it was open mall hours and that meant working a lot of nights and weekends. But I was used to working long hours, so it didn't bother me. Life was good.

There were seven people working in that office and we all had a good time while we were working. Planning trips for people was very exciting and rewarding, and it gave me a sense of fulfillment. I knew my customers liked the work I did for them too because they kept coming back to me and asking me to help them plan their trips time and time again. I can honestly say that I never had a bad experience as a travel agent. It was, without a doubt, the best job I ever had. I got to take some of my dream vacations, traveling to California, Florida, Hawaii, Jamaica, Cancun, Antigua, St. Lucia, and London!

◆　◆　◆　◆　◆

As time went by, my sisters grew closer to my mother while my relationship with her seemed to be moving in the opposite direction. I fully expected her to show up at my office asking me to book a free trip for her, but thankfully it never happened.

Most of the time it was a case of "out of sight—out of mind" for me. Whenever we all ended up at the same family function, my sisters were indifferent towards me. It was basically impossible to have a good conversation with my mother, so we all just continued to keep our distance from one another. Looking back at it now, I can see that the distance between us made it a lot easier for me when my story became public knowledge.

Judi and I on the other hand, always remained close. She was there for me through all the jobs and all the boyfriends. We were as close to being a true mother and daughter team as anyone could be. My cousins were all out of school by then, and even though we didn't see each other very often, we all kept in touch through Judi.

Judi and I talked on the phone a lot too. If she needed something from the mall, or help with an errand, she would call me and I would take care of it for her. After a while, she gave me the nickname "Princess." I was her princess and would do whatever she asked.

Then a friend of a friend told me about this guy named G. She said he was a nice guy, not bad looking, owned his own business, and that I should meet him. G and I finally met, and he was just about everything my friend said he was. By day, he ran a landscaping business — which meant that he owned a trailer, a few lawn mowers, and a couple of leaf blowers. By night, he was a bartender.

All these years later, I can definitely see the pattern I was stuck in when it came to men. I just couldn't seem to get away from guys like this! If I had taken the time to sit down and analyze my history with men back then, I might have run in the opposite direction screaming when I met him. But he seemed like a nice enough guy, so what the heck I thought. Why not give it a shot?

Dad

In June of 1990, I said yes to being a bridesmaid at my sister Keri's wedding. Months before the wedding, she started teasing me about her finding a husband and getting married before I did. I didn't care, but that didn't stop her from trying to rub it in. All that her constant remarks managed to accomplish was to show how immature she was. I simply hadn't found anybody I wanted to marry yet. I wasn't in a rush either. I had no idea if G was going to be the right guy, but he agreed to escort me to the wedding.

One of the people attending the wedding was my stepfather's cousin. I had known her forever. When she was married and raising four kids of her own, I used to babysit for her. We still had a good relationship, and she was one of the few people in my family who didn't make me feel like I didn't belong.

By the time the wedding rolled around, she was divorced and had a new boyfriend named Ron. When she introduced me to Ron at the wedding, she had a big smile on her face. He was kind of tough and rugged looking, but there was just something about him. Then I remembered finding some old letters with the name Ronnie written across the envelopes hidden away in the basement of my mother's house. Funny coincidence I thought. We exchanged pleasantries, and then I excused myself and asked her to meet me in the ladies room.

As soon as we got in the ladies room, I checked to make sure we were alone. Once I was satisfied it was just the two of us I turned to her. "Is Ron my real father?" I asked.

"Yes he is! Couldn't you tell? You look just like him!" She was smiling and there were tears in her eyes. She was genuinely happy for me.

"Oh my God," I said. "I've waited so long to meet him. I can't believe I just did. This is so cool. Is he a nice guy?"

"Yes he is. He's very mellow and laid back. You'll love him."

Well, you can imagine how fast my mind was spinning, but in a good way. *I might actually be able to have a relationship with my real father,* I thought. The mystery man I'd been thinking about for almost half my life was alive and well and standing in the other room. It was overwhelming. But as happy about this meeting as she and I were, we both agreed that the wedding reception wasn't the proper setting for a family reunion. So I asked her to tell him to call me at work the next day so we could arrange a get-together.

When we left the ladies room, I watched her walk over to Ron and whisper in his ear. All around me people were laughing, drinking, and dancing to Italian music. But I was lost in thoughts of my father. I was so excited. I just kept replaying different scenarios of what our first get-together would be like over and over in my mind.

I made my way back to the head table thinking about what my mother had told me all those years ago, "Your father died in Vietnam." Years later, when I finally asked her why she had lied to me about my father, all she said was, "You don't need to know."

Right then it didn't matter what she'd told me. Now I knew it was all a lie and I felt such a sense of relief thinking that I might finally get the answers I'd longed for. There was a chance—a real chance—I might finally be part of a normal family. I was cautiously and wildly optimistic all at the same time. I was eager to know my father, and truly hoped he felt the same way towards me.

The list of questions I wanted to know the answers to started running through my mind. Did he ever see me after I was born? Had he thought about me during all those years? What kind of family did he have? Where did he live? What kind of work did he do? Did I really look like him? Did he think we looked alike? Did I look like anyone else in his family? Did I say the right things when we met? What would his family think of all this? What would my family think of all this? How much does he know about me? Would he be disappointed when he got to know me?

I could sense a shift in my life, and that was great because I was more than ready for it. I felt entitled to the change and the truth that would come along with it. I had endured my idiot family long enough and had made it this far without their encouragement or support. I hadn't come through it unscathed, but I believed my life was about to change for the better.

I scanned the crowd in hopes of seeing Ron again and spotted him dancing. *What must he be thinking?* I wondered. I looked around the room and wondered if there were other people who knew who Ron was and that I'd just met my real father. It stood to reason that other people knew, but if that was true, why hadn't somebody told me? I definitely had mixed emotions about that.

Shifting my head to the opposite side of the dance floor, I caught my mother glaring at me, and wondered what she was thinking. She was not smiling. I stared right back at her until she turned away. This was going to be interesting.

I realized Keri must have known all along too. Obviously my mother had told her, but how long had Keri known? She'd been tormenting me for years saying that she knew who my real father was. Had she really known? It almost didn't matter. She had clearly enjoyed playing her mean little game at my expense. She'd used it to make herself feel powerful and special, but all it did was make her pathetic. I suddenly couldn't believe I was standing up for her at her wedding. I felt nothing for her.

I told G I had to speak to Judi, and left him to find her. She was by the dance floor swaying to the music, and I was barely able to contain the excitement I was feeling as I approached her. When our eyes met, I could tell by the look on her face that she knew I had finally learned the truth.

"Kathy, I'm so sorry, but your parents made me promise never to tell you," she said with an apologetic smile.

"I know Judi, it's okay."

"So what do you think?" She asked, her blue eyes regaining their sparkle. "It's pretty exciting."

"I'll say. I can't wait to talk to him. He's going to call me at work tomorrow so we can make plans to get together."

"Sweetie, I've known Ron since your mother and I were kids. He's a nice guy."

"Thanks Judi. Coming from you, that means a lot. I love you," I said, and hugged her.

"I love you too Princess."

Whenever I think about that day, there are two things I remember above everything else that happened. I remember meeting my father, and I remember that brief conversation with my Aunt Judi.

◆　◆　◆　◆　◆

The following Monday was a typical work day at the travel agency, with just a slight difference. My real father, the missing piece in the puzzle of my life, was going to call me! I knew how important this call was, and what it could mean to the both of us. My father would be gaining a daughter. And I would finally have a normal father *and* a chance to be a part of a normal loving family.

I hoped he would call first thing in the morning, and when I got to work I filled my coworkers in on what was going on. They were all supportive and excited for me. As the hours crawled by though, he didn't call and I began to get nervous. What if he'd changed his mind? Maybe he'd decided he didn't want a grown daughter in his life, or that he didn't want to be my father. Those thoughts kept bombarding my mind and heart until he finally called.

Because of his busy work schedule, we couldn't meet until that Friday night. We agreed on pizza and beer at his place, and I was surprised at the address he gave me. I knew exactly where he lived. It was only a few miles from where I'd grown up. I'd driven right past his home hundreds of times over the years.

You can imagine how slow that week went by. I usually have a lot of nervous energy anyway, and the waiting just about sent me right over the top. When something is on my mind, I have to analyze it from all angles and talk it to death, and I know I drove G crazy talking about meeting with my father. Judi was only a phone call away and we talked a few times that week too, but G took the brunt of it. The new boyfriend didn't seem to mind though. He responded like Mr. Wonderful.

The girls at work tried to keep me busy so I wouldn't have too much time to dwell on what lay ahead. I have to admit though, the extra days gave me time to think and calm myself down. By the time Friday rolled around, I was still anxious, but I'd relaxed a bit.

When I got out of work on Friday, I drove straight over to Ron's house. I was 28 years old, but I felt as if my life was starting all over again. I was being reintroduced to my rightful family, and all I wanted to do was to fit in.

I rang the bell and we hugged awkwardly at the door. Even though he was a stranger to me, he had the blessings of two people I loved and respected, so I wasn't the least bit afraid of the door closing behind me. I looked around nervously, and could tell he was a bachelor. Not because his place was messy or anything like that. It just had a comfortable rumpled masculine feel to it.

We made our way to the living room and I could see that he had spread out his photo albums on the coffee table. As I settled onto the couch, Ron offered me a beer. I said yes, and then we sat there nervously exchanging small talk about the past week and my sister's wedding. It was slow going at first, but after a while our conversation became more natural.

"It's finally nice to know you," he said. "It seems weird saying that to my daughter, but you were too young to remember me when you were a little girl. We would have met much sooner, but your sister kept playing this game with me. First, she told me you wanted to meet me, then after a few weeks she said you changed your mind. She went back and forth like that for quite a while. Each time I got my hopes up about finally meeting you, she'd call and give me the bad news. Did you know she was doing that?" he asked.

I shook my head. "No. I had no idea. I didn't even know who you were up until I met you at her wedding. I'm sorry, but she never told me anything about you at all." I could feel my voice rising as I got angrier. It was easy to imagine my mother and sister in cahoots with each other. As soon as they'd found out who Ron had started dating, they knew they had a problem. "Keri's been meddling and troublesome since she was a kid. She's close to my mother, so they must have talked and decided to try and stop us from getting together. I don't know why, but I'm sure they had their own super twisted reasons."

I was furious that my mother and sister had worked so hard to keep me from meeting my real father, but I wasn't surprised. Those two seemed to enjoy teasing and hurting others.

"Well, that's behind us now," Ron said. "Your cousin stepped in and put an end to it. She knew you and I would both be at the wedding and figured it was time the two of us met. Let's forget about them and concentrate on getting to know each another." And with that said, he ordered a pizza, and we started going through the photo albums while we waited for it to be delivered.

He showed me pictures of his parents when they were younger. His mother came from a big family that owned a dairy farm in Vermont. When she was a young woman, she came to Springfield and moved in with an older sister while she looked for work. His father was a mechanic who contracted polio and needed braces and crutches to get around. His parents met by chance, fell in love, got married, and had two boys and two girls. Ron was the oldest. His father passed away in 1985, but his mother was still alive and lived in the house he grew up in — right next door! He showed me pictures of his brother and sisters too, and it was nice to see what he'd looked like through the years. During summer vacations, Ron and his brother had been shipped to the family farm in Vermont. His parents wanted him to learn the value of hard work, but they also wanted to keep him and his brother out of trouble during the summer. Ron still managed to find trouble though, especially with my mom.

It was a strange feeling, seeing all those pictures of people for the first time and knowing that each one of them was a blood relative of mine. I learned that I had a half-brother named Scott. I had aunts and uncles and cousins too — a whole family of relatives who might actually be normal.

Ron even had a few pictures of me when I was a baby. I looked at them and couldn't help but reach out and touch them. I wondered if he'd ever looked at them over the years. Was he sad? Did he miss me? Did he even think he would see me again? Looking at him that night, with his rough hands and weathered features, it made me feel good that he had kept and preserved these tiny memories of me for all these years.

I really wanted to know more about the time Ron spent with my mother and how I fit into the story. Trying to get any information from my mother had been like trying to quench a thirst with a single drop of water at the bottom of a dirty glass. So when we took a break from flipping through the photo albums, I asked him. He needed some prodding, but he finally opened up — a little.

Ron and my mother had met in junior high. He would ride his bike over to her house when they were younger, but when he was old enough to get his driver's license, he would drive to her house and bring her to school in his father's car. That was around 1960. He said that my grammy seemed to like him, but my grandfather didn't, so he never spent much time at their house.

It sounded like they were typical 1960's teenagers. They went roller skating sometimes, and if my mom could sneak out of the house at night, they made their way to the Park Way Drive-In Theater. Another favorite pastime for them was hanging out with Ron's buddies, shooting the bull, and looking at cars.

There are a lot of people who believe that when a guy gets a girl pregnant, the proper thing to do is to marry her. From what Ron confided in me (I called him "Ron" because it was hard to think of him as Dad that first night) he would have quit school and gotten a job, but his mother told him that doing that, or getting married, would be a terrible mistake. She told him that if he quit school he'd end up working at a gas station pumping gas his whole life. That thought scared him enough to stay in school and graduate.

I can imagine my mother nagging him, but he never asked her to marry him. By the time I was born, summer vacation was almost over. Ron went back to school, enrolling in a co-op program that had him going to school for a week and then going to work the next week. His schedule alternated like that, but he had other outside jobs too. He worked picking apples, pruning trees, and doing other various farm chores. Nights and Saturdays, he worked at Truss Engineering running saws, pounding nails, and building trusses.

I learned other things about what happened all those years ago too. I wasn't surprised to find out that my mother didn't have many girlfriends. All the girls her age were still in school. They weren't at home being a mom. So the only people she had to hang out with were her younger sister and my Aunt Judi.

Ron said he spent as much time with my mother and me as he could. They took me with them when they went roller skating. In the winter, he took me sledding at Forest Park. They even made a small bed for me in the back seat of his car for when they went to the drive-in. Sadly, I was too young to remember any of this.

I could tell there were times when he was trying to be tactful, but all the tact in the world wasn't going to change who my mother was. I knew exactly how she treated people, so I wasn't surprised to hear how she'd treated him. It would be easy to blame her moods on the stress of being a teenage parent, except that she's had those same moods for as long as I've known her. I've experienced those moods firsthand.

Like I said, people always noticed my mother. What people didn't see was the way she was when she knew other people weren't looking. Ron admitted to having experienced her moods firsthand too. Sometimes, when she lost her temper, or fought with him, she'd scratch him bad enough to draw blood.

When I was three or four years old, Ron and my mother had a falling out and split up for good. My mother ended up going with another guy — my stepfather — to make Ron jealous. It didn't work. In 1967, Ron was drafted. He was 22 years old and spent the next thirteen months of his life in Vietnam.

By the time he'd returned home from the war, my mom had married my stepfather and now had a set of twin girls in addition to me. My stepfather had formally adopted me by then, and threatened Ron to make sure he stayed away from me. I was never told anything because someone decided it would be better if I didn't know my stepfather wasn't my real father. "Shhh.... Best not to confuse the child."

One of the reasons it took so long for me to figure out what really happened, and who my real father was, was because my stepfather's name was on my birth certificate. It was one of the first things I checked. I still don't know how they managed that.

Truth

As our conversation progressed, Ron asked me about myself too. He wanted to hear how my life had been going up to this point. In the days leading up to that night, I hadn't given any thought to if — or how — I was going to handle telling him about being molested and raped by my stepfather. I didn't want to bring it up because I wanted our first experience together to be special and positive. I wanted my real father to like me. But since he wanted to know, and I wanted to be open and honest, I told him the entire truth of what my stepfather had done to me.

His reaction wasn't what I expected. His facial expression never changed, and when I was done, all I wanted to do was to take it all back. In my mind, I was afraid that I'd made a mistake telling him, but he'd said he wanted to know about me, and this was a big part of my past.

When I'd finished, he didn't ask any questions or offer any condolences. It was almost like he wasn't even interested. He didn't wince, give me a hug, or pat my hand — nothing. No, the man I'd been thinking about from the moment I knew he existed, who was now sitting right in front of me, had just heard one doozy of a story, and barely blinked an eye.

Is it any wonder victims don't say anything? I'd poured out my secret and didn't get any kind of response from him. I wasn't even sure he believed me. Now I can look back at that night and cut him some slack for not knowing how to respond to what he'd heard. Most people don't know what to do or say when they hear something like this for the first time. It wasn't like he could go back and change it or fix it even if he wanted to. It wasn't like I wanted him to feel sorry for me either. It just would have been nice if he'd reacted a little bit — at least enough so that I knew he cared a little bit about me.

Still, I was glad I'd been upfront with him about my past. I couldn't hold it in and felt such a great sense of relief after it had all spilled out. That night took place in 1991, and he's never brought the subject up since.

In his defense, he was brought up in a society where such things were not openly discussed. I understood that part of it all too well. I can't say that I'd wish we'd talked about it more that night either. I was so happy to meet him, and in some ways glad that our new relationship didn't include discussions about that part of my life. Instead, we enjoyed the pizza and beer. When we were done eating, he showed me more photos of my new family.

It was getting late and I didn't want to overstay my welcome. I knew that Ron owned his own construction company and probably had to get up early the next morning. But one of the last things he told me was that over the years he would occasionally bump into my Grammy and she would fill him in on what was going on in my life. When he found out I was working at Friendly's, he stopped in for a meal every once in a while so he could see me.

"So you see Kathy, I never really left you. I was always around."

When I was finally home and in my bed that night, I couldn't sleep. I just rested with my eyes closed, happily reliving the best parts of the evening over and over again in my mind.

Building and Breaking

Shortly after that first visit with my father, I received a phone call from Keri. We hadn't talked since her wedding, but it wasn't like we talked on the phone to stay in touch with each other. The few phone conversations we'd had before the wedding were short and to the point, and all about making sure I was doing what I was supposed to be doing for her wedding.

When I answered, she got right to the point and said that as far as she was concerned, I didn't deserve to meet my real father. She accused me of wanting to meet him because I knew he had money, and that's what I was after.

I tried to explain to her that I wanted to meet him and get to know him because he was my real father, but I was wasting my breath. She started yelling and screaming at me, so I hung up on her. Like I said before, I was tired of people yelling at me for things that I didn't do.

It was definitely a bizarre phone conversation, and I was angry when I hung up, but also a little bit happy. She wasn't going to be able to change what happened. My father and I had finally met, and nobody in my idiot family could ever take that away from me!

◆　◆　◆　◆　◆

My father held a big cookout in his backyard so I could meet the rest of my real family. Everybody brought a dish, and while burgers and hotdogs sizzled on the grill, I mingled with the biological aunts, uncles, and cousins I'd been denied up until now. I met my grandmother who lived next door in the house Ron had grown up in. I got to meet my half-brother Scott too.

My "new" aunts talked about how they kept asking my mother to bring me over for a visit. She never did though. Instead, she totally cut me off from them. I never really understood why she would do that until I started writing about my life.

Now I think she was mad at Ron because he didn't marry her. Back then, that was what people did. If you got a girl pregnant, you married her. He didn't. I know my mother well enough to know she probably kept nagging him about asking her. When he still didn't ask, she tried to make him jealous by cheating on him. I can certainly understand why they broke up after that.

Maybe that's another reason why my mother has always treated me differently than my sisters. She blamed me for her and Ron's break-up. If I hadn't been around, maybe he would have eventually asked her to marry him. After that, maybe she'd decided that if she couldn't be a part of his family, then I never would be either. It might have all been a simple grudge she's held against me my whole life.

I didn't care at that point because 1991 was a good year. I'd inherited a large family, had a job I loved, and was traveling all over the world with Liberty Travel. Things were good with G, and as the months went by, my father and I got closer. One day he surprised me with an amazing gift. He told me it was so we could start making some new memories to make up for all the memories we'd missed out on over the years. His gift was a 1990 Grand AM. It was totally unexpected, and definitely a great memory to begin with. Good 'ole Dad.

◆　◆　◆　◆　◆

Eventually, I moved out of my efficiency apartment and into a condo G had found for us to rent. One night when G was working, Judi came over with a house-warming gift and we spent a few hours together just sitting and talking. That was one of the things I loved about my relationship with Judi. It didn't matter if we were talking on the phone, or sitting face to face, we never ran out of things to talk about. It was just always so easy to talk to her, and it was nice that she was willing to go out of her way to stop by the condo to check it out.

My mother never visited while I was living there. She hadn't stopped by any of the places I'd lived for a "friendly" visit since that first and only visit when she'd helped me hang curtains in my first apartment.

That was fine with me. At that point in my life I had no communication with my stepfather of any kind, and there was very little interaction between me and my mother or sisters. I knew they were all upset about me reconnecting with my father because one of my cousins told me. I didn't care. I was happy for the distance. Who needs or wants people like that always trying to interfere and make you feel bad?

◆ ◆ ◆ ◆ ◆

For so long I'd wanted to confide in my Aunt Judi about my childhood. I finally found the courage on a Saturday afternoon when Judi stopped by for a visit. I hadn't planned to tell her, it just happened. As usual, G was at work, and while Judi and I were sitting on the couch with our tea, I said that I wanted to talk about my childhood.

As I told her my story in detail, her eyes welled with tears and she kept whispering how sorry she was. I explained how going to her home had helped me get away from my stepfather, and how much I'd wished I'd been a part of her family instead. She said she'd wished I had been her daughter too. We cried and hugged each other, but she didn't leave. She stayed and we talked for hours.

It's hard to explain the sense of relief that came along with telling her. I had always felt like she loved me, but now I knew it was real. I never doubted that she loved me, but when you have a childhood like mine, it's always in the back of your mind that someone will look at you and know that you're different — that you're not *normal* like they are. But there was as much love in Judi's eyes after I told her as there was before I told her. She responded the way I thought a *normal* mother should react when she heard what happened. It was way past the time when she could have done something about it, but it was reassuring to know that someone could hear my story and still love me.

◆ ◆ ◆ ◆ ◆

Around that same time, I received a call from my father giving me a heads-up. He'd spotted G with another girl at a bar in Holyoke. I knew G had been working a lot, but I was working a lot too, so I didn't think too much about it.

When I confronted G about it, he denied it and said it had to be a mistake because he was working that night. I believed him. Ron hadn't actually gone up to talk to G when he'd seen him, so maybe it was just a misunderstanding. Maybe it had been really dark in the bar. I let it go, but a seed of suspicion had been planted and taken root.

Now I started paying more attention to our life together, and our relationship was never the same. For example, I threw him a surprise 30th birthday party only to find out shortly after that he wasn't 30. When I asked him how old he was, he replied, "How old do you want me to be?" I tried to get a look at his driver's license to verify his age, but he said it had slipped between the dash and the windshield of his truck. That was another lie. I found out from one of his ex-girlfriends that he was 28 years old and that he'd let his driver's license expire years ago.

Suddenly it felt like everything he told me was a lie. I found out there were times when I thought he was out landscaping, when he was actually sitting on his parent's couch watching TV.

Once again, my world was turned upside down and I was kicking myself for falling for another loser. What was wrong with me?! Part of me didn't believe there was really anything wrong with me, but I had to be doing something wrong. I didn't know how to stop what was happening, or how to fix it either. Unfortunately, our relationship wasn't the only thing I had trouble with.

◆　◆　◆　◆　◆

In 1993, I thought my job at Liberty Travel was going well, but then there was a major misunderstanding about something I was supposed to do. I didn't realize I was supposed to do it, and the owner didn't care that I didn't know. I lost my dream job as a result.

I suppose I could have tried to find another travel agent job, but it was one of those situations where you just don't want to go back. Instead, I went back to Mass Mutual. I got rehired for the same position I'd had when I originally started there over ten years ago—group accounting. It was a tough move because it made me feel like I was right back where I'd started.

As it happened, I ended up working with another aunt—my mother's younger sister, Jane. (Remember in the beginning when I explained that my Grammy was pregnant at the same time my mother was pregnant? My Aunt Jane was the baby my Grammy had shortly after I was born.) It wasn't like we were hanging out together outside of work or anything like that, but we had a good working relationship for at least a year. Then my mother found out we were working in the same department and that was that. My aunt stopped talking to me.

By that point, I'd pretty much reached my limit with everybody and everything. I was run down, tired all the time, and had nowhere else to turn. Out of desperation, I started seeing one of the in-house counselors at Mass Mutual. I wanted and needed an unbiased, professional opinion about issues like G. This was the first time I'd ever been to counseling, so I wasn't sure how it would work out, but it was convenient. I could see the counselor during regular working hours and the first ten sessions were free.

Our first meeting covered a lot of ground. My counselor said we could talk about anything, so I started by talking about my relationship with G. With all the questions he asked, it wasn't long before I was telling him about being molested by my stepfather as a young girl.

He offered some good advice about G. He then suggested that maybe my mother and stepfather could come in for a session so the three of us could work through this issue together. Right after the session, I called my mother. When I told her why I was calling, she said, "Counseling? For what Kathy? Nothing happened. I gotta go." Then she hung up on me.

I'd never actually stood face to face with my mother and told her what her husband had done to me as a little girl. And now I realized I was still a scared victim. I'd tried to tell her that day on the phone, but she hung up before I could really say anything. Needless to say, my mother and stepfather never came to counseling.

I didn't care. I still went because counseling was helping me deal with issues like the ones I had with G. It was also helping me confront the issue of being molested. It may not have been the first time I'd told the story of what happened to me (and it definitely wouldn't be the last!), but it was hugely important for me to tell my story to a trained professional. My counselor made it very clear to me that what had been done to me was not my fault. I was an innocent victim. He also suggested trying to get my mother to come in so I could tell her what happened, and explain that I needed her help as my mother. That never happened either.

Grammy

Things were as bad as ever with my idiot family, but they got worse. In early October of 1993, there was a fire drill at work. Since my Aunt Jane and I worked in the same department, I looked for her when we were all outside. I didn't see her anywhere, so I asked a couple of co-workers if they'd seen her. One of them told me that her sister (my mother) had come to pick her up at work because there was a family emergency.

When we were let back inside, I called my mother's house and was told my Grammy had passed away. My mother had come to Mass Mutual to pick up my aunt, but didn't even have the common decency to tell me about my grandmother.

I never saw my grandmother again — not at the wake or the funeral. No one told me anything about what was happening, and it was clear I wasn't "invited." Even if I'd wanted to, I couldn't bring myself to go to my mother's house for fear of seeing my stepfather. I knew what he did to me wasn't my fault, and I knew he was never ever going to touch me again, but knowing didn't stop the sickening twist I got in my gut at even just the thought of seeing him.

Nowadays, that twist isn't anywhere near as bad as it had been when he was molesting me. Now, it only lasts for a second or two while I remind myself that I will never ever be his victim again, that there's nothing wrong with me, and that he's the one who should feel disgusted and ashamed for what he did.

◆　◆　◆　◆　◆

Grammy's passing was one of those events I look back at and can only guess at what my family was thinking. In some ways it was just another example of dealing with my idiot family. But who does something like that? It was like they had decided not to have anything to do with me.

I think one of the reasons my family was intentionally cutting me out was because I now had a relationship with my biological father and family, and it pissed them off. Why? Well, probably because they were figuring out they couldn't control me anymore. But also because I was learning the truth about my life and they couldn't stand to see me happy about it.

I wanted to talk to my mother. Maybe I wanted to make sure she knew that even though I was getting to know the other part of my family, she was still my mom and I loved her. But I needed to talk to her about what my stepfather had done to me too. I didn't know how much she knew, and I wanted her to hear the whole story from me.

I also wanted to talk to her because I'd found out that my sister Meri's daughter, Roxy, was living with them, and I was truly afraid for her. The court had given my mother and stepfather custody of Roxy because her mother was unable to care for her.

When I finally got my mother on the phone, I steered the conversation towards what needed to be said, but she interrupted me before I could really say anything. "Kathy, nothing ever happened, and we have nothing to talk about."

It was always the same with my idiot family. "Let's all pretend nothing happened." It was so frustrating to reach out and try to have an honest conversation with my mother only to have her dismiss what I was saying and hang up on me—again. So in March of that year, I wrote her a twelve page letter instead. In the letter, I told her what her husband had done to me as a little girl. I expressed the guilt and shame I felt back then, and still felt on the day I wrote that letter. I also expressed concern for the niece now living in the same house I grew up in. Roxy was only four years old when I wrote the letter, but it didn't matter. I knew she was in danger.

I didn't trust my stepfather, or my sisters, to give the letter to my mother if I sent it to the house. Instead, I sent it certified mail with a signature required to where she worked.

I still have a copy of that letter, and reread it while I was working on this book. I couldn't believe how many times I told her I loved her. I said that as mother and daughter, we could work things out. I also said that I was reaching out to her, and all she had to do was to reach out to me. The letter was delivered and signed for, but she never responded, and that was the last attempt I made to contact my mother.

Despite my feelings for him, I called my stepfather too. I don't know what I thought it would accomplish, but I suddenly asked him why he'd molested me. His answer was terrifying. "Because you were such a pretty happy kid… and not my real kid."

My thoughts immediately shifted to my fears about Roxy living in that house with him, and I asked him point blank if he was doing anything to her. He said no. He told me he'd quit drinking — as if he could blame what he'd done to me on alcohol alone. I didn't believe him, and there was no way I was going to sit around and do nothing.

I contacted social services to file a complaint. I told them what my stepfather had done to me and explained that I was concerned for my niece's safety. I didn't hear back from them, so I called them back. It took a while to find out who the caseworker was, but I finally did.

"Kathy, you need to back off. Your niece is living in a loving home." That's what the caseworker said to me.

From that point on, that side of my family — the idiot side — did what they were best at. They closed ranks against me and pretended to be one big happy family to everybody else. It was very frustrating because I didn't know what to do, while they had no problem doing what they'd always done — call me a liar and a troublemaker.

There were days when I wondered if my life was always going to be filled with drama. I'd lost my Grammy and I missed her. She was one of the only people in that side of my family I'd felt close to even though we didn't talk much. After she died, they had her cremated, so there wasn't even a grave to visit.

◆　◆　◆　◆　◆

There was always some kind of drama at work too. It would have been nice to talk with my Aunt Jane about some of it because she still worked there and probably would have understood, but she still wasn't speaking to me either.

31

I was 31 years old now, and I really needed a change. In the past, I'd have waited around for something to happen to me, but this time I decided to take action. I wanted a solid relationship and decided to give G one last chance. I also wanted a more permanent address, but one of our ongoing issues as a couple was that I worked and saved for the future while G lived for the day without any thought for tomorrow. I was tired of paying rent and not having anything to show for it. It was time to buy something.

Our options were limited, but after searching the market for what was available, we decided to look at mobile homes. In other parts of the country, people would have called our new neighborhood a trailer park. But in New England, it's referred to as a mobile home park. As if the word "park" meant your house didn't have rusty wheels.

I settled on a small blue and white unit that had potential, which means I purchased a dumpy trailer with a rusty hitch. It didn't matter. It was mine, all mine. G didn't have any money, so I put the money down and financed the rest through Mass Mutual. It had three big rooms, a side porch, a shed, and a clothesline. The previous owner even left the washer and dryer.

That entire spring, G and I spent all our spare time gutting and totally rebuilding it. G's father was retired by then and often stopped by to lend a hand, run small errands, or just to keep us company. G was a good carpenter, and when we were finished it was beautiful. Everything was brand new. It smelled like a brand new house, and for about $400 a month, it was the best deal around.

The mobile home park was neat and clean, and everybody looked out for everybody else. Many of the residents were elderly and had been living there for years. We got to know our neighbors, and soon after we moved in, the mobile home directly across from ours went up for sale.

G told his older brother Gary about it. G and I had been together for about three years now, so I'd known Gary for a while. He'd been living in Rhode Island with his wife and kids, but now he was going through a divorce and wanted to have more to show for himself than seven boxes in the back of his old hatch-back. He had child support to pay though, and the idea of buying a house with wheels didn't appeal to him. But when he heard how much it would cost, he called the real estate agent for a viewing.

When Gary saw it, he was pleasantly surprised. The mobile home had four big rooms, all of the appliances, including a washer and dryer, a huge porch, and a small yard with a shed. Beautiful pine trees throughout the community gave the place a "country" feel. It really was a no-brainer. He made an offer, put down a modest down payment when his offer was accepted, and moved in. A few days later, I left a house-warming gift by his kitchen door, a scented Yankee Candle called "Home Sweet Home."

G was still working nights at the bar while I was working days, so I was home alone almost every night. One night, not long after moving in, Gary called and asked for some help with curtains. His parents had given him some odds and ends to get started, but he still needed a few things. That night was the first time we'd ever spent any time together when we weren't just talking about his brother.

I already knew that Gary was a hard worker and I had a lot of respect for him simply because of that. In order to pay his child support, Gary grabbed up as much overtime as he could at his regular job, and then picked up an additional part-time job delivering the morning paper. He had over 150 customers, and was now working seven days a week, but he never missed a child support payment.

After hanging the curtains and going through the rest of what his parents had given him, we went to Friendly's for coffee and just talked and talked. From that night on, whenever he needed a hand around the house, he'd call and I'd go over.

One day I was surprised to see that he'd brought home a puppy. "Benson" was a mini-schnauzer, and Gary said he got him to alleviate the loneliness. Years later, he confided in me that he knew puppies were a bonafide "chick magnet." He also knew I liked animals. Yeah, I know how it sounds, but he and Benson were best buddies.

Things were okay with G, but we were working opposite schedules and didn't get to see each other as much as I would have liked. I visited him at the bar on a few occasions to say hi, but he always seemed agitated that I was there, so I stopped going to see him. Instead, I started going over to Gary's to play with Benson. Gary and I would throw Benson's toys around and he'd chase them all over, banging into everything. We had a lot of fun with that little puppy.

On Christmas Eve, it was Gary — not G — who accompanied me to a Christmas party at a friend's house. It wasn't a date. We just went as friends. After the party, he went home and I met up with G at the bar.

On New Year's Eve, G said he had to do inventory at work, so Gary invited me over for a movie and munchies. We drank champagne, and exchanged a friendly kiss when the ball dropped. I didn't realize until much later that nobody does inventory at a bar on New Year's Eve, and I'm glad I didn't sit home alone waiting for him that night.

I liked talking and doing things with Gary, but there wasn't anything going on between us. He was G's brother. On the other hand, I was beginning to get the feeling that something might be going on with G. I didn't know if he was cheating on me, but I didn't like the way things were going. Out of frustration, I forced a confrontation with him and asked him what was he doing with his life and where he thought our relationship was headed. His response was to drag me to the mall to look at engagement rings.

I guess that was his way of trying to show me what he wanted out of his life, and I know there are women who might have been thrilled at the gesture, but I wasn't one of them. It wasn't like he asked me to marry him — he didn't. He just took me to the mall to buy a ring. Then, thirty minutes after we got there, he said we had to leave because he had to go to work. And no, he didn't buy me a ring while we were there.

Right then and there, it was over for me. I think G believed that an engagement ring would make everything okay, but I also think he knew our relationship was basically over too. The only problem was that neither of us said or did anything about it. Right after that, G started coming home drunk and being really loud, or not coming home at all. It was clear that things were never going to work out between us, so I decided it was time to take a stand and told him he had to move out. G apologized, and I really think he was sorry, but it was too little, too late.

After G moved out, I felt a huge sense of relief. He may have been a good guy, but he wasn't the guy for me. Fortunately, I had purchased the mobile home without any financial help from him, so I didn't have to worry about moving. I was also making enough money to keep it. He took a few things with him when he left, but my home was still my home.

Gary

Winter mornings are cold in Massachusetts, and I got into the habit of going across the street to say "Good morning" to Gary and Benson while my car was warming up. Gary had finished his morning paper route by then, and had breakfast waiting for me. A girl could get used to that.

I was getting used to a lot of things with Gary. Neither of us had made a move on the other when I was with G, but I'd be lying if I said it hadn't been easy to hang out with Gary. It had been easy, and now, our relationship was changing.

In the spring of that year, while I was stopped at a stop sign on my way to work, I was rear-ended. I hate to admit it, but I wasn't wearing a seat belt (I do now!) and I got bounced around quite a bit. A policeman showed up and made his report, but the only damage we could see was a slight dent in the bumper.

I was shook up though, so instead of going to work, I turned around and went home. Over the next few hours, my neck started hurting. When the pain became unbearable, I called Gary at work and asked him if he would bring me to the Emergency Room. X-rays showed that I had several cracked cervical vertebrae. By the time we left the ER, I was in a neck brace and had a prescription for pain meds.

Now I could barely move and had no idea how I was going to cope with my situation. It wasn't like there were family members who could drop everything to stay with me. But Gary solved the problem for me. When we got back from the ER, he propped me up on his couch and told me I could stay with him while I was recovering. He asked me what I needed from next door, and within a few minutes, he was back with the items I had rattled off to him.

Even with the pain meds, those first few days were rough. I had excruciating pain in my arm, could barely move, and couldn't do anything for myself. Gary was there to help me, but it was hard not to be able to take care of myself. It was awkward at first too. Gary was just so great though, and for the first time in my life I felt like I could trust someone. It could have turned into a really stressful situation, but our feelings for each other continued to grow deeper.

Slowly, the pain, stiffness, and swelling went away, but I found out that I would need an operation to remove the damaged discs in my neck. The doctor was wonderful. He said the small incision he needed to make at the bottom of my neck would blend right in with my wrinkles, making it virtually unnoticeable. Gary said my face dropped when I heard the doctor say I had wrinkles on my neck. I thought I still looked 21!

A few weeks before my surgery, Gary went to visit his father. His father had been in and out of the hospital for years due to poor health, so it wasn't unusual that Gary visited him in the hospital that day. I found out later that while he was visiting, Gary mentioned that since G was now out of the picture, he would like to start dating me. His father and I had always gotten along, so he told Gary that he didn't see anything wrong with it. That was all Gary needed to hear.

Sadly, Gary's father passed away a few days after that conversation. At the wake, G noticed a floral arrangement from Gary and me, figured out we were together, and called him a scumbag. Through gritted teeth, their mother warned them not to create a scene at their father's wake. After the funeral though, Gary's mother told him that neither of us was welcome in her home again.

On the day I went in for neck surgery, Gary, my Aunt Judi, and her husband Uncle Moe sat and waited for me to come out of surgery. Gary and Judi talked and got to know each other better while drinking lousy hospital cafeteria coffee. The surgery went well, and when they wheeled me into my room later that day, all of them were by my bedside. It was quite emotional. I fainted on the way to the bathroom and Gary, my "Mr. Wonderful," caught me.

During my recovery, Gary continued to take very good care of me, and I was able to see how a "normal" person lived and worked during the five months I was out of work. Gary worked Monday to Friday, 8 – 5, with occasional overtime. During his lunch break, he drove home to check up on me. I spent all my time resting and playing with Benson.

Gary was home every night and all weekend long. He happily took me to my doctor's appointments and we became even closer. It was different being with Gary. We had been together for a while and I never felt like there was a reason to wonder what he was up to. I trusted him, and I felt safe with him. We were already basically living together, so the next step seemed logical. Why pay two mortgages? He was thrilled the day I told him he could move the rest of my stuff over to his house if he wanted to. Soon after that, I put my mobile home up for sale.

I'm not exactly sure when Gary first met Ron, but I warned him how it might go the first time they met. My father definitely has his own opinions. He is never wrong, and he's got his own way of doing things. As for what I said to my father beforehand, I told him I might end up marrying this guy, so could he please be nice to him.

Gary remembers going over to my father's house with me on a Sunday morning with a dozen donuts. My father was watching NASCAR and reading the Sunday paper. It was hard for me to tell if either of them was impressed with the other.

◆ ◆ ◆ ◆ ◆

Shortly after I had permanently moved in with Gary and Benson, I felt it was time for Gary to know about my past. I had told G, but I'd told him because I felt like I had to. I wasn't sure if Gary and I were going to be together forever, but if we were, he would need to know at some point.

When I'd told G, I hadn't told him everything. It was more like I told him bits and pieces of what happened, waiting to see how he'd react. I can't remember exactly how he reacted, but I didn't go into detail. It was just too uncomfortable.

Telling Gary felt different. I didn't feel like I had to tell him. I wanted to tell him. We'd known each other for a long time by now, and had already gone through a lot together. I didn't want to hide this secret from him. I already trusted him with everything else about my life, and I felt like I could trust him with this too.

After he heard my story, he looked at me and told me he already knew. His mother had said something about it to him in passing when he first moved back home. He told me that he saw the way I interacted with other people, and how warm and friendly I was even though my childhood had been so terrible. He said he'd watched me put up with his brother for all those years and knew that if I could live through that—and my childhood—and still turn out to be the person I was now, then I was very special and he would do whatever he could to win me over. That's when I knew Gary was a keeper.

I slowly started to introduce Gary to my extended family, which is to say Judi's family. He was quiet and shy with my cousins. All they ever talked about was sports, and because Gary wasn't really interested in sports, they didn't have much to talk about. Still, we were invited to all their kid's birthday parties, family and holiday get-togethers, etc.

Needless to say, there weren't a lot of invitations from Gary's family. His mother still didn't want anything to do with us, and the rest of his family was really spread out. Gary tried to see his kids as often as he could, but his ex-wife made it very difficult. Years later, we found out his kids never saw the child support money he was sending. Instead, the money had been used by his ex to support her, her live-in boyfriend, and all their bad habits. As soon as his kids were of age and Gary no longer had to send checks, the boyfriend moved out. His kids had just believed he was a "deadbeat" dad because that's what their mother had told them.

We spent time with my father's family too. We went to family reunions, picnics, and graduations, and spending Christmas Eve at my father's brother's house became a yearly tradition. It wasn't like I had escaped all the drama, but I was beginning to understand what it must be like to be part of a regular family. Granted, our branch of this family was small, just Gary and me and Benson, but our small family was part of Judi's bigger family, and my real father's family too. It was nice. It was like I was part of a real family where everything was kind of blissfully normal.

Ups and Downs

Life in the mobile home park was good. Our neighbors were terrific. Gary and I took long walks and talked the whole time. That was something I'd never done with any of my other boyfriends. After I'd fully recovered from my surgery, we worked hard to make his trailer more like a home. We painted, wallpapered badly, and had both a new kitchen floor and carpeting installed. We decorated the porch. On weekends when the weather was nice, we'd sleep out there on a futon. We even had an inflatable pool to soak in during the hot summer months.

I got up early with Gary to help him deliver the morning newspapers, and by 5:30 a.m., we were back home drinking coffee and reading our own paper. On weekends, we hit tag sales and flea markets, always on the lookout for great things to decorate our home with.

Things were good. So good in fact, that I started to wonder about a serious future with Gary. I wasn't going to rush it though. Not with my track record. We talked about me going back into counseling too. It was clear that waiting for anyone in my idiot family to step up and acknowledge what happened was a waste of time. Not one of them was willing to listen to what my stepfather had done to me, but not one of them ever challenged what I said either. All they ever said about it was that it never happened. I'd given up any last hope that my mother and I would ever be able to talk about it too. As far as they were all concerned, I was an outcast. As far as I knew, everyone I grew up with hated me.

When I told my Aunt Judi about my past, she'd asked me not to tell anyone about it, but it wasn't like when Grammy had said "Shhh." Judi didn't want me to talk about it because she was concerned that my stepfather might do something crazy if I started talking about it. Many years later, I found out that after I'd told her what had happened, she quietly started talking about what my stepfather had done. We had a big family, and she wanted people to know so they could make sure their kids were safe from him. Of course that meant my mother had heard the whole story too, and chosen the monster over me. It wasn't like I didn't already think that, but it still hurt to realize she chose to support his lies rather than to believe her own child.

◆　◆　◆　◆　◆

The female counselor I started seeing was warm and friendly. We talked about my abuse and my past problems with old boyfriends. She seemed nice, empathetic, and competent. I felt like I was making progress, but after I'd seen her about six times, I was blindsided.

One day out of the blue, G called me at work. He told me he knew I was going to a counselor and then, almost verbatim, repeated back to me intimate details about our relationship that I had discussed with my counselor. It was frightening how much he knew about what I'd shared in confidence. When I asked him how he knew all this, he said, "I have my ways of finding out."

I was so mad, and felt completely unsafe and violated. I quickly called my counselor but had to wait until she was available. When I finally got hold of her, I relayed the conversation I'd had with G. She assured me there was no way anyone had access to my confidential information. I kept telling her that what he said was too exact for him to have guessed. I told her there was no way he could possibly know I was seeing her, so it had to be a breach of confidentiality on her end. All she kept saying was, "that's not possible."

When Gary and I thought this over (and over and over) we came to this conclusion: The counselor employed an office worker whose job it was to take the counselor's recorded notes and type them up. Based on how detailed the information was, the person transcribing the notes must have known I was talking about G, and told him everything I'd said. It was either that, or the counselor had told him herself.

Either way, a terrible breach and disservice had occurred, and her response to my concerns wasn't good enough to earn back one ounce of my trust. If I hadn't been so stunned and unnerved by the experience, I would have realized I should have reported what happened. I just never went back to see her again. Even after all these years, what happened still infuriates me. If it could happen to me, how many other people did it happen to? Hopefully, that counselor will read this book and recognize herself.

Counseling was no longer an option, but I had other things in my life that were good. Gary and I were invited to family parties and get-togethers at Judi's, and always had a lot of fun when we were there. Judi was such a good cook and her big house was the perfect spot.

By now, two of Judi's four sons were married and had kids of their own. Inside, I was dying to talk about what my stepfather had done to me so I could warn them to keep their kids away from him. I didn't though. I just kept reminding myself that Judi had asked me not to talk about it. I trusted her, and knew she would never let him have any time alone with her grandchildren—probably anyone's children. As long as Judi was around, I believed the children would be safe. It wasn't like anyone would believe me anyway.

It was my stepfather's cousin who had introduced me to Ron at Keri's wedding. She was living with him now. We'd always been friendly in the past, but when she heard what I said my stepfather had done to me, like most of the family, she distanced herself from me. Shortly after that, she decided I was no longer welcome in my real father's house.

I could never understand that. I'd been visiting him, in his house, for years. She'd been there all along, and now she didn't want me there? I don't believe Ron's ever doubted what I told him. I just think that instead of starting something with her and her big Italian family, he let her have her way and started coming over to our house instead. Whatever.

Now it was like my family was split. On one side was my idiot family. On the other was Gary, Judi and her family, and my father and his family.

◆　◆　◆　◆　◆

As I mentioned before, I had been a shy quiet child. As an adult, I was pretty much the same. I avoided confrontation, didn't want to make waves, and just wanted everyone to get along. I remember one day Gary and I were sitting at the kitchen table going over some bills. There was an error on one of the bills, but rather than contest it, I paid it.

I told Gary I'd rather just pay it than cause trouble. He couldn't believe I was letting it go. He could understand because he knew about my past, but he wasn't happy, and that bill generated a whole discussion about how I might be just a little too submissive. He thought I needed to stand up for what was right and not take any crap about it. He said that I had a right to be heard. He made some good points, but the person he was describing would never be me.

◆　◆　◆　◆　◆

Now that Gary and I were getting more serious, I decided it was a good time for me to get a second job to save more money. Waitressing had always worked before, so I quickly found a job at a popular restaurant. My hours at the restaurant were simple. All weekend. I pulled a double shift on Saturday and a half-day on Sunday. I was putting in overtime at Mass Mutual when I could too. Unlike all my other boyfriends, Gary worked just as hard as I did, working two jobs and grabbing as much overtime as he could. For Christmas that year, he gave me a hope chest. That was a good sign.

When Gary was working the Sunday paper route, he would pick up the papers Saturday and sort them on the porch. For a long time, I helped him deliver them. We'd get up between 3:30 – 4:00 a.m. in every kind of weather. It was easy to do because we both wanted to have money in the bank for our future. I don't know how we did it, but we delivered daily newspapers for almost five and a half years.

There were times when it felt like all we did was work, but we both had the same idea. We knew that working hard now would pay off later. We'd both spent too much time with the wrong people. Now we were working so we'd be able to enjoy our time together.

Talking

I could always talk to Gary about anything. One night we were lying in bed and talking by candle light about what my Aunt Judi had just told me. Judi was never one to complain, but that day, she casually mentioned that she'd gone to see her doctor and found out that she had breast cancer. What I didn't know right then was that she'd been diagnosed with breast cancer back in 1986. She'd been worried that something was wrong — again — but it had taken her a while to get up the nerve to go see her doctor. By the time she had, she was already in stage three.

Gary and I talked about Judi and how good of a person she was. She always put her family first. With a husband, four sons, daughters-in-law, grandkids, and me, she was always on the go. She worked a full time job too, but still took care of everyone else first. So much in fact, that now her health was suffering because of it. We prayed and kept our fingers crossed while she started treatments.

It was so wonderful to know I could talk to Gary about anything, but then he started dropping hints about the possibility of us getting married. I didn't know what to think at first, so instead of taking him seriously, I'd respond like he was joking. "You're kidding, right?"

That was the nervous part of me responding to him. Was I ready to get married? He'd already been married once. Would his second marriage work? I didn't know what to think on the inside either. I'd grown to think of Gary as marriage material, but was I marriage material?

Normally, I would have talked to Judi about it, but for some reason I didn't. I knew she'd be excited for me, but I don't think I was ready to believe it yet. The only person I talked to was a friend who only had good things to say about Gary, and about us getting married.

Even when Gary got down on one knee and proposed to me at the Storrowtown Tavern in West Springfield, I wasn't sure if he was being serious. Then he presented me with a beautiful diamond engagement ring. I was totally caught off guard, but of course I accepted!

Over dinner, he told me he'd decided I was "marriage material" shortly after we started going out. He'd known where to buy the ring because he'd heard Judi and I talk about the store she always got her jewelry from. He chuckled when he told me he made sure my diamond was bigger than my cousin's diamond. I listened to everything he said, but I kept holding my hand out and looking at my beautiful ring too.

Forever

The following year was very busy. Gary and I were still both working full and part-time jobs, and now we had a wedding to plan. I was 35 years old, and Gary used to kid me about how he was saving me from being an old maid. It's a good thing for him I was starting to develop a sense of humor. But he also did so many thoughtful things. One day, after wedding-dress shopping, I returned to my car to find a rose Gary had left for me. I still have that rose. It's safely tucked away in my hope chest.

While I was doing all the "girly" things to prepare for our wedding, Gary had something else important to take care of before we got married. He had to have a tattoo altered to hide his ex's name and added mine in beautiful script. No one had ever had my name tattooed on their body for me before!

We planned the entire wedding ourselves. We wanted a small and intimate wedding and closed our guest list at 65 people. The night before I got married, I really wanted to have a girl's night with just Judi and me. Gary was fine with it, and kind enough to spend the night at the Ramada Inn so we girls could be alone.

Judi and I went to the Holyoke Mall and stopped at Hannoush Jewelers to get our rings cleaned. We talked and laughed through our dinner at Ruby Tuesday, and talked and laughed some more when we got back to my place. We pampered ourselves with facial masks, and took pictures of each other all gooped up. I couldn't have asked for a better night, and as I fell asleep, I thanked God with all my heart for my wonderful Aunt Judi.

Gary and I were married on a gloriously sunny autumn morning in October. Judi and my father both walked me down the aisle. It was perfect. And no, none of my idiot family attended—they weren't invited.

◆　◆　◆　◆　◆

Four months after we got married, on Gary's birthday, we bought our first "traditional" home—meaning it had a basement instead of an axle. It was an old and neglected ranch that needed a lot of work, but the price and location were right, so we grabbed it. There was a farm across the street, and we had a beautiful view of rolling hills with horses and cows. Gary was so close to where he worked that he was now able to come home for lunch and let the dogs out.

It took a lot of time and work to turn that house into our home, but it was worth it. We even fenced in the yard for the dogs. Yes, we still had Benson, but we also had Bridget now too. We'd gotten her thinking that she'd be good company for Benson, but she had her own mind about things and didn't put up with any of his playful nonsense. They both loved their yard though.

All in all, we were settling into our life together, and it felt good. We were both still working a lot too, and that meant we were saving money. After Gary and I talked about it, I decided to buy a condo in Chicopee strictly as an investment. The tenants were so horrible that I sold it two years later barely making a profit. After that, we accepted some advice and coaching from my father, and Gary and I got involved in the stock market. We figured this would be an easier way to make money than being a landlord.

Within a few years, we had enough money to remodel the rest of the house. Once the house was finally finished, we stepped back and congratulated ourselves on doing such a good job. Then we looked at each other and said the exact same thing. "But it's too small!" And with that, we started making plans to look for a bigger house.

Revelations

One early Sunday morning while we were drinking our first cups of coffee and reading the Sunday paper, our doorbell rang. It was Judi. She was alone and very distraught. Once we got her settled down with a cup of coffee, she started to talk. She started off by saying that my Uncle Moe was not the person we thought he was. When she'd first met him, he was quiet and shy, but after years of encouragement, he'd become more outgoing and at ease with people.

I'd always had the impression that he talked more to others than he did to Judi, but that was the way some couples were. I hadn't really given it too much thought.

Alternating between laughing and crying, she went on to tell us how fake and phony he was, and that if she could do it all over again, she would not have married him.

All I could do was listen while my poor sweet Aunt Judi poured her heart out. My heart ached for her. She was the sweetest, most caring person I would ever know. She was the woman I considered my mother. It just wasn't fair that she was going through so much. I thought she had the perfect marriage. When I was a kid growing up, I dreamt of having a marriage just like hers.

She told us a lot of things that morning. She said that if she survived, she was going to leave her husband. She was stressed, but it was like she wanted to prepare me for what would happen if she didn't make it. She warned us that if she did die, we'd see what things were really like.

As she talked, I realized that for all these years, the smile she'd been putting on for the family had been a pretend smile. She wore it, always trying to make life better for everyone she loved. Now, she was sick, scared, and felt very alone. I understood what she was feeling. We had both been deceived by people in our family.

She had stopped by to tell us what was in her heart while she still could. I'm truly glad she trusted Gary and I enough to share what was going on. She was there for less than an hour, and then she laughed and told us she was on her way to Foxwoods. Judi and I never talked about that visit again. But her words of warning haunted me for years.

Aunt Judi

1999 was a long tough year. Even at the worst of times though, good things still happened. Gary and I had been saving money and "paying our dues" — along with our bills — for a long time. Gary quit delivering the morning newspaper, and I was able to quit waitressing. Now we had time to direct our energies elsewhere.

Unfortunately, Judi's fight with breast cancer was not going well. She tired easily and had to quit her job. She never wanted to talk about the disease or her treatments with me, but we were still there for each other. One day when Gary and I were visiting with Judi and her husband over coffee and cookies, Judi told us she had some news that we needed to hear.

On one of her recent visits to the medical center, Judi and her husband had run into the husband and wife who had lived next to us when I was growing up. Somehow, the subject of what happened to me had come up, and the neighbors told them that they knew what was going on because my mother had been friends with the wife. The wife said that on more than one occasion my mother came over to their house for a visit, and then burst into tears talking about what her husband was doing to me.

I couldn't believe what I'd just heard and was numb with shock. Gary was seething. My mother had known that her husband was sexually assaulting me? How could a mother knowingly allow that to happen? But it was worse than that. She didn't just find out and then put a stop to it. She found out and let it continue.

My Uncle Moe corroborated everything Judi told us, admitting that his brother was a child molester.

It's one thing to tell a horrible story like mine and hope the people you know and love will believe you, but it's nothing like hearing undeniable proof like this. It was such an overwhelming relief to have two of the people I cared most about hear firsthand that I hadn't made any of it up.

Now I understood why my mother wouldn't talk to me about it. She already knew. She wasn't ever going to admit it, but she knew. She made her decision and had sacrificed me to a monster. She kept me at arm's length my whole life to keep her precious household intact. Wow, she must be so proud. After the initial shock wore off, I got angry at my neighbors too. Shame on them for looking the other way.

By late summer, it was obvious Judi was not going to beat the breast cancer this time. There was nothing else the doctors could do except to keep her comfortably medicated. Hospice took over, and a bed was set up for her in the family room of her home.

I took every Wednesday off and drove to her home to spend the day with her. I sat next to her and we held hands as we talked and watched TV. She had difficulty swallowing, so when I fed her, everything had to be cut into tiny pieces. She knew she was dying and we talked about that too. She told me the outfit she wanted to be buried in and I promised her I'd make sure her wishes would be carried out. She slept a lot, and towards the end, she wasn't able to speak.

On March 4, 2000, shortly before noon, with her entire family at her side, my dear sweet Aunt Judi passed away. She was only 54 years old.

As the funeral arrangements were being made, I explained to my uncle which outfit Judi wanted to be buried in. When I showed up at the funeral parlor, she was not wearing her favorite mint green outfit. I know it sounds like such a small thing, but I couldn't help feeling like I was letting her down, and was helpless to do anything about it.

Over the years, Judi had collected Native American dolls. One Christmas, many years ago, I'd given her a beautiful doll named "Happy Heart." It was Judi's favorite, and she had it displayed in a place of honor in her arts and crafts room. When Judi was sick, she told me she wanted me to take Happy Heart after she was gone. I agonized over this for weeks after Judi passed, but Gary finally convinced me to call Uncle Moe and talk to him about it.

I called him three times, but he never called back, so I sent him a letter. His response was to drop off Judi's doll, in a paper bag, upside down and all messed up, on our front porch. He never even rang the doorbell.

As the weeks turned into months, I didn't hear from Judi's family at all. One of my cousin's wives and I had been close, so I called her to see how everybody was doing. She was nervous on the phone and didn't want to talk much. I just chalked it up to grieving and mourning. Everybody handles this type of trauma differently.

One day when Gary and I were out sightseeing, we decided to drive by Judi's house. We were shocked to see tire marks on the lawn leading up to the front door. The house was entirely empty! Cleaned out!

As soon as we got home, I called my cousin's wife again. She sounded just as uncomfortable and nervous as she had the last time we talked. When I asked her what had happened to Judi's house, she said she had to go and hung up on me! Over the next few days, I kept calling and leaving messages, but she never called back.

Over the years, I was able to piece together what happened. After Judi died, Uncle Moe never slept in their house again. He moved around, living with one son after the other for months. He finally sold the house and bought a smaller home in Springfield. He also found himself a girlfriend.

Judi and I had been like mother and daughter, and I thought I knew her family. I had loved my uncle and thought of my cousins as brothers. And yet all this happened without me.

Then I remembered a conversation Judi and I once had when she told me her sons were jealous of the time she and I had spent together, and that they sort of resented me because of it. It wasn't until later on that they had heard the story of my past abuse. That had tainted their Italian family pride, and I was clearly to blame for it. I didn't realize it at the time, but Judi's funeral turned out to be the last time I saw — or spoke — to Uncle Moe, or any of my four cousins.

Once again, I was being totally ostracized by a part of my family, and it hurt. How could they do that? It didn't make any sense to me. Why were all the men in that family such assholes? No more holidays, or birthday parties with my nieces and nephews ever again. It didn't matter that I was able to make sense out of why all these people were acting like this. It still hurt. Judi had been right to warn me, but it was of little comfort.

Loss

It was one of those gray days. The cemetery was no exception; its bare trees etched in stark contrast against the cloudy March sky. I wrapped my arms tightly around myself as I looked down at the patch of ground my beloved Aunt Judi was buried beneath. It hurt to think about her being there, but I did what I usually did when I visited her. I cleaned up the area around her headstone and talked to her about what was going on in my life.

I tried to remember her the way she had always been—laughing, blue eyes twinkling, full of love and warmth. I longed to speak to her the same way I'd been able to speak to her when she was alive, but that wasn't going to happen. I started to cry, and Gary put his warm reassuring arms around me.

Since Judi's passing, Gary and I had gone to the cemetery to visit her at least once a week. Being near her and talking to her helped me cope a little, but it still was hard. I missed having her in my life so much. She had loved me and saved me before she'd known what had been done to me. She had believed my story and continued to love me and treat me like her daughter even after I'd told her. She was the one who made me feel normal enough to belong to a real family. I hadn't just lost her, I'd lost the first family I'd ever felt like I really had.

I'd always felt protected by Judi too. She had told me not to talk about what my stepfather had done because she didn't trust my idiot family either. I hadn't talked and always felt safer because of it, almost like she was between me and them. Now that she was gone, and her family had abandoned me too, I was feeling more vulnerable than ever and started worrying about what all those people who didn't believe me might do.

I had visions of my stepfather trying to hunt me down to punish me for causing so much trouble in the family. We lived on a busy street where every car horn or tire squeal put me on edge because I honestly believed that people from that side of my family were out to get me.

I tried to distract myself and not think about it. In many ways, my life was better than ever. Gary was very supportive, and we had our own small family. Gary and I had solid jobs, a cozy home, our wonderful dogs, and a little money in the bank. Gary tried to assure me that my fears and concerns were just a product of my over-active imagination. We had the dogs for protection. They would bark like crazy if anyone was prowling around our house. We lived less than two miles from the police station which meant they could get to us quickly if we called. He tried his best to calm me down, but nothing he said alleviated my fear.

At one point, Gary had purchased an antique violin. He was taking private lessons, practicing for an hour-and-a-half every day, and thoroughly enjoying himself. His lessons were on Thursday nights, and even though he wasn't gone for very long, I was terrified every moment he was gone. It got so bad that Gary realized he needed to quit his violin lessons to stay home with me. I would want to go to bed earlier than usual too, and have him hold me. For added protection, we let the dogs sleep in our bed.

Even though Gary was with me basically all the time when we were home, I couldn't shake off my fears. They had always been in the background, but now that Judi was gone, I just couldn't seem to stop them. In fact, they seemed to be getting worse. Gary was so supportive, and when he suggested that it might be time to go back to counseling, I had to agree because things weren't getting better. There was no way I was going back to the last counselor I'd seen though, so we found a different person at a different location.

As this was my third time seeing a counselor, I knew what to expect. We reviewed my past and talked about my fixation on feeling like I was being followed or watched by that family — especially my stepfather — and how those feelings had intensified and gotten worse since Judi had passed.

Our sessions always seemed to focus on the same issues: my feelings of abandonment, and me trying to understand why my mother didn't (or wouldn't) believe me. In my mind, she was the one person in this world who should have stood by me, but she wouldn't even talk to me. She hung up on me every time I called her.

We also talked about what it meant to be a survivor, and that it was time for me to take control and reclaim my life. She was the first counselor to mention PTSD. It was a lot to take in, and I don't remember exactly why, but I stopped going.

I found the notes I'd written down during those counseling sessions while I was working on this book. There were some good insights in there; I just wasn't ready for them back then. Maybe I thought I was a lost cause. Or maybe it was because the one person I needed to believe me didn't, and no one else could substitute for her — except Judi — and now Judi was gone. Whatever the reasons were, I was in such a state of mind back then that I severed ties with a qualified professional who was trying to help me.

Decision

In the early summer of that year, my job at the insurance company was in jeopardy of being transferred to either Hartford, CT, or Greenfield, MA. Not wanting an hour commute to work, I quit my job and accepted a position as a receptionist for a small family-run business in Chicopee. It was a very good decision—I ended up working there for over fourteen years.

Gary and I spent the spring of 2002 finishing our remodeling projects, and every once in a while talked about moving into a bigger house. One day I was flipping through the newspaper at work when an ad for a "for sale by owner" caught my eye. It was just down the street and around the corner from where we lived. I called Gary at work and he drove by it on his way home for lunch. He said it was a "dump," but the yard was big and it was in a good location. I called to make an appointment to view the house. As soon as we walked in, we knew it was the right house for us. We wrote out a check for the deposit right then, and the house was ours.

Like our first home, this one required updating and some old-fashion tender loving care. We fenced in the yard for the dogs, put on a new roof, put on new siding, and installed new replacement windows. We put our wood stove in the corner of the living room, ripped out the electric heat, and converted to gas.

We were used to doing work like this though. It was comfortable. We wallpapered and painted and made it home. Unfortunately, thoughts of my idiot family were always bubbling just below the surface of my mind. It was also around this time that the Catholic priest sex abuse scandal started coming out. With each revelation of how deep their problem was, one specific thought kept popping into my mind. My young nieces were probably visiting my mother and stepfather in the very same house I had been sexually abused in.

With their innocence, they would believe they were going someplace safe with people who could be trusted. But now that Judi was no longer there to protect them, I was afraid something would happen to them. There was my niece Roxy to think about too. She was living in that house with my mother and stepfather as her legal guardians. I didn't want to think about it. I didn't feel strong enough to think about it, but I couldn't stop thinking about it. If I continued to keep silent, who would step in and do for my nieces and nephews what Judi had done for me?

I thought about when I'd first disclosed my abusive past to Judi and how she'd made me promise not to talk about it. Out of respect for her, I hadn't. But Judi was gone now, and things had changed. I had a future with Gary to look forward to, and I was feeling differently about my life.

Finally, after days and days of mulling things over in my mind, Gary and I took a trip to the cemetery to visit Judi. It was another gray day, and once again I cleaned up the area. As I stood there staring at her headstone, my eyes filled with tears. Barely able to speak, I said that I'd kept my promise to her and hadn't talked about what my stepfather had done to me. But now, things had changed. I acknowledged that I didn't know what was happening in my mother's house, but I knew what had happened to me when I was there, and I knew what my stepfather was capable of. I couldn't just sit by and do nothing, and even though I was still afraid, I was no longer willing to be silent, and had decided to take matters into my own hands. I asked for her blessing and support for what I was about to do, and hoped she would understand. I bent down and kissed her headstone, and we left.

Part Three

Finding a Mission

I remember how Gary used to describe me as "the cute girl with blue eyes and freckles," but I never really saw that part of myself because I was always struggling with what I felt on the inside. Certain things will always linger from my childhood, but I was suddenly very determined not to let them control me. I wasn't going to waste time trying to forget them either. You can't forget something like that anyway. It's always there in the background, but that was then and this was now. I lived through it. I was a survivor.

So what did I do? I started telling my story to friends, then neighbors, and finally co-workers. I told anyone who would listen, and realized that the more people I told, the better I felt. And do you know what happened next? People started to approach me with their own stories of abuse. It didn't take me long to figure out that I wasn't alone. I was a part of something… and it was huge.

Next, I went to the town police station and filed a report about my past so that if anything "suspicious" were to happen to me, at least it was on file and my stepfather would be considered a suspect. I wasn't as afraid as I had been, but I wanted certain things documented.

Most people were supportive of what I was doing, but a few were not. There were still those few who thought that what happened to me shouldn't be discussed in public. I respected their opinion, but I'd been quiet about what had been done to me for my whole life. I was done being silent. I knew what I wanted to do, and once I'd made up my mind, the fears and uncertainties about what my screwball family might do started to lose their hold on me.

I wanted to raise people's awareness of childhood sexual abuse. I just didn't know how to do it. There were no maps to follow. There were no step-by-step instructions or school courses. I didn't know anybody to go to for help figuring it out either. It was a topic I was all too familiar with personally, but all I had to guide me when it came to figuring out what to do next was my gut instinct.

We didn't own a computer at that time, so we started going to the library and using their computers at night and on Saturdays. The topics to research were endless. What is sexual abuse... examples of sexual abuse... when can you file a lawsuit for sexual abuse... criminal versus civil court... etc. Our brains started suffering from information overload. It wasn't like doing school research at all. I had to do things like refresh my memory about how government works. I was amazed at the information I was finding, and very committed to learning as much as I could.

After work, Gary and I would discuss ideas and make a list of what to research on the internet. Most of the time, we went to the library together. But when it was open late, I was happy to do research on my own. I wasn't as anxious at the library when Gary wasn't there because no one from that side of my family knew where I was, and there wasn't much chance of any one of them showing up at a library.

The more I learned, the more I realized how much there was to know. Sometimes I had to reread things several times over before they sunk in, but I kept at it. I tried to find books, magazines, or articles about childhood sexual abuse in the library, but there was nothing. It was as if the library had agreed to keep it a secret too. I searched every newspaper for articles pertaining to child sexual abuse. When I found one, I cut it out or made a copy (if it wasn't my newspaper) so I'd have it just in case I wanted or needed to refer back to it later.

One evening while I was waiting for Gary to pick me up, I stopped and read the bulletin board and saw that the library hosted different community events. I stood there looking at the list of events and wondered if they would ever let me speak to parents and their children about sexual abuse. I didn't know the first thing about talking to a room full of people, but I thought it might be something I could do—someday.

◆　◆　◆　◆　◆

In 2002 when I was starting my research on sexual abuse, one of the things I learned about was the statute of limitations (SOL) regarding this crime. Boiled down, the SOL is a state law that restricts the time within which legal proceedings can be filed. Each state sets its own limits on the amount of time survivors have to pursue their right to sue their attacker in a court of law. After the SOL runs out, victims no longer have any legal recourse. In the state of Massachusetts in 2002, a survivor had 15 years from their 16th birthday to file an initial criminal complaint against their attacker, which could lead to a criminal conviction and jail sentence for the perpetrator. Anyone who didn't file a criminal complaint before they turned 32 was out of luck.

I know 15 years sounds like a long time, but the crime of sexual abuse does not follow a timeline. It's not like you can look at someone who's been abused and say, "Well, it's been 15 years, so you shouldn't have any problem talking about it openly anymore" or "It's been 15 years and you haven't sought justice so you must be over it by now."

No two cases of sexual abuse are exactly the same. Even if the situation is similar, the person being abused is unique. Trust me, coming forward is not an easy decision. By the time I was 32, I had told very few people what my stepfather had done to me — and a couple of them were counselors. All the while, my idiot family was still spouting the party line: "It never happened."

Even if I'd known about the SOL before I turned 32, I'm not sure I could have filed. All I really wanted when I was 32 was to live my life like a normal person. It didn't matter anyway. I was 40 years old when I learned about the SOL, so it wasn't going to help me.

I learned that if a victim wanted to pursue a civil action that would lead to monetary compensation, they had to be at least 18 years old, and had until the age of 21 to file suit. A three year window… that was it.

I also found out that people who uncover repressed memories of being sexually abused have three years to file suit, no matter how old they are. But how was that going to help anybody? It's good to know someone can remember later in life and still be able to do something about it, but can you imagine how stressful it would be to first realize you'd been a victim, and then have to announce it to the world within a couple of years if you wanted justice for what was done to you?

It was hard for me to wrap my brain around the repercussions of the statutes of limitations. Someone could actually get away with raping and abusing children, and these SOLs were irrefutable proof of it. People who'd had no choice about what had been done to them would have to come forward and announce what happened to them in front of the whole world if they wanted to initiate proceedings against the monster who attacked them — whether they were ready to do it or not.

I wondered who'd picked those time frames. Did they ask a bunch of mental health professionals how long a victim would need before he or she would be able to handle what the courts were going to put them through? Clearly, the laws didn't care whether or not a victim would be ready to file within the time limits stated. It made me cringe to think of how many victims of childhood sexual abuse watched the clock quietly wind down, tick by tick, until their time eventually ran out. There would be no justice for them now, only lingering pain. And anger — lots and lots of anger.

I just couldn't believe that we, as a society, could agree to something like this, and I wanted to do something about it. How could we let a monster get away with something so hideous time and time again? Because the truth is, **if they are not caught, if they are not stopped, they *will* do it again.** I had experienced that truth with every assault.

Reaching Out

The more I learned about sexual abuse and SOLs, the more I feared for my niece Roxy. She would be a freshman in high school this coming September. The last time I'd been allowed to spend time with her, she was five years old and I had taken her to the mall. The next time I called to schedule another time to see her, I was told I couldn't ever see her again. I had a pretty good idea of why too. I'm sure my mother questioned her after our visit and found out I'd asked her if anyone was touching her in a way she didn't like.

I'd done all I knew how to do all those years ago when Roxy had moved into my mother and stepfather's house. I'd reported it to the people who should have been able to protect her. They were the same people who came back to me and told me to let it go, and that Roxy was living in a "loving" home.

I had a lot more information now though, and started putting together a plan. The first step was to contact Roxy's mother, my sister Meri. We hadn't spoken in years, but that was the norm for us. Her phone number was unlisted, but I was able to go on the internet and find her street address so I could mail her a letter. I kept the letter short, letting her know I needed to talk to her. I provided my phone number in the letter, and she called me a few days later.

That first conversation was awkward. My main objective was to gather as much information as I could about her daughter. But my sister has always had a hard time with life, and with the various medications she was taking, at times it was difficult for her to stay focused. She confirmed that she'd lost custody, and that my mother and stepfather were still her daughter's legal guardians. She said she'd tried to get visitation rights so she could at least see Roxy, but the courts hadn't allowed it. Our mother could have agreed to let her see her anyway, but she didn't allow it either.

Clearly our mother was determined to keep Roxy away from certain members of our family. Myself for sure, and probably Judi when she had been alive.

I found out that both Keri and Sheri had trouble raising their kids too. Keri, the sister who'd relentlessly teased me about knowing who my real father was, was now divorced, and her ex-husband was raising their daughter. Sheri's son was being raised by my mother and stepfather now too. I had no idea my nephew had been taken away and placed in that house. All this news was just more sad confirmation of how screwed up that part of my family really was.

Over the next two months, Meri and I talked on the phone at least once a week. Our conversations were always a little bit strained, but we were able to catch up on each other's lives. She told me about her boyfriend and the rocky relationship she had both with him and our family. I told her about Gary, but I was also very cautious with what I said. I didn't think she'd go running to our mother to tell her what I'd said, but I decided I'd rather be safe than sorry.

We even met at Friendly's for lunch on a Saturday afternoon so she and Gary could finally meet. I wasn't surprised to see Meri with her hair frizzed out and tattoos on her arms, but I think her appearance made Gary nervous. It definitely made for a bizarre first impression.

It didn't take long to figure out that my sister wasn't going to be able to do anything on her own when it came to Roxy. That didn't change my determination to do something though. I thought about what my Aunt Judi had done for me and I wanted to do the same thing for Roxy. I wanted to be there for her, but there was no way I would ever be allowed to walk through the front door of my mother's house to see her. If I wanted to provide Roxy with the same type of safe haven my aunt had provided me, I would have to get creative.

I could have tried to talk to my sister about what we might have been able to do together, but I honestly didn't think she'd be able to deal with it. My stepfather had most members of the family convinced they would suffer dire consequences if they did — or said — anything bad about him or his family. I was still struggling with that fear even after all these years, and it wouldn't have been fair to expect my sister to do something.

One of the things I decided to do was to start writing a journal I called "Roxy's Journal." There were so many things I wanted to say to her, but I knew it would probably be a long time before I'd be able to spend any real time with her. So I started writing in the journal hoping that when she finally got to read it she'd know that there were people who have always loved her and cared about her. It felt good to write it down too—almost therapeutic. In my first entry, I told her how concerned for her I was. I told her I'd contacted her new high school guidance counselor, and how nice she sounded, and how concerned she was for Roxy's safety and well-being too.

Over time, I had several conversations with her guidance counselor, but always respected that the conversations she had with my niece were confidential. After initially hearing my story though, the guidance counselor contacted DSS. After speaking with a DSS supervisor, a 51A was filed. Unfortunately, because I wasn't Roxy's legal guardian, I was never able to find out what the outcome was—or even if there was an outcome. I guess I should have been glad that I wasn't told to "back off" like I'd been told when Roxy was five years old. But I wasn't glad. I was hurt, feeling helpless, and pretty pissed off.

Finding a Voice

I needed to do something to keep moving forward. What I wanted to do was scream out my frustration because at every turn I ran into a roadblock. Why was this so difficult? I cursed my life and my weakness. I didn't know where to go for guidance, and I couldn't stand the fact that I was so helpless. There were no contacts or friends in high places that could pull strings for me. I was just a girl from Springfield. What could I do?

And then it dawned on me. One of the things I found during my research was a list of all the names, addresses, and phone numbers for all the politicians in my district. That list led me to a website that listed all of the politicians in Massachusetts, including my local State Representatives, Thomas Petrolati (D), and Gale Candaras (D). Like a lot of the research I'd been collecting, I wasn't sure what I was going to do with it when I found it, but I'd printed out all their names and contact information and still had them.

Out of desperation, I sat down with pen and paper and wrote a few old-fashioned letters. Within 28 lines on a single sheet of paper, I poured out my story. It wasn't poetry, and it certainly wasn't eloquent. It was a cry for help from a little girl whose past was being revealed through the trembling fingers of a grown woman. I exposed my abusive past and the frustration of my mother's refusal to listen to my story. I told of my niece being raised in the same house I grew up in, and how afraid I was for her safety. I also mentioned the statute of limitations, how unfair they were to survivors, and how they favored abusers. I ended the letter asking for their help, and added my name, address, and phone number below my signature so they could contact me.

Letter after letter was hand written during my lunch breaks, at night before I went to bed, and early the next morning before I went to work. Each envelope was hand addressed. We mailed them out in batches, each batch carefully dropped into the mailbox across the street from the bowling alley in Chicopee. The easy part was done. Now all I had to do was wait for them to respond.

Just out of curiosity, I tried to figure out how many people received one of those first hand-written letters. There were over 180. In fact, those letters were the catalyst for us getting our first computer. Once we had that, it made all my letter writing, research, and record keeping much easier. Another advantage of having our own computer was being able to work anytime — day or night.

I didn't get one response from that first batch of handwritten letters — not one. Not being an overly patient person though, I wasn't going to sit around and wait. Instead, I got more focused and started adding more information about sexual abuse. I started including articles I found in the newspaper, information I found online, and any other information that would help make it clear that survivors needed an extended time frame to report their abuse.

Each letter I wrote was better than the last, but they were still generating a zero response, so I started picking up the phone and following up on every letter I had sent to every state representative and state senator. I wasn't ever able to get through to them directly, so I started talking to their aides and building relationships with them. I also started emailing representatives. I was determined that if they didn't know who I was yet, then they were going to know me shortly.

At one point, I emailed State Representative Gale Candaras to see if she had received a letter I'd recently sent, but also with hopes of asking some questions I had regarding the statute of limitations in MA for sex abuse crimes. She promptly returned my email, very kindly letting me know I had spelled the word "statute" incorrectly. I had typed statue instead. What impressed me about Ms. Candaras was that she responded on a weekend night, on her own time.

Through the multiple emails we exchanged, my understanding of SOLs expanded. I learned that statutes of limitation were laws and that all laws have the ability to be changed. Gale helped me understand how lawmakers generate laws. She was also the first person to help me realize that I had the power to initiate change. Gale was extremely helpful in the early stages of my advocacy work, and her own belief that one person can make a difference inspired me to keep at it.

Wanting to get at least one more unbiased opinion about what I was trying to do, I contacted another counselor to discuss what was on my mind. I was still bummed about another 51A for Roxy going nowhere. There was my idiot family to consider too, of course. They were always on my mind—and not in a good way. So once again, I found myself in yet another counselor's office going over the same miserable story of my life, and at this point, I was sick and tired of talking about myself.

We reviewed everything of importance, and talked about what I could do regarding my niece until I finally accepted the reality that my options were limited, and that maybe I really had done everything I could legally do. I had contacted the police, DSS, and Roxy's school counselor. Unless Roxy was willing to speak up on her own, my efforts were useless. I couldn't prove anything. So slowly, I let go of what I couldn't do, and started focusing on what I could do.

Out of curiosity, one day I called Dial-A-Lawyer and explained my story of abuse to see what they had to say about my options for suing my stepfather. They told me the SOL had expired and there was nothing they could do for me.

2003

2003 was a busy letter writing year for me. I guess I thought that the more I put myself out there, the greater the chances were for getting a response. I sent a letter to the area director for the Department of Social Services but she never responded. I wrote a *Letter to the Editor* about abolishing the SOL so that survivors could pursue their abusers and bring closure to their ordeal, but it never made it into print. One attorney responded to one of my letters wanting to know how much money my stepfather had.

I even wrote a letter to President Bush asking him how I could go about changing the SOL. I thought I might at least get a generic White House response, but I didn't.

As far as Roxy was concerned, I'd given up on the legal channels, but I hadn't given up hope of somehow being able to help her. I found out Meri was going back to court to once again try and get visitation rights with Roxy. She called and asked me if I would help her by coming to court and telling the judge how things were in our house when we were growing up.

I agreed, even though there were days when I felt the weight of telling my story so often. It was hard not to remember how scared I'd been (and still was) of my stepfather, and how severely he'd twisted my mind. I can still remember how he would line all four of us girls up to get hit with his black belt. The whole time I was standing there I'd be thinking, *Dad won't hit me as hard. He loves me and I do special things.* Even now, the memory of it still makes me sick to my stomach! But it was also one of the reasons I was going to continue to do everything I could.

Shortly after Roxy started high school, my Poppie died. Of course no one called to tell me, certainly not my mother, and it was her father who had died. I heard about it from Meri. She didn't hear it from our mother either though. She had to hear about it from another relative. No doubt, our mother was mad at Meri for filing with the court to get visitation rights with her own daughter.

I wasn't invited to Poppie's funeral either. I suppose I could have gone anyway, but there was no way I was up to having a confrontation with anyone from that side of my family. I may have been determined, but I was also tired — bone tired.

◆　◆　◆　◆　◆

I heard from Meri that she had received her notice to appear in court for the visitation hearing. I was glad she was seeing this through and glad that I'd be there to support her. I also hoped my presence would reassure Roxy that I really did care about her. It had been so long since I'd seen her or spoken to her that I wasn't even sure she'd recognize me. As far as I knew, all she knew about me was what the people from that side of my family had been telling her for the last ten years.

Unfortunately, court didn't go the way I had envisioned. When I arrived and tried to enter the courtroom, the gentleman at the door looked at the paper attached to his clipboard and said my name wasn't on it. If my name wasn't listed on the paper, I couldn't enter! I explained the situation and why I was there, but he said that if I was supposed to be there, the court would have sent me paperwork to fill out beforehand. If I didn't get the paperwork, then I was not a party to this proceeding and couldn't go in. I told him I never received any paperwork, and that my sister was in there and needed me for her case. He was not swayed, and I wasn't allowed in.

What happened to the paperwork? That's still a mystery. With all the relatives I had working at the post office at that time, I guess I could have asked one of them what they thought might have happened to it. But yeah, that wasn't going to happen.

I felt so bad about not being there for Meri; more so when I found out that the court had denied her visitation rights — again. I couldn't even imagine what she was thinking about me at that point. I called Dial-A-Lawyer again to see what they had to say about what happened. They said what happened was in the past. Well it was more like: It happened, so what?

I'd seen Roxy leaving the building after the hearing. She looked so sad. She was surrounded by the family and even though they were ignoring her, they definitely weren't going to let me near her. So I wrote her a quick letter. All it said was that I hoped she was doing well, and that I loved her.

I left it with the school counselor to give to her, but Roxy never responded.

The same day I dropped the letter off, I was approached by someone who was able to tell me that DSS was looking into something my mother was trying to do. Roxy wanted to be a cheerleader, and to do that she needed to have a physical. My mother had decided she was going to take her to a different doctor. DSS saw that as a red flag and wanted to know why she was trying to change doctors. Like so many other things that happened, I never found out what the result of their "investigation" was.

◆　◆　◆　◆　◆

Sometimes it felt like everything was moving in slow motion. But then there were days when everything happened quickly. On Nov 5, 2003, I wrote an entry into my Roxy journal about my struggles with working to get the SOLs on sexual abuse crimes changed. I also wrote about contacting all the various doctors I'd seen over my life to get them to release my medical records so I could start building up my past medical history. In most cases, I was able to get copies of my records, but some of the doctors I'd seen had either retired or passed away and their records had been destroyed.

◆　◆　◆　◆　◆

I got a phone call from an upset Meri who told me she had to have an operation to replace the pacemaker that had been implanted in her when she was a child. The surgery itself wasn't a high risk surgery, but when I found out she didn't have a will, I suggested she should have one. I knew she didn't have much, but what she had was hers, and having a will would protect it. As difficult as she was to deal with sometimes, I still loved my sister and wanted the best for her.

We talked about a health care proxy for her too. She didn't trust our mother enough to give her power over any health or life decisions — and definitely didn't want any plugs being pulled too early. Meri had not been treated kindly by our mother either, so I became her health care proxy, and we both agreed that the less our mom knew about the situation the better.

◆　◆　◆　◆　◆

On Nov. 7th, I found out that my mother knew about the letter I'd written to Roxy. She'd yelled at Roxy's guidance counselor for passing it on, saying that I was harassing them. I talked with Meri that day too. She was getting more nervous by the minute about her upcoming surgery. She was also concerned about how she was going to get to Boston, so I offered to drive her there and back.

In another conversation the next day, Meri told me she had called our mother's house and Roxy had answered the phone. They started talking, but as soon as Mom figured out it was Meri on the phone, she grabbed the phone away from Roxy. Mom was rude to Meri on the phone and asked her what she wanted. Meri said she wanted to talk with her father, and told Mom she was going to Boston to have an operation. Mom's reply was that they already knew she was going to Boston with "Jackass," (which I'm pretty sure was me). Meri then asked Mom if she ever cared. She said no, and hung up the phone.

◆ ◆ ◆ ◆ ◆

I was worried about what was going on with Meri, so on Nov. 9th, I called one of her closest friends. He told me that shortly after Meri's conversation with our mother, Keri called her to remind her that I always lied about everything, and that's why nobody in the family likes me or wants to have anything to do with me. She then offered to take Meri to Boston, but before she did, she wanted Meri to sign over her monthly disability checks!

As much as I loved and wanted to help Meri, she was clearly being coerced by family members to do something that would benefit them. They didn't care about her. They definitely weren't looking out for her best interests either. She was just in a terrible situation which made her an easy target.

I had another conversation with Meri too, but it was a very different conversation than the last one we'd had. She told me I had to stop trying to contact Roxy through school, and that I had to let it go. She also said that Roxy was none of my business.

◆ ◆ ◆ ◆ ◆

On the 12th, I received an hysterical voicemail from Meri about sticking my nose where it didn't belong. She was talking about me prying into her daughter's life, but nothing had changed since our conversation on the 9th. I hadn't written any letters, or tried to contact Roxy in anyway. It broke my heart to listen to the message because it was filled with swears and threats. All I'd wanted to do was to help my niece, but at this point, Gary just wanted me to walk away and let them live their miserable lives however they chose.

It was tough to do, but I agreed with him. My idiot family was clearly full of bullies, and no one really knows when a situation may turn violent, so we went to the police department and filed a report so that Meri's threats would be documented.

This episode of family drama had played out over just seven days, but I still felt like I'd been dragged through a ringer. It wasn't like I could take time off to recover either. I had a full time job. Gary and I tried to take a brisk 2.5 mile walk every night after supper, and after that I'd sit down at my computer and do my advocacy work until it was time to go to bed. I started to feel my energy levels dropping, so I tried drinking an extra cup of coffee late in the afternoon hoping it would help wake me up.

◆　◆　◆　◆　◆

In addition to everything else I was doing, I was also following up on letters and emails, as well as continuing my research on sexual abuse. After a while, the extra coffee wasn't helping me stay awake. I was now tired all the time, and my legs were feeling crampy and tingly. We had a hot tub on the deck, and that usually relaxed my sore muscles, but then even the hot tub stopped helping. In fact I felt worse after I got out of it. Gary would massage my legs and that might help for a few minutes, but the pain and cramps would come back. There were more and more sleepless nights, and I was experiencing numbness in my legs.

Finally, I'd had enough and went to see my doctor. He did some tests and then sent me to the UMASS Medical Center where they did more tests. The results were sent to my doctor and his office contacted me to go over the results. He said the widespread soft tissue pain and tender points were associated with fibromyalgia. Fibromyalgia is thought to be the result of over active nerves. It's a condition that results in widespread pain and tenderness.

The exact cause of fibromyalgia is not known, but pain, fatigue, problems sleeping, stress, and anxiety are all symptoms, and I was experiencing each and every one of them. As I answered my doctor's questions about what I did during my days, even I was suddenly aware of how much I was doing. He also said the added stress of dealing with my family and my abusive past could be contributing factors. This was the final diagnosis after other possible conditions had been eliminated.

In a way, I was relieved my doctor was able to put a name to what I was experiencing. Now I could work on things that were sapping away my energy. Or so I thought. There is no cure for fibromyalgia. What my doctor suggested was a slight change in diet with more exercise as a way to manage the symptoms. Through a series of trials and errors, I figured out that eating sardines and walking kept the leg cramps at bay. Before bed, I stretched and exercised my legs. We figured out that if I didn't walk or workout for four or five days, my legs hurt. Some days were better than others, and from what I've read, it sounds like I have a mild case, but I have to keep to my routine. It's a good thing I like sardines.

Even with everything I was trying to do, I was still always tired and rundown. Many nights I would be asleep by 7 p.m. It didn't help that it was totally dark so early in the afternoon at this time of year either. The more I learned about my condition, the more I feared it could spread to other parts of my body. Right now only my legs were being affected.

Gary wanted me to put my advocacy work on hold. He said my health was more important than anything else, and didn't want me to do anything other than walk, workout, and rest. I was compelled to keep going though, and through the fall and winter of 2003/2004, I worked during the day, spent my evenings furiously typing away on my keyboard, and stuck to a strict eating and workout routine. We bought a treadmill and I used it regularly all winter. It was boring in our small dark basement, but it was necessary. Gary painted the ceiling, walls, and floor to brighten it up to encourage me to get down there every day. Eventually we set up a TV in front of the treadmill. That helped too.

2004

In early June of 2004, Meri called to talk about Roxy. Mom had told her that Roxy had been acting up and running away from home. From what Meri said, it sounded like Mom couldn't control Roxy any longer so she kicked her out, and now Roxy was in a halfway house as a result. I reminded Meri that according to DSS Roxy was in a "loving and caring home." I didn't say it, but if that was true, why would Roxy be running away — unless she had a good reason to run away. I had a pretty good idea of what that reason might be too, but again, I kept my mouth shut.

I didn't really believe Meri cared one way or the other about why Roxy ran away. All she wanted was for me to track down her daughter for her. This was a typical pattern with Meri though. Time would go by, and then she would call because she needed something. She knew she could call me because I genuinely cared about what happened to Roxy. Sometimes I felt like I was the only one who truly cared about her. I promised my sister I would look into it, hoping it would turn into another chance for me to connect with Roxy. Mom didn't know Meri had talked to me, or that she'd given me the address of where Roxy was staying.

The day Gary drove me to the halfway house where Roxy was staying, I was both anxious and nervous. It had been about nine years since I'd spent any time with her. Judging from what my sister had told me, I wasn't sure what to expect. She didn't sound like the sweet innocent child I remembered. My niece had spent almost her entire life in that cold and loveless house, and I knew what the people in that house were capable of doing to a child. You really can't prepare yourself for a situation like I was about to walk into, but it wasn't really a choice for me. Someone had to reach out to this child. Happy well-adjusted kids don't normally keep running away. Something was wrong.

When I arrived, I introduced myself and met with Roxy's social worker. She wouldn't go into detail other than to say that my niece was troubled, and wanted to distance herself from her grandparents. A few minutes later, Roxy walked into the room, and the niece I had been obsessing over for so long was standing right in front of me! I was overcome with emotion, and didn't know if I should laugh, or cry, or hug her, so I did of them all at once. From that point on, I honestly believed that both our lives would forever be changed. Now I could take her under my wing, just as my Aunt Judi had done for me.

Roxy was a young lady now, tall and feminine, but with the attitude and mouth of a tough street kid. She was clearly having a difficult time with her life, saying things like, "They just don't understand me" and "They don't let me do the things I want to do." In one way, her complaints sounded like the typical growing pains most young girls go through. Most girls aren't allowed to come and go as they please, but most girls didn't have grandparents like hers either.

All I wanted to do was to help her anyway I could. Of course she didn't really remember me, so I took it slow. I explained that I was her aunt, and that she and I had a close relationship when she was much younger. I let her know that both her mother and I cared about her, and were worried about her. I said I was sorry for not being a part of her life for so long, but explained that her grandparents hadn't let me see her or talk to her since our trip to the mall when she was five. As you can imagine, I did most of the talking, hoping I was making sense. It was hard to tell. After about an hour, I left with mixed emotions. Something didn't feel quite right.

Shortly after my visit with Roxy, I found out that she'd left the halfway house. I had no idea where she went and was worried about her, so Gary and I drove around my old neighborhood looking for her and/or her boyfriend J. Roxy had told me about J — where he lived and what he looked like — so we knew where to start. After driving around for a while, we saw someone who looked like he could be J. We stopped, and I leaned out the window and asked him if he was J, adding that I was Roxy's aunt. It was J, and I asked if we could talk for a few minutes. We went back to his house, and while Gary waited in his truck, J and I stood in his garage talking.

He said that he really liked Roxy, but that they hadn't been dating very long. I explained that when I called the halfway house to talk to her, I was told that she was no longer there. I hadn't been able to talk to her for the past few days, and I was hoping he might be able to help. He said he hadn't heard from her lately either.

We talked a while longer about how they met, and what kinds of classes they were taking in school. He seemed like a nice kid. We were pretty sure she would be in touch with him, so we made tentative plans for the four of us to go out for ice cream as soon as it could be arranged.

A few days later, Roxy called me to tell me there had been an "incident" at the halfway house and that she had been moved to a different halfway house. She said she was okay, and wanted to get together, so we made plans to go out for ice cream the next day. Gary wanted to know the details of the incident, but I didn't want to push Roxy for details at this point. I just wanted to continue to build a relationship with her.

The next day Gary and I picked up J and Roxy and headed to the Friendly's in the mall for ice cream. Roxy seemed like any other 15-year-old drama queen. J was content to smile and stare at her. Between Roxy's laughing and giggling, I tried to carry on a conversation with her hoping to get to know her. Gary and I both attempted to sneak in questions that might help us learn more about her past. She answered a few, but not all of them.

I divulged a little bit about myself too. I told her that I wouldn't go to her grandparent's house because I'd been touched the wrong way when I lived there. I explained that the family had broken ties with me because I'd spoken the truth. I said that was fine with me because I didn't want to be around people who didn't believe me. Both Gary and I did our best to encourage her tell us a little about herself, but it was like pulling teeth. Maybe most kids are like that today. We didn't know, and after a couple of hours, I could tell Gary was ready to leave, so we left the restaurant and walked around the mall for awhile.

It was nice being with Roxy, but strange too, wondering if — or when — she was going to tell me her grandfather had touched her. I just wanted to get to know her though, and make sure she knew that she could tell me anything she wanted to.

Walking around the mall with her was interesting. It's a kid's hangout, full of the kinds of stores teenage girls love—clothing stores. And this girl knew exactly what she did and didn't like. She told us where certain clothes could be bought and how much they cost. This kid knew her stuff and immediately I could tell Gary's radar was up. I didn't want to start a precedent on our first day together by lavishing her with gifts, but boy, was she persistent. She wouldn't let up about me buying her clothes. I finally gave in and said that on our next visit to the mall we could go clothes shopping. I looked behind me and saw Gary shaking his head. He was not smiling.

After dropping off the kids, there was no hesitation from Gary when he gave me his impression of the day. He said he thought my niece was telling more lies than truths, and that she was trying to manipulate me. I didn't disagree. Fortunately, we were both prepared for something like that. After all, she'd been living in my mother's house for ten years—ten very formative years. It was expected, and neither one of us was going to fall for her act.

Maybe it was a little unfair of Gary to sum up Roxy so quickly, but I had to agree with some of what he was saying. His last words on the subject of that day were, "That kid is trouble." My last thoughts for the day were about figuring out how Roxy could come live with us. I was already planning the Fourth of July picnic I would give so I could introduce her to my real family, just as my real father had done for me so many years ago. Within a short amount of time, Gary and I started talking about doing what we needed to do to have Roxy come and live with us.

When I asked Roxy what she thought about the idea of Gary and I becoming her foster parents and her coming to live with us, she sounded positive and excited, but I also thought she believed she'd have more freedom living with us. I didn't push the point because there were so many hoops Gary and I had to jump through before it would become a reality. In my mind though, I was already thinking like a parent and dreaming of us being one big happy family. I was still writing in my "Roxy Journal" too, but not every entry was positive:

June 27, 2004

> *Hi Roxy,*
>
> *It's about 9:00 p.m. and you called me this morning to apologize for not calling last night. I waited until 11:00 p.m. then went to bed. To say I wasn't upset would be a lie. My stomach was turning. I didn't know if something happened to you. Riding a bike home in the dark is something I wouldn't even do as an adult. There are so many wackos out there.*
>
> *Would you be bored living here? Would you just want to sleep here and spend all your time with J? I would want us to do things together as a family. School and chores are also important. With all the freedom you're used to, you must be*

used to going along on your own.

By this time I was beginning to understand I couldn't impose my will on my niece, even though I thought I knew what was best for her. I started to seriously doubt she'd want what I was offering too. She rarely followed through on anything she told me, and days would go by without her contacting me.

Gary doubted everything she told us and wondered what she was really doing. I gave her a journal to write her thoughts down in like I was doing. I told her about the journal I'd been keeping, and about how I believed it was an important moment in both our lives. As a little surprise, I slipped a nice card into her journal, but I doubt she even opened it. She never mentioned the journal or the card, and I didn't ask.

June 29, 2004

Hello Roxy,

Today I dropped off the waiver info that DSS needed, and they gave me the Commonwealth of Massachusetts Department of Social Services Child Specific Home Study Family Assessment paperwork to fill out, which I will do tonight. Roxy, I put the phone by my bed and hoped you would have called last night. You called during the day and left a message on the machine. I gave you my work number… didn't you want to talk to me? I hope this all works out — you deserve to be happy.

July 1, 2004

Happy July Roxy,

I dropped off the letter of interest today at 10:30 a.m. I called J and asked him if he told you I called yesterday. I'm feeling like you don't want any of this… I have been thinking and wondering about you for many years now. I wonder if you really meant all the things you said to me.

July 2, 2004

Hi Roxy,

Well, today after calling J twice and getting the brush off, Gary called him and J said the same thing to him. Gary also heard a girl's voice in the background, which sounded like you.

What do you want Roxy? I just don't know, so for now, I am going to sit back and wait. I will always love you and want what's best for you.

Love Kathy

That was the very last entry I ever wrote to Roxy. Days went by before I heard back from her. We never had that July 4th picnic. As for the journal, I kept it with hopes of sharing it with her someday, but she never saw, read, or heard one word from it. As the weeks passed, I heard less and less from her. Eventually she ended up going back to her grandparent's house and then the calls stopped all together.

Maybe the dream I had been replaying in my mind for all those years regarding my niece had been unfair to her. Here I was, this mysterious absent aunt coming out of the woodwork and trying to push my ideas of a better way of life on her. She wanted what she wanted though, and it was totally at odds with what Gary and I wanted to provide for her. I had to accept the fact that she wasn't interested in what we had offered. My heart was so sad, but I knew it was time to let go of my dream of helping Roxy escape a life that I couldn't wait to get away from. I'd tried my best with an open heart—my husband by my side—and for whatever reason, it was never going to happen.

But when one door closes another one opens, and Gary and I decided to start a family of our own. The first thing we had to do was consult a reproductive specialist because Gary had had a vasectomy many years ago. They told us there was only a 5% chance of a successful reversal. My problem was that I had too much scar tissue to become pregnant easily, let alone successfully carry a child to term. They also told us we were too old…. I was 42.

Okay, we thought, then we would adopt. We were fine with that option too. So between September and December we attended several informative meetings with other couples who wanted to adopt. During the last meeting we sat in on, the group hosting the meetings told us there would be an upfront cost of $60,000! When Gary raised his hand to ask why it cost so much, they said it was all administrative costs. That pretty much guaranteed we would be raising puppies for the rest of our lives.

It was a cold December night, and as we left the building after that last meeting, we heard the door behind us close and click shut on our dream of having a family.

2005

Needless to say, I once again buried myself in my SOL advocacy work. This was my calling, and this was where I could do the most good. I was stubborn enough to think I could make something happen, and stubborn enough to believe that surviving a childhood filled with sexual abuse had left me more qualified than anyone else to spearhead this work.

I'd met so many victims by this time that I understood I wasn't just advocating for myself anymore. I was advocating for the young—and the not so young—who weren't able or ready to advocate for themselves. There should never have been a time limit placed on reporting this crime. And no one should be denied justice just because it took them time to come to terms with what had been done to them.

Signs that I was on the right path with my advocacy work started popping up too. I opened our local newspaper on Feb 17, 2005 and this headline jumped out at me: *Officials seek change to sex abuse law. The state (MA) lawmakers want the statute of limitations to be removed following the recent clergy scandal.*

To say I was thrilled to read this would be an understatement. I had been working on this exact topic for about 2 years now, and this just affirmed my belief that we could affect a positive change in the law. So I started reaching out to the Boston politicians with mail, email, and phone calls. It was good to know they were working for change in their end of the state while I was working the western part of the state. They wanted to abolish the SOL due to the priest sex abuse scandal while I wanted it ended for anybody and everybody.

The newspaper article went on the say: "The statute limited prosecution of abusive priests in the Boston Archdiocese's sex scandal. The current 15 year SOL in rape cases prevented prosecutors from going after most others. Rep. Ron Mariano, D-Quincy, lead sponsor of the bill, said,

'Many victims of sexual abuse take years to come to grips with what happened to them. By then, it's too late to prosecute their abusers. We need to allow victims to deal with their victimization and come forward at a time that's appropriate for them.' Prosecutors were able to charge one priest because he moved out of MA in the early 1990's, a move that stopped the clock on the SOL, but for dozens of other priests, prosecutors were unable to bring a case because of the statute. Similar bills were introduced in recent years, but failed. State Senator Scott Brown, R-Wrentham, said that the current SOL has allowed many sex offenders to get away with their crimes, knowing they can't be prosecuted. 'This is something that has been going on way too long.' "

It would have been nice if I could have just emailed a copy of this article along with all the other information and articles I was collecting, but the amount of information I had to send out was too much for email. Email might be good for communicating and exchanging information, but people don't like long emails. They don't always like attachments either, and are less likely to read or print them out. If I mailed important articles and information through regular mail, then I knew they would be in someone's actual hands, and hopefully they would read them. I took it on as a challenge — to get as much mileage out of this article as I could — so I made physical copies of it and included it with all my mailings to Massachusetts lawmakers. It was one way to make sure everybody was aware that some very influential people were finally speaking up, and it made our cause that much easier for other politicians to support.

A week after the newspaper article appeared, I sent in a *Letter to the Editor* applauding the work being done in Boston to eliminate the SOL. It wasn't the first time I'd written a letter to the editor, but it was the first time I'd felt compelled to respond to an article. In my letter, I reminded readers that priests weren't the only abusers. This time, my letter was published, and it felt great to be a part of the conversation!

As for the packages I was mailing to state representatives, I took advantage of the fact that I could send more information this way. It was expensive too, because the money I was using to purchase office supplies, print copies at home, and pay the postage to mail them out was coming out of my own pocket. But like I said, I was determined.

Each of those packages consisted of a short one-page bio of my life, the newspaper article about the priest sex abuse scandal, and relevant information I'd pulled from the internet. For example, I included a list of the MA legislators petitioning for the passage of the SOL bill, along with a copy of a press release printed on Representative Ron Mariano's official letterhead that outlined the priest sex abuse scandal, and what should be done.

After a few weeks went by, I followed up with a phone call to each recipient asking if they had received the information I'd sent them, if they had any questions, and for their support in passing the new law. Those phone calls were squeezed in during lunch breaks at home, and nights after dinner. You'd be surprised at the number of politicians and aides I made contact with by phoning their offices on the weekend.

I didn't have to get Rep. Ron Mariano and his staff on board because he was the sponsor of the SOL bill, and over the years, I'd exchanged many emails with him and his staff. They were extremely helpful with educating me on the inner workings of government. According to one of their emails, "At any one point in time there are over 6,000 bills pending. Many never see the light of day just because of the sheer number pending, but those that get heard are the ones that garner the most attention. If time runs out on a bill, it has to be re-filed. If it doesn't get re-filed, it gets dropped."

This bill was so new by comparison to others, and there were so many bills, that it was just about impossible for every politician to know about every pending bill. I learned that this bill had been initiated two years earlier, but hadn't made it through. This time was different. This time, with all the press about the Catholic Church sex abuse scandal in the news, more people than ever were willing to listen to what people had to say about the SOL bills. That's where I came in. My job was to make sure this bill didn't get forgotten or dropped, and that every lawmaker was made aware of how important it was to every survivor of sexual abuse.

With my follow-up phone calls, I realized there were many politicians in Boston who were not aware of this bill, and I was thrilled to bring them up to speed. These lawmakers and their staff worked tirelessly. They were professional and always responded to my inquiries. Ron's office kept me updated as the list of bill co-sponsors continued to grow. It was very fulfilling to hear the names of new co-sponsors when they were people I'd spoken with about supporting the bill.

I received a very touching email from Ron's aid, Wayne Weikel. "Kathy, your work has certainly not gone unnoticed here in this office. It seems a bit patronizing for Ron or I to say that we appreciate your hard work, because in the end, we are not the ones who this legislation helps, but if it is possible to speak on behalf of those who fall victim in the future…Thank you."

This was more proof I was making a difference. Elected officials in Boston were starting to reach out to me, a girl from Springfield doing her advocacy work part-time while holding down a full-time job. People were noticing me and rallying along with me towards a common goal. I'd never received a kind word growing up, and now, whenever I got a "thank you," or a kind word was sent my way, it made me feel stronger and more confident about myself and about what I was doing.

Ludlow Representative Thomas Petrolati and his staff were also strong supporters of the bill, and very responsive whenever I called or sent an email. I would stop in at their office from time to time just to say hello and to thank them for their support. One of his staff members had a mini-schnauzer too, so we always exchanged dog stories when I stopped in. Every time I appeared in a newspaper article, someone in his office would laminate the article, and Tom would write a little note to me. It meant a lot to me that he would do that, and I have kept everything I've received from them. They are wonderful people, all doing their best for Ludlow's citizens. It was great meeting them, getting to know them, and sharing a common goal.

Little by little, I was starting to receive personalized letters from other senators and representatives too, thanking me for my work and pledging their support of the bill. What a fantastic group of people. You can say whatever you want about politicians, but they were there for me, supporting me and my efforts, and being there for me meant that they were there for every other victim too.

The newspaper ran an Associated Press article on March 7, 2005, in which then Massachusetts Attorney General Thomas F. Reilly said that he would support the bill that would end the SOL in sex abuse cases. "A predator of a child should never be out of the reach of the law," Reilly said. "When someone is brave enough to come forward and testify and confront their abuser, they should not be prevented because of any technicality in the law."

A week later I received a signed letter from then Governor Mitt Romney, thanking me for my work and informing me that he would send along the package he received to his staff. I treasure each and every one of these mementos.

One of the most amazing benefits for me personally with reaching out to all these politicians was the number of wonderful people I was meeting and adding to my ever-expanding circle of acquaintances. Occasionally, a politician, or his aide, would give me the name and email address of someone they thought I should connect with. It really was that kind of grass roots support system. I met genuinely wonderful and hardworking people who believed in the importance of the advocacy work I was doing. I connected with people who came from backgrounds similar to mine, and the emotional support we were able to offer each other was immeasurable. I also connected with people who might not ever be ready to speak up for themselves. They all inspired me with their strength though, and I became even more determined (if that was possible) to keep going—for them— even if it meant becoming the unofficial poster child for sexual abuse.

◆ ◆ ◆ ◆ ◆

An incredible and exciting part of life was opening up for me. The more people I met, the more I learned. Not just about how our government worked, or about statistics, or about childhood sexual abuse, but about the human spirit too. I was moved when people started contacting me to tell me their stories. No matter what time of day or night it was, if somebody called or emailed me, I was there to listen. There's just something about talking with someone when you know you don't have to pretend that it didn't happen, or that it wasn't as bad as it really was. It was a humbling experience, but an experience I drew strength from. It was a glorious feeling knowing I was doing something that would honestly and truly help people. I finally felt like my life was worth something, and I constantly thanked the universe for putting me here to do this kind of work.

With a flurry of emails and phone calls in mid May 2005, we had helped move both bills forward. The Criminal Statute bill had been HD 2854, and was now H3555. The Civil Statute bill had been HD 2849, and was now H909. All in all, very good news. The bills were making the journey forward to becoming new laws. It showed progress and promise, and everyone involved was feeling optimistic.

◆ ◆ ◆ ◆ ◆

I was skimming through the newspaper one day and came across an article about a Catholic organization called *Voice of the Faithful*. It was a group that had been started in 2002 in Wellesley, MA, in response to the Catholic Church's clergy sexual abuse crisis. The organization was continuing to grow, and now had a chapter in East Longmeadow run by John and Mary Lou Bowen. One of the organization's goals was to participate in the governance and guidance of the Catholic Church so that nothing like this would ever happen again. But it was also involved in pushing for legislation that would eliminate SOLs for sex crimes against minors.

At this point in my life I had no problem picking up the phone and talking to a perfect stranger, so I called John Bowen to talk to him about the work his group was doing. I talked briefly about my past, and about the advocacy work I was involved with. We talked about our common struggles with battling sexual abuse, and I asked him if there was anything I could do to help. After a pause, he asked me if I'd be willing to speak at their next meeting, saying that he believed hearing from a survivor of sexual abuse firsthand would be a strong reminder of how meaningful and important the work the people in this chapter were doing.

John was very nice, and even after I explained to him that I'd never spoken about my abuse in public before, he said it wouldn't matter. He assured me that my sincerity would show through in person—just like it did over the phone—and that would mean more to the people than anything else. So I agreed. I thanked him for his vote of confidence, and said that I was looking forward to meeting him and his group. Fortunately for me, their next meeting wasn't for a few weeks, so I had time to prepare.

If there's one thing most of us have in common, it's a fear of public speaking. I was no exception. Just thinking about it terrified me. I had never spoken in public before and I was scared, but my desire to reach a group of people far outweighed my fears. This was just another way to get the word out. For 20 or 30 people to hear from a survivor was going to be an eye opening experience for many of them.

Still, I wanted to do a good job, so I talked to co-workers who regularly spoke at meetings and conferences to get their ideas and perspectives on the best way to approach speaking to a group of people. I went online too, but found more information than I could handle. I knew there were people who could just stand up and start talking, but I wasn't comfortable with this kind of "shooting from the hip" strategy. I didn't want to leave anything to chance, so I enlisted Gary's help, and together, we sat down to compose my first speech.

We talked about what I wanted to accomplish with my speech, and what highlights I wanted to hit. After going back and forth with ideas, he went upstairs to his office and came back down a few hours later with my first speech. (Did I mention that Gary is the writer in our family? Without his hard work, this book wouldn't exist!)

The speech was basically a longer, more detailed version of the bio I was mailing out to politicians, but it also included a part about how concerned I was for the safety of my young niece now that she was being raised in the same house, by the same people I'd grown up with. I rewrote the speech so it would be in my own familiar handwriting and practiced reading it over and over again to myself, and then aloud until I felt comfortable with the material. I practiced reading it slowly so I wouldn't lose my place, or my audience. I wanted every word to carry weight and have meaning. It came in at about five minutes.

Voice of the Faithful meetings were held at St. Michael's Church hall in East Longmeadow. When I got there, I was very nervous, but then I looked around. The atmosphere was comfortable, and it was an older audience of about 30 individuals. Before I had too much more time to think about it, John introduced me as their guest speaker, and I was standing in front of them.

I started by thanking them all for the opportunity to share my story, and felt a wave of peace and reassurance fill me. If this was public speaking, it wasn't too bad. As I read my speech, I made sure to look up and make eye contact with people in the audience. At certain points in my story, they responded with gasps at what they were hearing.

I finished my speech by thanking John, and the members of the group, and then it was over. I received a warm applause from the audience, and then left so they could continue their meeting. And that was it. I'd given my first public speech and thought, *I did it!*

When something new and amazing like this happens, you hope the positive energy you put out is enough to help people feel inspired to take action. I hadn't written my speech in an attempt to get the audience to gasp at what my stepfather had done to me, but when they did, it reminded me of how important it is for people to know the reality of sexual abuse. It's not a bedtime story, and for some people, hearing a survivor's story is an experience that can inspire them to become stronger advocates too.

A few days later, I called John Bowen to thank him again for the opportunity to speak. He told me how pleased he was with how it went, and we promised to keep in touch. And delivering my first speech? It was a piece of cake, and I was ready to say yes to the next person who asked me to speak.

◆　◆　◆　◆　◆

Through John and Mary Lou, I learned about the pastor of St. Michael's, Father James Scahill. Father Scahill was an outspoken supporter for the community of survivors of clergy sexual abuse. And even though this didn't make Father Scahill very popular with his clergy peers, he worked tirelessly to try and help heal the wounded relationship between his church and his community. He listened to his parishioners' concerns and reached out to counsel and support survivors of abuse. Priests take a vow of obedience and even though his views were publicly denounced by one of Massachusetts' Bishops, he continued to stand for what he believed to be in the best interest of his people.

In 2004, Father Scahill received the *Priest of Integrity* award from *Voice of the Faithful* for his honorable pastoral service. *Voice of the Faithful* president James Post said, "Father Scahill demonstrated exemplary courage and principled leadership by speaking up for victims of abuse, and insisting the church do the right thing in responding to them. When he spoke out, he could not have contemplated the hardship he would face, or the criticism he would bear. But he did not flinch or forsake those survivors of clergy sexual abuse. And looking back, we can see the power of his actions — they are a beacon of integrity for all to see."

I was raised in an Italian Catholic family, and I took my sisters to church every Sunday. When I wanted to attend a Catholic high school, my parents wouldn't pay the tuition so I worked as a waitress to pay for it myself. So I was very much aware of the strict Catholic way of life, and how priests and nuns were supposed to act. I'd never heard of a priest quite like Father Scahill, and since we were both working towards the same goal, I decided I wanted to meet him. The more we banded together in pursuit of our common goals, the better our odds would be. I contacted his church and spoke with his assistant, Patty. She said she would give him my phone number so he could call me. When he called me back, and then decided I wasn't a fanatic, we had a nice conversation. He also invited me to the rectory for a visit. I was so excited!

When I arrived at the rectory, Father Scahill answered the door himself, and guided me to an office with a set of chairs by a window. When I sat down in one of them, he smiled and mused, "Why does everyone assume I should sit in the fancier chair?"

I looked at the chair I'd sat in, and he was right. One chair was definitely fancier than the other, and I'd sat in the less fancy one. Father Scahill had a down-to-earth manner that put me at ease right away. I thanked him for seeing me, and we got right to the point of my visit.

He wanted to know a little about me so I shared my story and told him about the advocacy work I'd been involved in. He listened. That meant a lot to me. I'd never dreamed I could have a conversation with a priest about sexual abuse. We both discussed our work to eliminate the SOLs on sexual abuse, and offered each other our support. He gave me his cell number and asked me to keep him updated with any information I got, and said that I could speak to Patty too.

He certainly made an impression on me that day, and it was a visit I've never forgotten. Yes, I'd made another contact, but more importantly, a contact with a regular guy who was genuinely friendly, approachable, and actively fighting to support victims of sexual abuse.

As I was leaving Father Scahill's office, I told him about the first hearing for Bill 909 — an act amending the civil statute of limitations — that I'd just heard about. It was scheduled for September 21st in Boston. At the hearing, supporters would be able to tell their stories and ask lawmakers to support the bill. He said he wouldn't be able to attend, but he certainly wished everybody good luck with their efforts.

Rep. Tom Petrolati, couldn't make the meeting either, but had his aide, Jack Ryan, send an email to Rep. Ron Mariano, sponsor of the bill, plainly stating that he was in favor of passing this legislation, and requested that he be recorded as a supporter of this important proposal.

Jack sent me an email to keep me in the political loop and went on to say, "Your story, and asking for our help, only strengthens our resolve to see this bill passed. I hope this gives you some comfort in knowing we are with you in this matter."

Comfort? Are you kidding me? I was elated! I did my happy dance all over the room! That email made me feel like the neighborhood wimp who all of a sudden has the entire football team as her new best friend. It was really happening, progress was finally being made. But with only two days notice, it was going to happen without me. I couldn't get the time off of work.

On September 23rd, Jack sent me a follow-up email full of extremely useful information regarding the hearing that had taken place. Everyone in attendance had considered the hearing a success. There were approximately 50 citizen supporters, many of them testifying in favor of the bill that would extend the civil SOL. He listed all the supporters who testified — survivors, survivor's spouses, a psychologist, a former police chief, legal advocates, and a psychiatric nurse who specializes in working with sexual abuse survivors.

There was no public opposition, in any form, at the hearing!

Also listed in the email were the names of the House and Senate Judiciary Committee members present. But more importantly, the names of the members who were not present were listed too. As soon as I saw that list, I knew those were the people we needed to focus on. Those were the people we needed to reach, educate, and convince that this was a meaningful bill to support. It was time to start focusing on the fence sitters. We knew who they were, and we had all their contact information.

The very next day, I received another email, this time from one of my new acquaintances, Bonnie. Bonnie Gorman and Susan Renehan were co-chairs of the Coalition to Reform Sex Abuse Laws in Massachusetts. Susan had heard about my advocacy work and reached out to me. It was great to connect with another group of people working towards getting the bills passed, and I was happy to be added to their email list and help them in any way I could.

In this email, Bonnie included a list of judiciary committee members, along with their email contact information, and asked us to email them personal letters asking them to support the bill, and for their favorable vote and a recommendation that the bills be sent to the full legislative body for a floor vote. It was critical for the legislators to move these bills out of committee, and they needed to hear our stories and be reminded of why they needed to support the bills.

This is what we were working towards:

- An Act amending the Criminal Statute of Limitations (House 3555, Senate 1058)… This bill will give District Attorneys more time to bring criminal charges against rapists and child molesters.
- An Act amending the Civil Statute of Limitations (House 909, Senate 1057)… This bill will remove time bars that prevent adult survivors from pursuing lawsuits against pedophiles that victimized them when they were children.

It was nice being part of a group of people who all shared the same goal. We were connected through our emails, but most of my co-supporters lived in the eastern part of the state, so we hadn't had opportunities to meet. Every once in a while though, I'd pick up the phone and call one of my new friends. We'd talk about our work, go over the latest SOL news, and review any upcoming events or meetings. We also talked about whatever else was on our minds.

Of particular interest then was an SOL Advocacy Day planned for Tuesday, January 10, 2006 at the State House in Boston. I had no idea what an Advocacy Day was, but I knew it was another opportunity to promote legislation on the passage of both the criminal and civil bills which would change the SOL in favor of the victim. I knew that there had been some support for the bills when they were first presented in 2004, but not enough to get a vote, so the bills had never made it out of the judiciary committee.

In this current session, it was the Catholic Church clergy sex scandal that inspired a wider coalition of political support for the bills, with over sixty legislators having signed on as co-supporters. This time there was an excellent chance of the bill making it out of committee, but, as always, we had to strike while the iron was hot. This rally was to show legislators how much public support there was for these bills.

In one of her emails, Bonnie asked me if I would speak at the rally. Without hesitation I told her it would be an honor to be allowed to tell my story. This time I had a whole two weeks to prepare!

The rally was scheduled for 11:00 a.m. with a press conference to follow. After that, advocates were free to mingle, and to try to meet with representatives and senators that were available. It promised to be a huge event with plenty of media coverage.

Many people from Western Massachusetts are nervous and wary about driving around Boston, and I am no exception. So I contacted John and Mary Lou Bowen to see if they were attending the Advocacy Day Rally in Boston. They were, so I asked if I could ride along with them. Of course they said yes. This was going to be a great day!

◆　◆　◆　◆　◆

While I was working full time and busy with my advocacy work, Gary was working harder than ever too. He had been working for the same family-owned company for over eleven years, and was their inside sales manager. Now the company was going through changes, and not all of them were good for Gary. They were continuing to grow and decided to move their operation to Rocky Hill, Connecticut. Prior to that, Gary had been able to come home for lunch. Now he left for work at 6:00 a.m. and didn't get home until after 6:00 p.m. As a result of the owner's decision to consolidate manufacturing and operations, Gary's staff almost tripled overnight, which meant his work load just about tripled too. It was a difficult time for him and his co-workers. He had worked closely with the same people for eleven years, and while some of them were kept on after the move, most were let go.

If there's one thing that bothers Gary, it's having his routine messed with. Not only had his hours gotten longer, but now that his job and staff had expanded, there was too much work and not enough time to get it all done at the office, so he started bringing it home to work on. Neither of us was very happy with the adjustments we had to make, but we did what we had to do. I added most of what needed to be done around the house to my to-do list. When Gary brought work home with him, we worked in our upstairs office together.

It was a tough transition because Gary used to love his job. We would talk about it during our after-supper walks. Within a few months of the company's changes, I could tell he wasn't enjoying it. I didn't know it at the time, but he was already thinking about leaving his job once his new staff was fully trained.

Sure enough, in October, Gary landed a job with a family-owned business in Enfield, CT, working in their inside sales and service department. He swore off management forever, and was looking forward to being closer to home. It was still too far away for him to come home for lunch, but it was only a 25 minute commute. Soon, our life settled back to normal, and we were both happy he'd chosen quality family time over a stress-filled career.

2006

As the Boston rally approached, I found out that I would be speaking for three to five minutes. As I started to prepare what I was going to say, I did the same thing I'd done with my first speech. I thought about what topics were most important to touch on. My story was a big part of it, but so was how I became aware of the SOL bills, and what I'd been doing to contact legislators. I wanted to stress that the time to act was now. I tweaked my original speech, and once it was done, I kept reading it over and over until I was comfortable with it.

A few days before the rally, the Boston Globe ran an article that discussed the Catholic Church and their priest sex abuse scandal, along with the SOL bills. As amazing as it may sound, not all lawmakers were in agreement. For example, the House Chairman of the Committee on the Judiciary had some concerns about the proposed SOL bills. He said, "I have some strong reservations about changing statutes of limitations. I think they serve a very strong public purpose. Sometimes the rationale behind them is not necessarily appealing, but they do play a very important role in our judicial systems. We have to be deferential to the statute of limitations and very cautious when dealing with proposals to change them."

Okay, I respect his right to have an opinion, but chances are extremely good that he hadn't lived through the same kind of childhood I had. And what about the survivors who came forward to bring the clergy sex abuse scandal to light? Where was justice for them if the SOLs weren't changed? All I could do was hope that the voters in Massachusetts who were reading about the Catholic Church's sex abuse scandal understood that there was a lot more to it than just the politics of the cover-up. It was about people who had been sexually abused as children by adults they should have been able to trust without question. These bills were a way for the judicial system to provide sexual abuse survivors with a way to safely stand up and face their abusers. And that's what we were pushing for, a change that would allow survivors to legally pursue those who did them wrong when they were innocent children.

Another comprehensive and informative article about the upcoming State House rally ran in The Register, our local newspaper, that day too. I had called the paper's editor a couple of weeks ahead of the Advocacy Day to tell her about the rally, and hopefully get some local coverage for it. We talked for a while, and then she decided to feature both my personal story and the clergy sex abuse scandal. It made me happy to see my story and my mission in print. I wasn't naive enough to think I could single-handedly wipe out childhood sexual abuse, but I did hope that the attention I was putting on the problem would help reduce the number of attacks.

◆　◆　◆　◆　◆

There was no doubt that the SOL bills were my top priority, but I had another idea starting to kick around in my head too. It seemed like every parent I talked to said the same thing, that their children weren't taught anything about sexual abuse — not even what to do if something confusing happened to them. I knew what they were talking about because I certainly hadn't ever been taught anything about it. It doesn't do me any good to think about how different my life might have been if I'd been taught either, but it got me thinking about it even more.

We needed to change the way we talk to our children, and teach our children, about sexual abuse. Even with all the SOL advocacy work I was doing, and believed in with all my heart, we were focused on dealing with situations where the damage had already been done. It hurt to think about all the children who needed our help right now, and it made me mad that people still thought that ignoring the problem was an acceptable solution.

The SOL bills were very important because they were a chance for adult survivors to seek justice in the court system — if that's what they wanted. Doing everything we could to get these bills passed was something we were doing for survivors who hadn't grown up with people they could have talked to, or who could have realized it when something wasn't right. Seeking justice through the courts would be another part of the healing process for them, and a way to get closure. Each survivor who took advantage of one of the new SOL bills would be paving the way for the next. Their actions would increase awareness too, and encourage other survivors to speak up. Because you know what they say, "Your secrets will kill you."

The more people who heard about me and my story while I was advocating for the SOL bills, the more chances there would be for educating our children about sexual abuse too. By educating our children, I mean teaching them the difference between good and bad touching, and about how to speak to a trusted adult if they aren't sure, or are confused about something. Of course, it has to start with adults, and I hoped that hearing my story would increase their awareness, even if it was only one adult at a time.

I could clearly see teaching young children early in their school careers about how to be safe and aware of themselves and their bodies. If they were taught in school about body safety (or whatever you want to call it) there would be fewer adult sexual abuse court cases in the long run.

◆ ◆ ◆ ◆ ◆

When I woke up on the morning of January 10th after a fitful night's sleep, I felt a mixture of emotions as my mind started gearing up for all the things that were going to happen during the day. I was excited and nervous, and a little overwhelmed, but deep down inside, I was calm and at peace. I felt strong and in control because we had worked and planned for this day when our voices would be heard in the state capital. I was ready, and I said to myself, "This is it. Today's the day!"

Gary had wanted to take me to Boston and be there to hear me speak, but he had just started his new job and didn't want to ask for the day off. So all he could do was give me a hug and a kiss, wish me luck, and then head off to work. I was too keyed up for breakfast so I just had coffee, put on my best dark suit, kissed my dogs goodbye, and headed for the park and ride to meet up with John and Mary Lou.

By 8:45 a.m., I was sitting in the back seat of their car headed for Boston. As soon as we got on the Mass Pike, I felt my anxiousness ratchet up another notch and was glad I was with John and Mary Lou rather than driving there on my own. They talked about their 29 years living in Boston, and how they'd gotten involved with the SOL bills. They were both very knowledgeable about the current laws, and I was impressed by the fact that they hadn't stuck their heads in the sand and tried to ignore the situation like so many other people who didn't have a personal stake in it had done. Instead, they had seen an injustice, rolled up their sleeves, and got involved.

When we got to Boston, John pulled into a parking garage. As soon as we were on the street, he started pointing out landmarks and telling me their history while I started snapping pictures. Once we were inside the State House, I took even more pictures. We made our way to the Grand Staircase on the second floor where folding chairs had been set up in front of a podium.

The air was electric! Politicians mingled while news teams jockeyed for the best place to set up their cameras. There were a lot of people coming and going and it was thrilling to be a part of it. A few minutes after 11:00 a.m., someone walked to the podium and everyone quieted down. It was beginning — it was really happening!

Average Age of Abuse:
12.3 years old
Average Disclosure Age:
44.7 years old
Average Yrs Before Disclosure
32.3 years

The obligatory thank yous and "it's nice to see everyone here today..." were being expressed while I was secretly starting to sweat in my suit. This was the big time! The speaker explained why we were all here and laid out the agenda for the day. The next hour was dedicated to the speakers and would be followed by a news conference. Then we would break to meet with our local lawmakers to try and drum up support for passing the SOL bills.

Then I heard, "Ladies and Gentlemen, Kathy Picard." I stood and started walking to the podium, but it felt like I was moving in slow motion. Fortunately, I made it there without tripping or bumping into anyone. The polite applause died down and I started by thanking a few people before getting right into my speech.

This felt different than when I'd been the guest speaker at the *Voice of the Faithful* meeting. I was feeling the nerves a lot more today, so I just pretended I was practicing at home in front of my dogs, and that helped me relax enough to not sound like a blithering idiot. I focused on my speech, trying to look out into the audience like I had done before, but mostly my eyes were on the handwritten script in front of me.

Five minutes later, I was done reading and the audience was applauding. What a rush that was! It was perfect. I had stood and contributed to a worthy cause, and from that point on, I was a different woman. I was more confident and focused, and more determined than ever to see this to the end.

After all the speakers had their say, it was the politicians turn to speak, and the news conference began. I listened for a while, but I'd made plans to meet some of my new friends and allies, so I started looking around for them. Because I'd been one of the speakers, most of the people I'd been looking forward to meeting and talking to found me first. We hugged and got teary-eyed and had our pictures taken together. It was fabulous. We talked about our advocacy work and what a worthy cause it was. Because of these dedicated people, today was possible, and by the looks of things, very successful.

Rep. Ron Mariano, Kathy, and Rep. Tom Petrolati

As the news conference wrapped up, we said our goodbyes and then set out to track down our legislators in hopes of having a personal chat. When I met the sponsor of the bills, Rep. Ron Mariano, I asked to have our picture taken with Rep. Tom Petrolati. That picture ran in The Springfield Republican a few weeks later. It was a good thing. More exposure meant more opportunities to tell my story and advocate for change.

It may have been an emotionally draining day, but the ride home was soothing, and once I was settled in the back seat of the car again, I dozed off and on for the rest of the ride home. We parted company at the park and ride, promising to keep in touch. On my short drive home, I replayed the day over in my mind and couldn't wait to tell Gary about it. It felt like it had been a very busy day, but a very successful day filled with lots of positive energy. Things looked promising for the bills. It was sad to think that the buzz over the priest sex abuse scandal had probably helped tip the scales in favor of passage, but that was the reality of the situation, and we were all cautiously optimistic.

As soon as I walked through my front door, I started talking to Gary about my day. He very kindly listened to everything I said while we prepared, cooked, and ate supper, and even while we cleaned up after. By the time we were done, I was talked out and too exhausted for our nightly walk, so I went to bed early.

As I lay there comfortably drifting off to sleep, I thought about the people we were trying to reach. For the most part, they weren't people living within a close-knit loving caring family with a father, mother, son, and daughter — although they needed to be aware too. I was thinking about the single parent, the foster child, the counselors who see kids every day, and adult survivors like me. I wanted to reach people in situations that left them on the fringes of their own lives, people who didn't know what to do or where or who to turn to, regardless of how old they were. I wanted them to know there was hope.

Follow-up articles on the Boston rally appeared the next day in all the major newspapers. And even though the event had taken place in Boston, I'd made the local papers, and received some flattering emails about what a compelling speaker I was. I even got a "You Go Girl!" email from The Register's editor.

When I got to work, my co-workers informed me that I'd made the 11:00 o'clock news. I had no idea I was going to be on the news. I'd been so tired the night before that I was asleep by 9:00 p.m.! I went online though, and sure enough, there I was, speaking. It was strange, but very nice to know I was being heard.

I liked hearing about it. I liked the attention too, and even though I was nervous beforehand, I liked standing in front of a crowd and speaking. But Gary was always there to remind me that we were working towards something important. It wasn't about "us," and we were both determined to keep my growing notoriety in perspective. We were doing this for a reason, and agreed that we weren't going to let things go to our heads and get wrapped up with inflated egos. (Okay, I confess that part was more about me, but I really appreciate the fact that Gary wrote it so it sounded like we both had to work on it.)

◆　◆　◆　◆　◆

I received an email from Bonnie Gorman letting the group know that an important judiciary hearing about repealing the SOL bills was slated for March 14th. In it, she asked all supporters to attend the meeting, and to contact their local media outlets and let them know about the meeting so it would get more press coverage. The judiciary committee would soon decide whether to send the SOL bills to the floor for a vote — or not — so we needed a big push the first two weeks in March. Time was running down for this year's session, and it was crucial to contact all the lawmakers and ask for their support.

So of course, I went right into action. I put together dozens of my packages, like I had in the past, and asked Rep. Tom Petrolati to hand deliver one to each member of the judiciary committee. After several days, I followed up with emails to make sure those packages were received. If I didn't get a response to my email, I followed up with a phone call. Consistency and follow through was just as important as the initial contact because it showed others you cared enough about the issue to put the work in.

Then something totally unexpected happened. On Feb. 13, 2006, I received a letter from The Massachusetts Commission on the Status of Women. I almost tossed it straight into the recycling bin thinking it was probably a request for a donation, but for some reason I opened it. Inside was a cover letter informing me that I had been selected as one of the Unsung Heroines of Massachusetts for 2006! I was totally taken by surprise. It sounded like a really good thing, but I wasn't sure what to think. How did they even know who I was?

The second page answered my question. It was a copy of the nomination form that had been filled out by Rep. Gale Candaras. I'd been in contact with her so many times over the past few years that we were on a first name basis. It felt really good to know that Gale thought my advocacy work was worthy of an award. Part of me was starting to get really excited, but part of me still wasn't sure what to think. Did they really give out awards for what I was doing? I needed more proof that the letter I was holding was the real deal, so I emailed the organization. Sure enough, it was legitimate, and they were going to give me an award! I'd never heard of such a thing. I believed the advocacy work I was doing was important, but it had never occurred to me that I might receive an award for something I was doing part-time.

I learned that the Massachusetts Commission on the Status of Women, MCSW for short, is an independent state agency whose mission is: *To advance women toward full equality in all areas of life and to promote rights and opportunities for all women.* I found out that nominations have to come from a State Legislator, and that the nominee has to live in the Legislator's district. I was very honored to realize Gale had nominated me as the representative from her district, and immediately contacted her to thank her.

She was one of the first legislators I had reached out to for help in the early stages of my advocacy work, and the first to respond with encouragement for what I was trying to do. Gale has been an inspiration to me since our first conversation. She has always made herself available, and knowing she would be there when I needed help has pushed me to do things I might never have otherwise tried. Gale is proof that one person can make a difference because she has made a difference in my life. Because of her, the quality of my life is better.

The awards ceremony was scheduled for March 3rd, and would take place in the Great Hall inside the Boston State House. Since I was going to be there anyway, I decided to make the most of my trip by trying to set up a few quick one-on-one meetings with members of the judiciary committee. Being able to share my story with decision makers, and talk to them face to face about how important the SOL bills were, was an opportunity I wasn't going to let slip away.

Gary heard me on the phone speaking with people about scheduling meetings and listened to me talk out the day in detail. He smiled at me and said, "Wow, you aren't the same girl I married. Who are you and what have you done with my wife?"

And it was true. I was no longer the shy quiet child/adult. I wasn't living the life of a victim now. Granted, members of my idiot family were still able to pull my strings, but when they weren't occasionally invading my time or space with their crap, I was doing more than just standing up for myself, I was standing up for people who were still carrying the weight of being a victim around with them. I was on a mission. I was living my life on much firmer ground because of it, and it was wonderful.

From the very beginning of my advocacy work, my goal was to raise awareness of childhood sexual abuse. It's an ugly topic, and a dirty little secret too many people sweep under the carpet just so they can go on with their lives as if everything is "okay." But keeping the secret doesn't change anything for the better. It certainly doesn't help the children. The only people who benefit from silence and ignorance are predators.

◆　◆　◆　◆　◆

When I started my advocacy work, I quickly realized that getting my story out was going to be a big part of it. Up to this point, Gary and I pretty much lived the same way our close family and friends lived. We were all working class people who paid our bills, worked hard to keep a roof over our heads, and did our best to fly under the radar. None of us were big on the idea of drawing attention to ourselves, but now I was realizing that if I wanted to be successful with my advocacy work, I was going to have to talk about my life even more. Fortunately, I'd always had the ability to speak with certainty. Now it was just a case of getting used to saying "I know this happens because it happened to me" on a larger scale.

Now I was beginning to get some press coverage and I started thinking about how to use the media to reach more people. I didn't really know where to start or who to call, so I just picked up the phone and called The Republican, the largest newspaper in Western Massachusetts. After being transferred around, I finally ended up in the voicemail box of a reporter named Tommy Shea. I left a long detailed message about why I was calling and said I hoped he would call back soon. Tommy did call back, and we talked for some time before I realized I was being interviewed right over the phone.

Our conversation was relaxed and he gave me plenty of time to tell my story and explain what my advocacy work was all about. Of course I mentioned being nominated for an Unsung Heroine of Massachusetts award. Why not? I was proud of that distinction. I had been nominated because someone thought my work was making a difference. It gave my work weight, and I'd already noticed that people perked up and listened when they heard about it. I also felt like it gave both me and my work credibility. Looking back, I understand that I had credibility from the beginning—credibility and truth go hand in hand. But now I had hopes that my expanding credibility might open doors that would have otherwise remained closed.

When the article appeared in the newspaper, Gary and I were so impressed with Tommy's work that Gary emailed him to thank him for writing such a good story about his wife. I was feeling pretty good about the article too, and contacted The Register's editor to keep her updated on what was going on with the bills, and to tell her about the award I was receiving. She liked what she heard, and said she'd like to do a follow-up article—with pictures—after the award ceremony.

◆　◆　◆　◆　◆

March 3rd was a beautiful day for the ride to Boston. This time I rode in with Gale and Darlotte, one of Gale's staff members. I knew what the agenda for the day was, but this was the first time I'd ever been given an award as an adult, so no matter what else happened the rest of the day, I knew for certain this would be an experience I would always remember.

When we arrived in Boston, we immediately headed for Gale's office. We left our coats and purses there, and I finally got to meet all the wonderful staff people I'd been talking to and trading emails with over the past few years. It was nice to be able to connect more faces with more names, and everyone made me feel like an old friend. From there we headed towards the Great Hall.

I had never seen a room quite like the Great Hall before. It looked like the hall of a castle taken right out of a fairy tale. It was huge and regal looking with its glass-domed ceiling. The walls were yellow brick, and there were beautiful stained glass windows. The walls were also lined with tiered rows of multicolored flags, each one representing one of Massachusetts' cities and towns. Rows of chairs had been arranged on the gleaming marble floor, giving the massive room a dignified and elegant air. It felt like a true honor to be part of a ceremony taking place in this room. Now that Gale and Darlotte had gone off to do their thing, I picked a chair with a good view—not too close to the front—but close enough so I wouldn't miss a thing.

Before too long, people started filling the seats, and when the MCSW chairwoman stood at the podium, the room grew quiet. She began by welcoming all parties and gave a brief overview of why we were all there.

Lt. Governor Kerry Healey spoke next and gave a moving speech, but I couldn't tell you what it was about. I was just too nervous and excited to remember. The next speaker talked about the importance of the great work we all do.

Then, MCSW committee members began reading the names of the Heroines alphabetically. When each name was called, the person stood, everyone clapped, and the award was presented. As they got closer to calling my name, I asked the person next to me to take my picture as I stood. I just wanted to make sure the moment was captured and it wasn't just a dream. (When Gary saw the picture, he said I was glowing, but it was probably just the flash.)

After all the names had been read, and the awards handed out, we all headed to the Grand Staircase for a group photo. As we all gathered on the staircase, I looked around at the women I was surrounded by. We might not have known each other, but we were all striving to make our communities a better place to live. It was a humbling experience to stand among them, and I was truly grateful that someone thought I deserved to be a part of this group.

After the group photo, people broke off into smaller groups, taking more pictures and talking excitedly while the media interviewed various politicians and award recipients. It was a very festive and supportive environment. I mingled around a bit and had my picture taken with several other women from the group, but I had an agenda for the rest of my day.

During the weeks prior to the ceremony, I'd made calls to certain judiciary committee members and made arrangements to stop by their State House offices for a brief visit. But as I made my rounds, none of the legislators were in. I left my name with a staff worker at each office, and actually got to speak with one aide. At least I'd made the effort. With advocacy work, consistency is a necessity. It's all about not giving up, because the more you try, the greater your chances for success.

As I was walking back to Gale's office, I came upon Senator Scott Brown's office door and couldn't resist. I've met many politicians over the years, but never a real-life GQ model. When I walked in, I introduced myself and asked if I could speak with him for just a minute. As he emerged from behind the closed door, it was easy to see why he'd been a male model. He was tall, trim, and very good looking. I introduced myself, we shook hands, and then I told him why I was in Boston and the reason for my visit to his office.

I know how busy politicians are and that everyone wants a piece of their time, so I kept it short but he was very friendly and talkative. He listened as I told him my story and talked about how important the SOL bills were to victims of sexual abuse, myself included. I asked for his support, and he gave me his word he would support the SOL bills. Not a bad way to end my visit to Boston.

Back at Gale's office, we ordered sandwiches and sat and ate while we talked about the day's events. When we were done, Gale presented me with an official citation for my advocacy work. I was completely taken off guard, and kept staring at it to make sure it really had my name on it! One of the staff members took a picture of Gale presenting me with the citation.

It had been a most memorable day, and I was very happy with the way everything had gone. I'd met some wonderful people, received both an award and a citation, and had a great meeting with Sen. Scott Brown — who promised to support the SOL bills. To me, this day was proof that no matter where we come from, or what our background is, we all have something we can contribute to make a difference in other people's lives.

There are people who would be tempted to think that maybe now I could look back on all the years of sexual abuse my stepfather had inflicted on me and think it was worth it because of what I was now accomplishing with my advocacy work. They'd be wrong. Yes, I was definitely starting to feel like I might be able to make a difference for other victims of abuse, maybe even prevent or stop someone's abuse, but nothing was ever going to make what he did to me "okay." Nothing.

All the good things that were starting to happen now weren't happening because of what he did. They were happening because I wasn't willing to settle for being a victim anymore. I was becoming stronger and more determined. It was who I was now, and today, I'd had the privilege of spending time with other strong and determined people. What an honor! What a day!

◆　◆　◆　◆　◆

The date for voting on the bills kept getting shoved back because the House was tied up with a budget debate. As frustrating as this was, at least the bills were still under consideration. And it was back to emailing and calling the lawmakers in Boston to inspire them to get off their duffs and do the right thing.

◆　◆　◆　◆　◆

There was new family drama to deal with too. My sister Meri claimed her clothes were being stolen right out of the dryer by tenants in the apartment complex where she lived. After hearing about this for some time, Gary and I purchased a washer and dryer and had it delivered and installed in her apartment. It was a simple solution that made her life easier, and everyone was happy. She promised to pay me back a little each month, and she did.

Around the same time, Meri's boyfriend got drunk one night and pushed her around. She called the cops, and they arrested him. To make a long sad story short, he ended up going to jail on a domestic abuse charge. For some reason, their car had been towed away, and now the towing company wouldn't release it until the bill was paid in full. So I drove her to the jail to visit him a few times. When he got out, they tried to make it work, but it was useless. He moved out, and the last I heard he'd moved down to Florida.

I heard from Meri a while later, this time because a law firm in Needham, MA had been sending her letters — which she threw in the trash. Apparently she had an old credit card with a balance that hadn't been paid off, and now, the creditor was seeking legal action. Once I'd heard the whole story, it was clear she was in quite a mess.

I contacted the law firm and agreed to help my sister get organized and pay off this debt. She gave me power of attorney because she didn't understand any of it. It took a few weeks to get all the paperwork figured out, but once everything was in place, she gave me her payment each month and I sent it in for her. That way I knew it would be handled properly. I asked the law firm to remove the interest charges from her account, and to not post any new interest charges in the future. They agreed, but they refused to drop the forty dollar court cost. All this work and follow up for $1104.59.

I loved my sister and would have done just about anything to help her out, but sometimes she was her own worst enemy. No matter how many times she screwed up though, I seemed to be the only one who was ever there for her. Not even her own parents would lend a hand.

◆　◆　◆　◆　◆

On Sept 8, 2006 Bonnie forwarded us a much anticipated email. The House voted on new compromises to the SOL language. It was now on its way to the Senate for review. Attached to her e-mail was the State House News with an article titled: *House Loosens Sex Crimes Statute of Limitations.*

"The House accepted legislation Friday that would eliminate the statute of limitations on sex crimes against children in cases where outside evidence corroborates the alleged victim's charges… The House and Senate earlier had compromised on extending the statute by 12 years, to 27 years, from the time the alleged victim turns 16… The House added the language through an amendment… Also closing loopholes associated with sex offenders and the laws that punish them… We have to place our trust in the hands of the district attorneys who will be prosecuting these crimes."

This was positive news, and it looked like we stood a good chance of having these bills passed. Sure enough, on September 21, 2006, Lt.

Governor Kerry Healey signed the bill that changed the criminal SOLs into law. And even though the new criminal law couldn't help me (I missed the deadline by one month!), I was elated that it had happened! As the political world is all about compromise, so too was the passing of this bill. Our objective had been the total elimination of the SOLs, but instead, survivors got an extended period of years in which criminal charges could be filed against their abusers. It wasn't a total victory because the bill that would have changed the civil SOL hadn't made it. But it was still a win and we were thrilled to take it!

◆　◆　◆　◆　◆

I guess I could have decided to take a break and just enjoy the win, but when you spend so much time working on something like this, it's hard to stop. Instead of relaxing, you feel like there's something you're forgetting to do. I was used to always working on something anyway, so I decided to take advantage of my momentum and started looking around for something else to expend some of my energy on. It didn't take long to come across an article in the newspaper about educators offering a series of seminars discussing adolescent safety and communication techniques being held at the Monson Free Library. It sounded interesting, and I've always liked reaching out to people doing things like this, so I contacted the library coordinator to find out more about the seminars.

We had a very nice conversation. She explained the purpose of the seminars, and I told her about my childhood and how it had affected my life, my advocacy work, and my involvement with the SOL bills. After hearing my story, she mentioned that she had a friend who might be a good contact for me, and with my permission, passed along my contact information.

That same evening I heard from the woman, and about her organization, *The Family Violence Intervention Coalition*. The main focus of this organization was to link eastern Pioneer Valley communities that have domestic violence task forces with communities who do not have those resources. Towards the end of our conversation, she asked me if I'd like to speak at their regional meeting in October to discuss my involvement with the SOL legislation. As usual, I said yes, and over the next few weeks, she and I put together an agenda while Gary worked on my speech.

October is Domestic Violence Awareness Month, and on October 16, 2006, I was standing in front of another roomful of people telling my story.

I told them what it was like being victimized by a family member while I was growing up. I emphasized how my family rejected me and harassed me after I came forward as an adult survivor of childhood sexual abuse. I talked about the counseling I underwent, and how my advocacy work helped me deal with my abusive past.

It's hard to explain how healing and energizing it is to stand in front of a crowd of people who care that something like this could happen. They understand that I'm not the only person with a story like this. And even though it might not be possible to stop it from ever happening to anyone else ever again, this group of people was very committed to doing what they could. When my speech was over, hands went up, and I answered everyone's questions.

Later that evening, a man and woman approached me and shared their stories of abuse with me. They weren't ready to talk about their experiences publicly, but they thanked me for the work I was doing, and for all the work I'd done to help get the new legislation passed.

I understood where they were coming from. Those first steps can be very hard to take. But who knows, maybe someday they will be ready to step forward and bring their abusers to justice. It felt very good knowing they had that option. All in all, it was a good night spent with good people.

◆ ◆ ◆ ◆ ◆

I enjoyed working with this woman. We made a good team, and she started looking around to see where else our talents might be able to do some good. She found out there were plans to host a speaker's forum in the early spring of 2007, and on November 9th, she emailed me good news. We were going to be speaking at Westfield State College on March 17, 2007 as part of their "Free Speech Speakers Series Spring 2007." Our topic: Domestic Violence – Public Policy and Public Health.

In addition to covering a brief clinical description of the different ways people respond to personal trauma and victimization, her part of the presentation also pointed out the need for law enforcement, the criminal justice system, and mental health resources to develop a consistent and compassionate protocol for responding to victims.

As a survivor of childhood sexual abuse, my role was to tell my story, to talk about the counseling I had sought out over the years, and how I had helped to get the SOLs for prosecuting sex crimes against children extended.

Other than that, 2007 was a normal and uneventful year. In my life, that was a good thing!

2008

April is Child Abuse Prevention Month, and I found out that there were several events taking place on the Asnuntuck Community College campus. I knew someone who was a professor at Asnuntuck—Jim Wilkinson. Jim was a former co-worker at Mass Mutual, and the founder and president of Amberwhistle.

The Amberwhistle was named after Amber, a nine-year-old girl from Dallas, Texas, who was abducted from her neighborhood in 1996, and was later found dead. This tragedy led to the creation of the AMBER Alert (America's Missing Broadcast Emergency Response) program which Massachusetts adopted in October 2002.

An Amberwhistle is a whistle attached to a wrist band that when blown by a frightened child can reach between 115-120 decibels, plenty loud enough to attract the attention of nearby parents, neighbors, or friends.

When Jim and I met, he brought along a few whistles. Sure enough, the noise it produced was piercing. Each whistle came with helpful information about things like coming up with a family password. That way, if a child is approached by a stranger who doesn't know the password, the child knows not to go anywhere with that person. Another idea was to make sure your neighbors knew about the whistle so they'd know what to do if they heard it. Jim left some whistles with me and I told him I would be in touch when a new project came up where we could work together.

In theory it was a good idea. The problem was money. I couldn't get the whistles for free, so I needed to find the funds somewhere. I usually paid for things directly related to my volunteer work, but the whistles were quite expensive. Still, I wanted to purchase as many as I could to pass out to kids for free, and after wracking my brain for a few days I turned to the

Zontas of Quaboag Valley for help. My friends at Zonta invited me to give a brief presentation on the Amberwhistle Program during their March 10th meeting. As always, they were wonderful, and within a few days a check arrived in the mail.

◆　◆　◆　◆　◆

The other thing Jim and I had talked about when we met was my interest in participating in the events Asnuntuck was planning for Child Abuse Prevention Month. I shared my idea, which was basically a presentation on protecting children against sexual abuse, advice on helping those suffering from abuse, and sharing resources that are available to kids and their families. The presentation would be followed by a Q&A period. He liked my idea, and with his help, I was scheduled to speak at 11:00 a.m., on April 16th, during Child Safety Month's: The Week of the Young Child.

I don't know why, but it still amazes me when things just fall into place. Not only was I going to be speaking to a great audience, but for the first time, Gary was going to be in the audience too. He worked down the street from the college and would be able to break away to catch my presentation. It was exciting for both of us because even though he knew my material front to back, he'd never seen me interact with an audience before.

It was a good turnout. There were plenty of questions afterward, and Gary couldn't believe how natural and relaxed I seemed, literally standing right under the spotlight where the podium was set up. He said I made good eye contact, and that the sincerity in my voice, and the audience's reaction to my story were very moving. He also said he was blown away by my handling of the questions. Gary has always been totally supportive of me and my work, but now he was also firmly convinced I was doing the job I was meant to do.

For days after speaking at Asnuntuck, I was jotting down notes and talking with Gary about an idea I'd been mulling over. That's how the big things take shape in our house though. One of us gets an idea, thinks about it, and then presents it to the other. When it's time to really start talking about it, we pour ourselves a cup of coffee, sit at opposite ends of the couch facing each other, and start talking. That's when the fun begins. We toss the big picture out there for each of us to see, dissecting and discussing, and going back and forth over every little detail of the idea. We analyze the best way to implement it, and try to figure out how much time, energy, and money it will take. We call this process "talking it to death," and we just keep on talking until the topic is exhausted and we've come to a decision.

Knowing that we can do this means the world to me. To know your partner has your back, and has faith and confidence in you, can make the difference between success and failure. It's our teamwork that has paved the way for me to accomplish more things than I'd imagined were possible. Now I was ready to bite off a big new challenge, and on April 29th, I officially kicked off my campaign to organize and promote my very first Child Safety Event. Mine would be like no other. Think circus, and you'd be really close to what I had in mind — minus the elephants.

◆ ◆ ◆ ◆ ◆

During that summer, I received a phone call from Sally Johnson Van Wright. She worked at the Women's Correctional Center in Chicopee, MA, and wanted to know if I'd be willing to speak to the inmates for their Leadership Enrichment Program. Of course I said yes.

I'd never imagined speaking at a prison before, but in a lot of ways it made perfect sense. As soon as I started thinking about the women, I knew that many of them would be from broken homes. They probably struggled with relationships and had given up on their dreams. I wondered how many opportunities they'd let slip by simply because they didn't know how to choose a different path. And while jail might not be rock bottom, it sure wasn't a fun house.

I'd never been in jail personally, but that didn't mean I didn't have anything in common with the inmates I was going to be speaking to. I'd grown up abused and neglected, both physically and mentally. I'd been hurt, confused, and damaged too. It wasn't a stretch to think that a majority of the women had had a tough time growing up too. If my Aunt Judi hadn't stepped into my life, who knows what would have happened. I could have just as easily gone down a different path praying without hope that someone would help me.

I knew I couldn't be their Aunt Judi, but I could be me, showing them firsthand that we don't have to let what other people do to us define us. Maybe speaking to them would provide them with the hope that they could do something with their lives in spite of what had happened to them too. At the very least, I was physical evidence that a person can always choose to do something good, and that none of us is destined to be defined by our past. For inmates who had children, I hoped they might better recognize how helpless and vulnerable children can be, and become better parents, making better choices, as a result.

On July 11th, I pulled into the parking lot at the Western Massachusetts Regional Women's Correctional Center and was immediately hit by how serious this facility was. Gray rectangular buildings, some topped with razor wire, dotted the property. As soon as my car stopped, a prison guard approached and asked if I was a lawyer. When I told him I was a guest of Sally, he tried to reach her on his radio. She was teaching a class so I was escorted to the waiting room. I'd never been in a place like this before. There were guards everywhere and lots of activity. I didn't have a reason to be nervous about being there, but I was, so I sat with my eyes down pretending to study my notes.

Sally finally came into the waiting room and introduced herself. It was nice to finally meet her after months of phone calls and emails. She took me through the sign-in process and a security checkpoint where I received a badge I had to wear while I was inside. Sally also gave me a brief tour of the prison that ended in the meeting room where I would be speaking.

Once all the inmates had arrived, the group began by reading the Women's Correctional Center's Mission Statement followed by the Leadership Institute Vision Statement. Then Sally introduced me, and I jumped right in and started talking. To me, it was evident they were listening, and I once again wondered how many of them had histories similar to mine. After I concluded my story, I answered their questions. One inmate broke down and told us her story of abuse. I knew from Sally that these women were all in counseling and I hoped that something I'd said that day might be able to help them, but I'll never know if I did or didn't. That's just the way it is sometimes.

◆　◆　◆　◆　◆

With my presentation at the correctional center behind me, I was now able to focus my full attention on my safety event. When I started planning the event, I wanted it to be more than just a conversation about sexual abuse prevention. I wanted it to encompass as many aspects of safety as possible, so whenever I had an idea, I picked up the phone and started making calls. As the event drew nearer, it started growing. Before I knew it, I had commitments from the Chicopee Police Dept.'s SWAT Unit and Underwater Response Team, the Chicopee Fire Dept., Ludlow K-9 officer Mike Whitney and his dog, Smokey the Bear, McGruff the Crime

Prevention Dog, the Massachusetts State Police, and The Amberwhistle Program with Jim Wilkinson.

Charlie Ramos would be there with the Iris Scan Program — a system used to positively identify an individual. The Chips Program offered DNA sampling, finger printing, and child video documentation. Baystate Dental offered to do teeth impressions and hand out free tooth brushes. The Chicopee Library got involved, as did Villari's Martial Arts Center and the Buffalo Soldiers Motorcycle Club of Springfield. The Laflamme family of Chicopee donated pumpkins for kids to decorate, the Lupa Zoo of Ludlow agreed to send their mobile zoo, and DJ Chris from one of the local radio stations was ready to keep the energy flowing by pumping up the music.

Author and parenting expert Bill Corbett agreed to be a guest speaker and share parenting tips from his book, "Love Limits & Lessons: A Parent's Guide to Creating Cooperative Kids." The Shriners Hospital and the Red Cross each signed up for a booth too. I booked Clowning for Kidz, a bounce house, a cotton candy machine, and a real train that kids and their parents could ride. Starbucks agreed to donate coffee and hot chocolate for the volunteers — which was another thing on my list.

As the event continued to grow and take shape, I realized I was going to need volunteers to help me pull it off. So I reached out for volunteers, asking Ron, Scott, and my sister Sheri, my friends, and the Chicopee Senior Center. I also got the surprise of my life when the Knights of Columbus (K of C) in Chicopee offered to host the event in their building — complete with dining hall, kitchen, and a humongous parking lot! I was absolutely stunned and never, ever expected such a generous donation. This was a huge facility in a highly visible location with plenty of traffic.

I am truly grateful for every donation that helps get information about childhood sexual abuse into the hands of people who need it, but it was hard not to be overwhelmed by so many total strangers saying, "We would love to help you" and then come through with such amazing donations. I truly believed that what I was doing was important, but working on this event proved to me that other people believed it was important too. Of course it also made me wonder… if all these people were ready to help with an event like this, then why were the school systems so hesitant? It was obviously something the community was willing to support.

The event was scheduled to open at 10:00 a.m., but there was a lot to be done so Gary and I arrived at 6:30 a.m. Gary went to Starbucks to pick up the coffee and hot chocolate while the volunteers started to arrive.

Everybody pitched in and did their part, and without a hitch, the event started.

For the safety portion of the event, kids needed to visit at least five stations to learn about safety. When they accomplished this goal, they each received a certificate of completion with a gold stamp, signed and dated by myself. The kids were so proud of their awards.

There were indoor and outdoor activities going on simultaneously all day long. The music was great, the clowns had the kids laughing with all their antics, and there were smiles all around. Almost 200 kids participated that day, and we promised to hold a similar event the following year. The event was over at 2:30 p.m. and considered a huge success by everyone in attendance. The local TV station and newspaper had stopped by, and our volunteers told us about all the positive feedback they got from parents. But best of all, the kids had a fun time learning things that would help keep them safe. It was everything I wanted it to be—and more. It was a really fun day, and thankfully, it didn't rain!

The one thing I hadn't expected to happen that day was for my sister Sheri to arrive with her daughter Ann. I'd told her about the event, but I never knew what was going to happen when it came to my sisters. Still, I was glad she showed up, and it was exciting to have her there to see what I'd accomplished. Ann earned her certificate—which I got to sign and hand to her personally—and I was proud of my sister for doing something that would help keep her daughter safe. And even though it was a bit awkward, I introduced her to my brother Scott.

I talked to her later that night too. She said she was glad she'd gone, and glad that her daughter had gone too. We talked about setting up time to go walking together, but only managed it a few times.

2009

I was always on the lookout for knowledge and information pertaining to all aspects of childhood sexual abuse so I'd be ready to help if someone asked me a question, wanted more information, or just needed someone to talk to. Sometimes information literally landed on my doorstep, which is how I learned about the *Children's Trust Fund*. They had done a bulk mailing and I received one of their brochures in the mail.

I read that brochure several times over the next few days. Their mission is, "To prevent child abuse and neglect by supporting parents and strengthening families." To accomplish their mission, they offer a variety of training for professionals working with families. One of the trainings they were offering at that time through an agreement with *The Committee for Children* (the developer of the course) was called "Talking about Touching." It was a research-based training for adults who wanted to learn how to teach kids basic personal safety skills that could help them stay safe in dangerous or abusive situations.

The training curriculum taught adults how to teach a personal safety program in the classroom, as well as how to train other adults to teach the safety program. Among other things, adults learned how to create a safe environment for discussing sensitive topics, the appropriate way to respond to children who have been abused, and how to identify, report, and handle a child's abuse disclosure. The audience for the program was kids, pre-k through third grade. When "touching" was discussed, it was in the context of general safety rules.

It sounded like a great training. The big problem was that they didn't offer it locally. The next class was in Seattle, WA, so in addition to the cost of the training and the classroom presentation resource kit I'd have to purchase, there would be airfare, hotel, and meals. Gary was used to me reaching into our own pocket for resource material, office supplies, gas for my car, and anything else I needed, but this was going to cost a lot more than driving downtown to photocopy a bunch of resource materials.

I thought about the people and groups I'd approached for help in the past, and remembered the one question I got asked over and over. Was I a 501(c)(3) — a tax exempt non-profit organization that can accept unlimited contributions which the donating party could then write off? I was not, and started thinking about it. If I became a 501(c)(3), it would be easier to get donations. I also found out that as a 501(c)(3) I would be eligible to apply for government grant money to fund my advocacy work.

So Gary and I came up with *Little Voices Matter*, which at first was a website that served as a platform for my mission to "Educate people on sexual abuse, increase awareness of the problem, and provide training for mandated reporters such as teachers, counselors, social workers, and law enforcement. Also, to sponsor children's safety events, form counseling groups for victims, and advocate for legislation that protected and supported the rights of victims of childhood sexual abuse." I then selected an attorney from town and began to set myself up as a 501(c)(3) under the name of *Little Voices Matter*.

◆ ◆ ◆ ◆ ◆

As much as I loved my role as an advocate, not all aspects of my advocacy work were met with outstretched arms and positive feedback. There were still people who took one look at me and ignored and dismissed me as a lightweight. There were also people who agreed to help but then disappeared, never coming through with the assistance they had promised.

I understood where some of them were coming from. I had no formal training for what I was pulling off, and before I became adept at PowerPoint, my presentations were very basic. And while sharing my story will always be meaningful and purposeful, it's not exactly what you'd call entertaining. I'd gotten used to seeing people uncomfortable with the topic squirming in their seats, and used to the few who would come up to me afterwards to tell me that I shouldn't be talking about things like this in public.

In retrospect, maybe the simplicity of my presentations was a good thing because the people who didn't turn off to the way I presented were creative and inspiring people realizing the importance of what they were hearing. They were the people willing to work together to make all of our communities a safer place to live and raise a family. They too, were well on their way to making a difference in their own way, and I was very grateful to meet each and every one of them.

Still, Gary and I had a few lively discussions about my presentations. I call them "my presentations," but Gary had a lot of input as well. He couldn't understand how repeating my story over and over again wouldn't get stale and boring and turn people off. So, in order to avoid that fate, we worked to keep changing things up to try and keep it fresh and interesting. That's why partnering with other people and groups was so inspiring — it opened up new avenues and opportunities for all of us.

The only place I still wasn't able to make any headway was with schools. Once again, I was going to make a pitch to the Ludlow School Committee. This time, before I spoke to the committee and the superintendent to discuss the possibility of teaching some kind of child safety in the classroom, I did a little impromptu research. I asked my friends and neighbors with kids in school if their children were taught anything about personal body safety, good touch — bad touch, or any other safety topics along these lines. They all said no. I wasn't surprised. Whenever I give a speech, parents always ask me if something like this could be taught in schools. Teachers have approached me too, saying that they wished this information was available to their students.

Everyone agrees it's an important topic, but for some reason, nobody wants to talk about it. Is it really such a big deal to teach a child about boundaries that could prevent them from being molested or raped? It's not like you explain it to them by saying something as ridiculous as "Do this or else you'll get sexually abused or raped." You teach them about boundaries the same way you teach them how to share, how to play nice with other kids, and what to do in case of a fire.

I'm truly grateful for every parent who takes the time to make sure their child is safe because that child might be able to help one of their peers stay safe too. But we know for a fact, that it isn't always taught in the home. It's strange that schools are willing to identify children who aren't getting other things at home — like enough food to eat, parental supervision, and help with their homework — but they aren't willing to step up to the plate when it comes to something like sexual abuse, which absolutely interferes with a child's safety and security.

When my husband and I were young kids in school, about twice a year, we would have a guest speaker in the auditorium. They were usually local celebrities like an anchorperson from the local TV station, a sports figure, or a musician. They would talk about their years in school, their life experiences, and how teamwork and support is so important. There was usually a theme too, and whether by accident or design, it was always geared towards being a learning experience for the kids. That's all I wanted to do, talk to groups of school kids. I didn't want to reinvent the wheel or give them another class to study.

According to the 2009 statistics from the Centers for Disease Control and Prevention, one out of every four girls and one out of every six boys will be sexually abused by their 18th birthday. If I could address a group of kids within the safe confines of their own school, I truly believe they would benefit from hearing about things that could keep them safe. Sure, there would be kids who would act just like members of the school committee — as if this wasn't something they needed to know about — but statistics have taught us otherwise. Sadly, for too many children, hearing someone like me speak might be the only lifeline ever extended to them.

I had ten minutes to speak to the school committee, and a lot of material to cover. I put together a package for everyone at the meeting, which consisted of my bio, sexual abuse prevention ideas, and the statistics of the registered sex offenders in our town, as well as the surrounding towns and cities. When my time was up, I answered questions. They thanked me, and said they would be in touch.

After a week of waiting had passed, the suspense was killing me so I called the superintendent. She was polite and right to the point, stating that they didn't need my help, and that they felt their curriculum was sufficient.

I was persistent over the years with this particular superintendent about the importance and value of this kind of information, but she never budged. Neither has the new superintendent. I've never had any luck with any of the schools I've approached in Massachusetts. Even as I write this in 2016, after all the awards and years of advocacy work, I've never been invited to speak at an elementary or junior high school. It looks like the only way the children attending public school in the state of Massachusetts are ever going to learn even the simplest things about personal safety in school is if it's made mandatory by the Massachusetts Board of Elementary and Secondary Education as the result of a campaign spearheaded by concerned parents, teachers, and advocates.

It was Gary who finally convinced me to stop hitting my head against the brick wall of public school committees and superintendents. He suggested that if I wasn't able to share my message with kids in public schools, then how about reaching out to places like The Boys and Girls Club, the YMCA, the library, and local colleges. He pointed out that those organizations were always looking for new ideas and volunteers to bring something fresh to their programs. This is one of the reasons I am so grateful for Gary. Somehow, he always manages to ask the right questions.

◆　◆　◆　◆　◆

I was also always on the lookout for places and audiences who could benefit from hearing my story and information. I don't remember what made me think of it, but I realized that if I could speak at the Women's Correctional Center in Chicopee, MA, I might be able to speak at a men's prison too. So I contacted the Carl Robinson Correctional Institution in Enfield, CT and was put in touch with one of the counselors. He thought it was a great idea, and sent me literature about the facility. It's a medium security prison that offers a wide assortment of programs aimed at counseling and educating their approximately 1400 inmates.

One of the ongoing programs the facility offers is called V.O.I.C.E.S. – Victim Offender Institutional Correctional Educational Services. This program is designed to use volunteers to help broaden the inmates understanding and sensitivity to the impact their crimes have on society.

I wasn't told specifically how the inmates were going to be selected, and of course, it went through my mind that there could be child molesters in the group. The thought of it did intimidate me a little bit, but it didn't stop me. I tweaked my "regular" speech to include what I had felt as a victim of sexual abuse both when it happened, and now as an adult. I wanted them to hear that the physical and emotional effects of molesting a child can last a lifetime, hoping that this perspective would help them understand the trauma of being a victim—or as I say now—a survivor.

I was instructed to dress appropriately and not show up in anything too sexy or revealing—as if I would! I took the day off from work because I thought I might be a little rattled afterward. When I got to the prison, I was buzzed in and escorted through hallways and rooms until we got to the classroom. Aside from me being the only woman in the room, it went exactly as the women's event had, except that this time I passed out questionnaires to the inmates after I spoke.

One of the comments I received was, "I didn't know that talking about it could help ease some of these symptoms. This brought back some memories, and this information is somewhat helpful in dealing with these memories. I think you should keep on telling your story. It could save someone's life one day."

It had been another good event, and I hadn't been *too* rattled. Of course that might have been due to the fact that there had been three prison guards stationed in the room while I was speaking. Their presence had definitely gone a long way to relieving some of my apprehension, but at first, their uniformed presence had been a bit unnerving too.

As a little girl—thanks to my parents—I learned to be afraid of cops. My parents wanted all four of us girls to think of cops as the people who would arrest us and throw us in jail if we didn't do what we were told. Needless to say, my stepfather added his own twist to it when he was alone with me to make sure I believed that if I ever talked to the police about what he was doing, they'd tear our family apart and it would be my fault. It didn't help that he was also an auxiliary police officer.

The only policeman I really knew at that point was Police Chief Lou Barry. I'd first met him when I was organizing my 2008 safety event. Since then, we'd become good friends and kept in touch. One of Chief Barry's many jobs was teaching a criminal justice class at Holyoke Community College, and one day, he called and asked me if I would be willing to share my story with his students. He believed that hearing a firsthand account from a sexual abuse survivor would be extremely valuable to these future police officers. How could I say no to my friend Lou?

There was just one problem. I still had a tough time with police officers, and now I was thinking about speaking to a room filled with them. Eventually, I told Lou about my irrational fear and started the process of unraveling the misconceptions my parents had engrained in me. One of Gary's brothers is a K-9 Police Officer, so talking to him really helped with the process too. I was determined to work it out, and prepared myself to speak to his students.

There were about 25 future police officers in the class, and as I stood in front of them, a small part of me wondered if they'd believe my story. It also briefly crossed my mind that they might be mad at me for talking about this—just like my parents and family had been when I'd started disclosing my abuse. As a young girl, those thoughts alone were enough to frighten me into silence, but fortunately, that wasn't the case now.

I wanted these people to remember my story, but I also wanted them to know what to do if they went out on a call where abuse was obvious, or maybe even when they just had a gut instinct that something was wrong or off. It's so important to be understanding, sympathetic, and patient with victims on the verge of disclosing because they can be very confused about who to turn to, and who to trust. Hopefully, the person they finally pick doesn't over or under react to what they hear — and that's a tough thing to do when it comes to abuse. My goal for each of these students was for them to feel confident about their ability to offer some kind of assistance whether the abuse was evident or suspected.

I still speak to Lou's students, and every time I stand in front of them, I'm grateful for the chance to do something for the victims of abuse I can't physically reach my own hand out to.

◆　◆　◆　◆　◆

I decided to make the trip to Seattle to take the *Talking about Touching* training program, and on the first day of class, met my five fellow classmates. At the end of the class we each received a certificate, and I left feeling like I'd gained information and knowledge that could help me accomplish bigger and better things. Experiences like this always inspired me to keep striving to reach my full potential.

For this year's Child Abuse Prevention Month, I contacted our local ABC affiliate TV station about doing a story on the topic, and was asked if I was willing to be interviewed in person. The thought of it made me nervous, but I immediately said yes. This was going to be my first time on television, and the first time I would tell my story in front of the entire Western Massachusetts region. I had no idea what it was going to be like, but I knew it was the perfect opportunity to raise awareness of childhood sexual abuse, and hopefully get people inspired and involved to help keep our kids safe.

The reporter who came to do the interview was a woman. The interview itself didn't take that long, but it was weird because the cameraman didn't just film the interview. He filmed me doing things like microwaving a cup of hot water for tea, sitting at my computer and looking at the *Little Voices Matter* website, and then of me playing in the backyard with the dogs. I wasn't sure how they were going to put it all together, but it turned out okay, and once again, I was getting my message out to a larger audience. All because of a simple phone call.

Now it was time to get down to working on the details of planning this year's safety event, scheduled for Oct 4th. My challenge this year was that I had agreed to do a second safety event at the K of C in Ware on the 24th. I used the same blueprint I'd used for last year's safety event to plan the first one. There were a few new vendors and a great bunch of new and returning volunteers. And thanks to all the generous donations and contributions we received, it ended up being another successful event.

The Ware safety event had a Halloween theme so kids and adults came dressed for a party. Because the venue was smaller, we scaled it down, but you couldn't tell based on how much fun we all had. We discussed Halloween safety tips, every child received a pumpkin, and the Ware Fire Department passed out red plastic fire helmets. The Ware Police Department finger-printed the kids, John and Magi Bish ran an identification program, and Charlie Ramos from the Hampden County Sheriff's Department was back with the Iris Scan Program. We also had Clowning for Kidz, and Mrs. Pickle. Other vendors included Baystate Mary Lane Hospital, the Ware Family Center, the Salvation Army, the WIC Program, and the Ware Domestic Violence Task Force. We offered free raffle prizes, and hot dogs and hamburgers were available at the outdoor dining pavilion. Every child received a sundae cup from Friendly's Ice Cream, and in spite of the light drizzle, everyone smiled and had a good time. Every child received a certificate too, representing all the valuable safety lessons they'd learned that day.

◆　◆　◆　◆　◆

As strange as it may seem, there are times in life when more actually becomes less. I'd planned and executed two more successful events (obviously with a lot of help), but there was the 501(c)(3) to deal with too. When I had first envisioned becoming a 501(c)(3), I had pictured it as something that would help me generate enough donations to keep me perpetually busy with my advocacy work. I enjoyed writing my speeches with Gary, emailing and calling people on the phone, setting up events, participating in events, and speaking and educating people about childhood sexual abuse. The adrenaline inspired by the importance of what I was doing had me doing more every year. As a non-profit, I should have been able to do even more — at least that's what I'd thought.

I spent months, and Gary and I spent thousands of dollars, setting up *Little Voices Matter* as a 501(c)(3). It had taken a lot of thought and time to select the eight board members too. Scheduling board meetings was always a challenge, as was the fact that everybody had their own ideas about how things should be done. In addition to that, I still had my fundraising and advocacy work to do — all while working a full time job.

People kept telling me that I needed to focus on managing *Little Voices Matter* so I could turn over some of the advocacy work to someone else. I was buried under piles of administrative paperwork, getting very discouraged, and too soon, the realities and politics of running a non-profit started getting in the way of my advocacy work. So, less than a year after becoming a legitimate 501(c)(3), I shut it down. I didn't want to be a figurehead, a pencil-pusher, or an administrator. I just wanted to keep doing the meaningful and purposeful work I'd been doing all along. I apologized to my board, and gratefully, they all understood.

At least I know I tried. It was sad to let it go, but I knew I had tried my absolute best to make it work. It just wasn't for me. But now, I could get back to the advocacy work I loved.

2010

One of the things that's been strange about looking back at my life is seeing just how much plain ordinary time went by. Our lives were normal—whatever that means. Gary and I were both working. We had a routine that worked for both of us. We had days filled with reasons to smile and days without them.

Back in 1985 when my Aunt Judi's oldest son had married Gina, it had been a big tadoo. He'd been the first of all the kids to tie the knot, so their wedding was a big Italian wedding. It wasn't long before they had a daughter, and then a son, and I was excited to have a niece and nephew.

Unfortunately, after the story of my abuse started to leak out, just about everyone on that side of the family decided it was my fault that there was a big black smear on the family name. It was all lies as far as they were concerned. And when you get right down to it, I can almost (almost!) understand why some people might have thought it was all lies. Back then, in my mind there were only 2 people who knew the truth, and it was his word against mine.

And then my Aunt Judi had listened and believed me. I knew she was watching out for her grandchildren, nieces, and nephews, and any other children who might be within reach of my stepfather. But when she passed away in 2000, all my cousins started distancing themselves from me too. I'd called Gina a few times to try and talk to her, but she was still married to my cousin and had been pulled into the ranks of people determined to keep me out.

Sadly, Gina's mom passed away in July of 2010. I remembered her mother as a wonderful woman, and I knew that she and Gina had been very close. Needless to say, no one in the family let me know she'd passed, but I'd found out about it anyway, and left a message on an online guestbook that had been set up. Shortly after that, Gina surprised me by contacting me. The last time we'd spoken had been at Judi's funeral in 2000, and that first conversation was definitely a little awkward.

She started by thanking me for leaving such a nice post in the guestbook, and said that she'd thought about me often over the years. I learned that she was separated, but not yet divorced, and that she knew about my abuse because my Aunt Judi had told her. It was nice to be able to have an open conversation with her, and we've been close friends ever since.

◆　◆　◆　◆　◆

In August, Sheri invited me to join her and Ann to celebrate Ann's birthday. Of course I said yes. Ann decided she wanted to have a girl's day at the beach, and then like a normal teenager, she invited her boyfriend. So it was a girl's day at the beach — plus one.

The day was gloriously warm and breezy. We brought a cooler filled with food and drinks, and when we weren't swimming or walking along the beach collecting shells, we lounged on blankets stretched out under a large beach umbrella. We spent the day swimming, talking, laughing, and just plain hanging out. When we got back to my place, we had cake and sang "Happy Birthday."

Of course, I had taken pictures the whole day, and a couple days later decided to put them all on a DVD. I added the Happy Birthday song for background music, and gave a copy to my niece when I was done. I still look at my copy from time to time when I get lonely for family.

2011

In the ongoing struggle to totally eliminate the SOLs, Rep. Ron Mariano sponsored a bill supported by CORSAL (Coalition to Reform Sex Abuse Laws) called the *Protection from Sexual Predators Act*. At this point, it did not have a regular bill number yet, but was known as House Docket No. 00689.

The proposed bill had multiple key points, one being that it would entirely eliminate the criminal statute of limitations for indecent assault and battery, and rape for all minors. Of particular interest to me was that it would also eliminate the civil SOL for past and future childhood sexual abuse claims so that abuse survivors would be able to prosecute their abuser in a court of law regardless of their age.

Boston attorney Carmen Durso sent out an email in January outlining the proposed bill. In the email, he said that a group of volunteer law students would be assigned the job of contacting every legislator and asking them to sign on as co-sponsors of the bill. He also wrote that, "It would be useful for others to also contact them." That was all I needed, and just as I had done in the past, I started sending out emails that I would later follow up with phone calls.

◆　◆　◆　◆　◆

I received a phone call at work one day congratulating me on being nominated for an award. I learned that each year, the high school I graduated from, selects one of the school's alumni to receive the St. Joseph's Medal. Someone had contacted the committee anonymously, told them about my advocacy work, and said that I would be a good recipient for the award. The caller went on to explain that this award is presented to a nominee who has excelled in their professional life—or made their community a better place in which to live, holds to their Catholic values on a daily basis, and is generally an upstanding citizen. Of course I was elated, and honored to be considered for the award.

Later that same day, a committee member called me to ask which Catholic Church I attended. That was a tough question to answer, and I had to explain that I wasn't going to church because I couldn't support the way the Catholic Church hierarchy was covering up the abuse of children. I was then told that my nomination would be rescinded. I was disappointed, hurt, and upset, and not being one to keep secrets, I told my friends and co-workers about what happened… I might have even put it on Facebook.

Days later, I received a phone call from Kevin Cullen, a columnist with The Boston Globe. Somehow he'd heard about the St. Joseph's Medal story and wanted to interview me. I was only too happy to talk with him, and his article appeared in the January 23, 2011 copy of The Boston Globe.

I'm not sure who tipped off The Boston Globe, but I'm glad they did. Receiving the award would have been nice, but not because I'd "won" it. It would have been another opportunity to shed even more light on sexual abuse. In the end, Kevin's article generated more attention than any award I could have ever received.

◆　◆　◆　◆　◆

One day in February, I opened my email and saw an email with the subject line "Greetings from Yokohama Japan." It was from a guy named Jose who had read about me online and wanted to talk. His girlfriend was in the military, pursuing her master's degree at the same time. They were in a committed relationship, and when she was stationed in Japan, he went too. He talked about how much he loved her, but explained that there was one big problem. She had been molested as a young girl and was now experiencing problems with her personal relationships—especially her relationship with Jose. He didn't know what to do to help her, and needed someone to talk to.

We emailed back and forth a few times, and even spoke on the phone twice — which was difficult given the fact that Yokohama is fourteen hours ahead of our east coast time. I understood that he needed to talk and listened to him tell me their story. I told him my story too, and gave him some resources to follow up with. He knew it wasn't going be easy and that it would take time, but he loved his girlfriend and was willing to do anything he could for her.

When the earthquake and tsunami hit on March 11th, the first thing I thought of was Jose and his girlfriend. I tried calling him but couldn't get through. My emails went unanswered too. And then finally, after a few weeks, I received a short email from him saying that they were both fine.

I reached out to Jose recently to see how they were doing. The experiences they'd shared and worked through had strengthened their relationship. They had now been married for three years, and had a beautiful baby boy. He told me that talking to me had been a great help, and that they would both forever be grateful. I was just grateful that I had been in the right place at the right time to connect with him.

◆ ◆ ◆ ◆ ◆

Out of the blue, Gina came home one day in early fall to find a message on her answering machine from Uncle Guilio, my stepfather's brother. He'd left a message for me on her machine because he didn't have my phone number. She immediately called me and played the message for me over the phone.

"Have Kathy call me. I want to reach out to her to expose my brother (my stepfather) as a pedophile."

He ended the message with his cell phone number. I was stunned and asked Gina to replay the message a few times because it was hard to believe I'd heard it correctly. I knew Guilio and my stepfather had never really gotten along, but something must have happened for him to decide to reach out to me. And for him to call and leave that message, whatever had happened had to be a big deal. Obviously his message was a big deal on its own, but why now, after all these years?

The last time I'd seen Uncle Guilio was at my Aunt Judi's funeral. He'd always been an intimidating guy to be around. He was a big burly Italian, and I was a meek little girl. We might have said hello to each other at the funeral, but that was it. I wanted to know what he had to say after all these years, but I wanted to be cautious too. I wasn't willing to start messing around in family matters if that was what was behind his sudden decision.

I needed to find out what was going on though, so I contacted an attorney and told her what happened. She said it was a law enforcement matter and suggested that I contact the police. I did. A police detective spoke to my Uncle Guilio three times, but never was able to get him to disclose any knowledge of abuse. I believed something was there, but for whatever reason, Uncle Guilio wasn't ready to give it up. Still, there was finally a crack in the family armor, and if I was lucky enough, and Guilio was pissed off enough, there was a chance I could find out what he knew.

◆　◆　◆　◆　◆

Over the years, I've had the privilege and good fortune of meeting many "ordinary but extraordinary" people who always seem willing to step up and do what they can. We might come from different ethnic, cultural, and educational backgrounds, but it's always nice to connect with people who have the same desire and goal—to do what they can to prevent child sexual abuse, and to offer help to those survivors who are seeking it. It was also inspiring to realize how many family members and friends people had who were willing to lend emotional support any time of the day or night. I could always count on Gary's support, and support from my father's side of my family too, but I was truly ashamed of the truth that not one of the relatives from the idiot side of my family would ever voluntarily lift a finger for someone unless there was something in it for them.

This was just one of the many reasons I continued to keep my distance from them. I hated the fact that I had the same last name as them too. It was like it tied me to them in a way I couldn't get free of. True, I'd changed my last name when I got married, but it still bothered me. And then Gary came up with a really good idea. Why not legally change my maiden name?

After a few days of talking about it, I called the Springfield Probate Court to find out what it would take to change my last name. It turned out to be a very easy process that didn't cost anything. The clerk mailed me the forms I needed to fill out. Aside from those forms, all I needed was a copy of my birth certificate and marriage license. My birth certificate had my mother's maiden name listed as my last name. It had been changed to my stepfather's name when he adopted me. In a way, this change would be doing the same thing, except that this time it would be my real father adopting me.

I was excited about the process and could clearly envision dropping my maiden name and replacing it with my biological father's last name. When the forms arrived I couldn't wait to fill them out. Some of them had to be notarized, but when that was done, I called the clerk to let her know they were on the way back to her. I also asked her if I could get a picture taken of the judge, me, and my dad after the change had been finalized. "Of course!" she said.

I could barely wait to tell my dad, but wanted to tell him in person so I could see the look on his face when I told him how proud and excited I was to take his last name. In my mind, I was already planning a small celebration at a really nice local restaurant once the change was official. I knew exactly when I was going to tell him too. For years, we'd been getting together on Sundays, and now that he was no longer seeing my stepfather's cousin, I was once again visiting him at his house. So this coming Sunday, we'd be sitting and drinking coffee, and I'd tell him that I was finally and officially going to be his daughter!

I'd wanted to surprise him, and I did. He didn't exactly jump up and down with joy like I was prepared to do, but he said he thought it was a good idea and that he was on board with me doing it.

Several weeks later, our usual weekend visit turned out to be on the day before we were scheduled to go to court for the name change. We were just talking like usual when my father blurted out, "Everyone I've told about this adoption thinks there's a money motive behind it."

I was too shocked to really hear what else he said, but the gist of it was that there were other ways to accomplish a name change. I didn't know that. I only knew of the way that had been explained to me by the probate court clerk. I was stunned and embarrassed that people would say that I was only changing my name as a way to somehow get access to his money. It was a lot worse trying to absorb the fact that *he* seemed to be questioning my motives too.

He said, "People are wondering why you would want to make a change like this after all these years."

I explained that it didn't have anything to do with money. It was about getting rid of the name of the man who molested and raped me. I had been so excited, but now, something so special and symbolic had been flipped around to make me appear ugly and manipulative. Unfortunately, Gary had gotten dragged into it too because the name change had been his idea.

We had planned to drive to the courthouse together the following day, and before I left, I asked him if he wanted me to cancel the change. He said no, and that he still wanted me to have his last name, but I cried all the way home just the same.

When I got home and told Gary what had happened, he suggested that we should get out of the house and start doing some early Christmas shopping. We did, but the conversation with my dad rattled around in my head the whole time. By the time we got back home, I'd decided that my dad didn't really want to go through with the name change. If he was glad that I was changing my last name to his, why would he say those things? Why would he question my motives? I couldn't be sure if he believed that I didn't have any reasons beyond just wanting to have his last name, and couldn't go through with it knowing he might. So at around 6:00 p.m. that night, I called him and told him I was going to cancel the change.

He said, "Okay... well... I'll call you later on in the week." And that was that.

◆　◆　◆　◆　◆

My 30th high school reunion was held at the Marriott Hotel in downtown Springfield at the end of November. I hadn't ever attended one of the reunions, but this one felt different. 30 was a big number, and somehow significant in that it coincided with a stage in my life where I was happily married, gainfully employed, and doing advocacy work I loved. A bunch of us had been Facebooking for weeks now, checking out what we all looked like, and speculating about who would be there. I was excited.

The ballroom was decorated and music from the 70s and 80s filled the air. Gary and I checked our coats, got drinks, and found a table. Soon though, I wanted to walk around and socialize, so we did. I talked to people I hadn't talked to since high school, introducing Gary to all of them. I talked to one classmate who had asked me out, and we laughed when he reminded me that I'd told him I couldn't go out because I had to "wash my hair."

After making the rounds, we went back to our table where we were joined by some of my recent Facebook friends/former classmates and spent the rest of the night reminiscing, drinking wine, laughing, and taking pictures.

The last time I was with these "kids" felt like an entire lifetime ago. It hadn't all been fun either. Even now, there were people in this room who looked at me and I could almost see them deciding I was still the same quiet insecure girl they remembered. But they didn't know me now, not really. Nobody could ever see or know what was inside of me, except for me. And that night, surrounded by former classmates, it was a different me inside, and I had fun. All of my experiences, all that I was, helped me get to a place where I truly felt like I had finally achieved equal footing with my peers. I felt at peace, but just as importantly, I felt accepted.

2012

In February, Lou Barry again asked me to share my story with his class of prospective law enforcement officers at the Police Academy in Springfield. Once again, I said yes. And now that House Bill No. 469—the latest version of the civil SOL bill—was in play, I wanted to incorporate it into my presentation, and contacted the House Chairman of the Judiciary Committee's office for an update. The chairman was the individual who got to decide which bills would—or would not—move forward for consideration of becoming a new law. It was still only February, but I knew the chairman had until March 21, 2012 to decide the fate of the bill. Right now, it was still being debated.

Time was ticking by, and once again, emails regarding the bill were flying between the bill's supporters. Attorney Carmen Durso, an attorney who works with sexual abuse survivors, and Jetta Bernier, the executive director of *Massachusetts Citizens for Children* had joined forces with CORSAL—Coalition to Reform Sex Abuse Laws—and set up a rally for March 14th at the Boston State House. I was contacted about the rally through both CORSAL and *The Enough Abuse Campaign*.

In addition to attending the rally, we were asked to step up our own individual letter, email, and phone call campaigns. No problem for me. I was happy to contact every politician in my community. Then I moved on to every Senator and Representative in the state. I knew I wasn't the only person doing this, and that was a good thing. We wanted to make as much collective "noise" as we could. After all, it's the squeaky wheel that gets the grease!

◆ ◆ ◆ ◆ ◆

As always, life was ticking along, and one day I received a phone call from Meri. Someone had complained to the property manager of the place where she lived that she had a washer and dryer in her apartment. Because residents weren't allowed to have them in their apartments (they were supposed to use the coin-operated appliances in the basement), she was told to get rid of them. If she refused, the manager told her she could argue about it with their attorney. She called me to ask if I was the one who had called the manager and ratted her out!

She sounded jittery on the phone, and repeated herself a few times. Then she said that our mother had suggested she should hire an attorney. There was no way that was going to happen. There was no way she could afford it, but my radar went up immediately when she mentioned our mother. It meant that my sister was once again on speaking terms with her, and I needed to be careful about what I said because it would definitely get back to her. Had my mother been the one to suggest that I'd made the call to the manager? I know that might sound a bit paranoid, but experience had taught me too well that even the simplest of comments could be turned against me.

I hadn't called the manager, and told her that a few times. Why would I? This was the same washer and dryer Gary and I had bought her years ago after she'd been complaining about having her clothes stolen. I reminded her of that, but she was so stressed that I'm not sure she really heard me. It turned out to be a short conversation that ended with a quick "Good-bye" rather than our usual "I love you."

◆　◆　◆　◆　◆

As the deadline for House Bill No. 469 approached, one of the people I called was The Register's editor. I asked her if she could put something in the newspaper about the upcoming bill, and on March 9th, The Register published an article that explained what the bill was all about, and how important it was for people to contact their legislators and ask them to support it. Sy Becker from Channel 22 interviewed me on March 10th for the exact same reason — to drum up support for the bill.

On the day of the rally, I rode to Boston with Gale Candaras. After parking, we joined the other "ralliers" at the *Massachusetts Citizens for Children* offices, which were right across the street from the State House. There, we were each given sealed packets addressed to specific legislators. Each packet contained a cover letter from Jetta Bernier outlining the importance of abolishing the SOL, a book written by Professor Marci Hamilton called, *"Justice Denied: What America Must Do to Protect Its*

Children," information outlining key facts about childhood sexual abuse, and a copy of House Bill No. 469. At 11:00 a.m., we all walked across the street for a press conference. Both Attorney Carmen Durso and Jetta Bernier spoke to the crowd. From there, we went and delivered our packets.

It's hard to believe, but even with our combined efforts, and a growing tide of public opinion on our side, there were *still* key lawmakers who had their doubts about the merit of changing the SOL.

The current civil SOL had been chosen to protect "alleged" abusers from claims initiated by adults with less than accurate memories or questionable motives. The logic was that memories fade, people die, and over time, it becomes harder to find the kind of "physical" evidence courts want to see. In today's terms, it sounds like they had picked a time limit based on when the case could officially be classified as a "cold case."

Right now, I was one of those cold cases. One of my friends has a letter written to her by her abuser apologizing for what he did to her between the ages of 5 and 14. But because of the current civil SOL, she couldn't sue him in a court of law. He was untouchable—even with a hand-written letter admitting his guilt.

On Tuesday, March 20th, more than 100 of Massachusetts' 160 legislative leaders endorsed the measure to make changes to the outdated law, and the bill was favorably voted out of committee. Bill No. 469 would now be known as H 4326 in the House of Representatives, and Bill No. 02409 in the Senate. The people had been heard, and now we had a small but significant victory to celebrate!

◆ ◆ ◆ ◆ ◆

I was still visiting with my Dad a couple of times a week. I called him one day and got the surprise of my life to hear that my mother had contacted him. As far as I knew, they didn't have anything to do with each other beyond running into one another at a wake or funeral for someone they had both known. And even then, they might be friendly to each other, but no one would ever mistake them for friends. So for her to call him was extremely unusual.

She had called him to say that she had some boxes filled with my stuff and wanted to drop them off at his house. I was shocked to find out that she'd held onto any of my personal belongings for all those years. I couldn't even imagine what there was to hold onto.

After she'd dropped them off, I went over to his house and asked him how it went. He said they talked a little, and she said things might have been better for her if they'd worked things out between the two of them instead of splitting up. Pretty soon, he began to think she might be hitting on him, and when he made it obvious he wasn't interested, she left. The last thing she said as she was leaving was to make sure that he didn't give me her cell number.

Like I would ever call her? I hadn't spoken to her for about 12 years and had no plans to call her in the foreseeable future. Still, I was happy for the boxes. They held things like school report cards, my first communion card, pictures, and awards I'd won as a kid. It was interesting and intriguing looking through all the stuff because it reminded me that there had been other parts of my life worth remembering.

Sometimes, it's tough doing so much advocacy work. In 2012, I was still working hard to make my day in court a reality. But that kind of focus comes with a price. No one can talk about their experiences as a victim without reliving a little piece of it whenever they tell their story. I was used to telling my story, and truly believed telling it would make a difference. I wasn't going to stop either… but I paid a price for it.

There's a part of me that will forever "flinch" when I see certain phone numbers come up on the caller ID, or recognize an email address in my inbox. There are noises that scare me, smells that make me nauseous, and colors I have to close my eyes to. And even though my court case will one day be a part of the past too, I will never escape the memories of what was done to me.

That's why the things I found in those boxes were nice. They helped me piece together the picture of a *normal* girl. My teachers wrote comments on my report cards that I'm sure they wrote on other kid's report cards too. "Kathy is a good worker and a very conscientious student"… "She is pleasant and well behaved." It was comforting to know there was a part of me that was normal back then in spite of what was happening.

◆　◆　◆　◆　◆

Now that both the House and Senate had taken up the SOL bill, it was up to our elected officials to find a way to play nice and do the job of refining the wording of the bill into something the majority could live with. While this was going on, online articles chronicling the struggles survivors have to deal with started popping up all over the internet. People were speaking up and doing their part to make sure readers everywhere understood how important it was for victims to have a way to seek justice. The result was that the bill to abolish the civil SOL in Massachusetts was getting a lot of attention.

People were beginning to grasp the truth that the only protection and benefit the current SOL provided was for sexual predators, and things were looking good for the bill. We were optimistic about it passing, and I wanted to be prepared for when it did. It was time to start looking for an attorney to represent me in the suit I was planning to file against my stepfather as soon as the law was passed.

I contacted the attorney Gary and I have gone to over the years to see if he would be interested in taking on the case of suing my stepfather in civil court. He said that he no longer handled such cases, but gave me the name of an attorney who did. When I called that attorney, we spoke for less than ten minutes, which mostly consisted of me giving him a brief history of my background.

When I finished, his first question was, "Does your stepfather's family have money?" When I let him know they didn't, he apologized, and said his firm was very busy and that he would need to get paid for his work. I thanked him for his time, and that was the end of that, but I was very upset with how the conversation had gone.

I'd spent years of my life working and pushing to help get this law passed, but had never even considered the possibility that the law would pass, and I still might not be able to sue my stepfather because there wasn't enough money in it for an attorney to take the case! It was a very discouraging thought, but in reality, I'd only talked to two attorneys. There were more out there. I just had to follow my normal course of action — stick with it!

A week before my birthday, I received a rude all-caps email from Sheri. In it, she accused me of sending her husband a newspaper featuring an article about me. The newspaper had found its way to her doorstep, and she was convinced I'd put it there — or had someone else put it there for me. The email went on to accuse me of "wanting" her husband, and of course, lying about everything. It ended with her letting me know that if she found out I was trying to contact her husband, she'd get a restraining order against me. I didn't bother to respond because it wouldn't have made any difference even if I did. She'd just keep saying that I was lying.

◆　◆　◆　◆　◆

Throughout the years, I've met a lot of victims of sexual abuse. Sometimes they reach out to me directly, but sometimes I meet them through someone else. That's how I came to meet Jordan Chmura. One of the police academy's cadets had heard my presentation, and later heard Jordan's story. Wanting to help, he called Chief Lou Barry for my contact information, thinking I might be able to help Jordan in some way. After a few emails, Jordan had my contact information. Now it was up to her to decide if she wanted to talk to me.

On Wednesday, September 12, 2012, at 8:13 p.m., 15 year old Jordan sent me an email. "Hi. This is Jordan Chmura." My life hasn't been the same since—in a good way.

The next day we emailed back and forth and exchanged phone numbers. We were on the phone for two hours, during which I let her do most of the talking. She was quiet and shy on this first call, and I was careful not to push too hard. I knew from my own experience that her story had to unfold at her pace. Over the course of the call, Jordan slowly revealed that her friend's father had sexually abused her starting when she was 11 years old, ending when she was 15. One of the things he liked to do when he was "done," was to kick her with his steel toed shoes.

The one big difference with Jordan is that she found someone she felt safe enough with—her dance teacher—to disclose what was happening. It started with Jordan crying. Her dance teacher asked her what was wrong, but wasn't willing to accept Jordan's answer that "nothing" was wrong. Her dance teacher continued to pay attention, and after some time, figured out that Jordan always seemed to react when one particular person showed up at the end of dance class to pick up his daughter. Then, with courage and kindness, she provided a safe space for Jordan to talk about what he was doing to her.

Charges were filed against him, he was arrested, and in front of a judge and witnesses, he admitted his guilt. There was no jury trial. He received a seven to ten year sentence with ten years probation when he's released. As of 2016, he's still in prison.

We talked about many other things during that first phone call too. She talked about wanting to become a pediatrician, a writer, and a motivational speaker. She sounded intelligent, and her grades in school were excellent. I told her about my past and about some of the work I do. All in all, it was a very good conversation, so we decided to meet face to face a few days later. I picked her up at school and we went to Panera Bread. We talked for hours there too. She was such a smart brave girl for coming forward and putting her abuser behind bars. She admitted that it had been frightening to face him in court, but she'd done it anyway.

Jordan and I became quick friends. We had something terrible in common, but it was great that we could be normal friends anyway. And almost right from the beginning of our friendship, we talked on the phone every night. I hoped that our conversations gave her the same chance to feel "normal" that my conversations with my Aunt Judi had given me.

Another person Jordan had built a relationship with was Tricia Caron, a licensed therapist, who in addition to her private practice, maintained an office at the high school Jordan attended. Twice a week, Jordan and Tricia would meet and talk. Shortly after I met Jordan, she and a friend of hers approached Tricia about starting a support group for abused kids at the high school. Tricia thought it was a great idea, and volunteered to be the support group counselor.

Jordan thought Tricia and I should meet, and I was invited to one of the support group sessions. I arrived early so I could meet Tricia — who is a fantastic person. About eleven kids came to the group session. I spoke for almost thirty minutes, and then together, Tricia and I answered all their questions. I passed out literature and gave them each my contact information.

As of spring 2016, that support group still meets at the high school. There's a new counselor supervising it now, but it's still going strong, supporting kids who have and haven't been directly assaulted. It's such a great example of how meaningful a positive school experience with the subject of sexual abuse can be. Not every kid in the group has been abused. Some of them know people who have been abused and they want to understand, and know what they can do to help.

Wouldn't it be great if more schools could embrace this idea? They say that "our children are our future." Personally, I'm just as grateful for the kids who go to the group as I am for the support group itself. They can make a difference. They can help their peers in ways adults can't. I just wish more schools could see this and actively support the organization of more groups like this.

◆　◆　◆　◆　◆

One morning I was reading the newspaper and came across an article about the Stewart family of Granby donating land to the town for a new library. I was telling Lou Barry about it, and he said he knew the Stewarts. As he talked about them, I realized it was John Stewart's family. John and I had met years earlier when he was a law student at WNEC and I worked in the law library. So I looked up the firm he worked for and sent off a short e-mail, telling him what a wonderful thing his parents had done for their town. John emailed me back to thank me, and we made plans to get together for lunch to catch up.

2013

Sometimes it's a wonder we get things accomplished in this country considering how long it takes to get things done! The Protection from Sexual Predators Act of 2011 — a.k.a. the current version of the civil SOL bill — had been re-introduced in 2011, amended twice in 2012, and ended 2012 without ever making it out of committee. When the bill to change the SOL for criminal sexual abuse passed in 2006, I was just as excited as everybody else. But that bill was never going to help me because too many years had passed. The bill that had to pass for me to seek justice was the one I was putting every ounce of my free time and energy into working on — the bill that would change the civil SOL for sexual abuse so I could sue my stepfather.

As I've said before, I've never regretted telling my story — not once. If telling my story will help, then I'm going to tell it. But it was different since the criminal law had passed. This new bill would affect me directly. I cared, and I was scared. It was like my story was one more piece of evidence of how important it was for this bill to pass. I tried not to think about the bill not passing, but I had to be realistic too. It had failed to be put up for a vote before, and in the back of my mind I couldn't help but wonder if I'd done enough — or if my story had been enough. What if people didn't believe my story? What if the people who hadn't gotten involved or signed on to support the bill believed I was the liar my family always said I was?

I knew my story was not the "one" story that was going to make the bill pass or fail. I'm not any more special than anyone else. But I knew that if the bill failed to pass, I wouldn't be the only one who would suffer as a result. I'd put so much of myself — so much of my life — into something I truly believed in. If the bill passing meant that I would be able to seek justice for what was done to me, what would it mean if it never passed? What would that mean to all the victims who were still too nervous or scared to talk?

The anxiety and stress I was feeling as a result of all these thoughts was beginning to take its toll. As usual, Gary was wonderful. I talked his ear off for sure, but realized I needed to talk to a counselor again. And this time, counseling would be different. I had matured and was in a much better place. My issues were different. It was the stress I needed help with — that and the anxiety and worry about the bill passing.

I knew who I wanted to talk to too. Back in 2007, Gary and I had needed to work on our relationship, and had found Bart Nierenberg. Bart was, and is, the ideal counselor. He exudes peace and serenity, and has both a calming demeanor and a soothing voice. His advice has always been spot-on, and he already knew my story. I felt safe talking to him, and safe coming and going from his office — which was also important to me.

During the week leading up to our first session, I wrote down notes on topics I wanted to cover with him. I didn't want to waste his time, and I wanted to get as much out of our sessions as possible. I knew I was stressed about dealing with my obnoxious and invasive family, but there was another stressful thought brewing too. If the legislation passed, I was going to sue my stepfather, and that meant I would be face to face with him, and the rest of my idiot family, in court. Those people were going to be there, like some kind of scary demented gang determined to trash me. That scared the hell out of me.

◆　◆　◆　◆　◆

Gina called me one day to tell me that my mother had stopped by her house for a visit. Gina said she looked drawn and very depressed. She was wearing sweat pants, slippers, and no makeup. While she was there, she confided in Gina that she and her husband (my stepfather) were living two separate lives. According to her, they even went food shopping separately, and she was pretty much just staying in her bedroom.

She complained that my stepfather had had numerous affairs over the years, and said she hoped he would die soon. Apparently, she was in the process of giving away many of her personal items because she had breast cancer and was getting prepared to die.

Obviously, everyone's first instinct when they hear something like that is to be sympathetic. And yes, my mother had lost two sisters to breast cancer, but Gina and I had no proof she had cancer beyond her saying so. This could just be another one of her manipulations to get attention for herself. If she wasn't getting any attention from her husband, she would get it any way she could. My mother had always made it about herself, and it was very possible that this was just more of the same.

◆ ◆ ◆ ◆ ◆

One person I was very grateful to have been introduced to in 2013 was William N. Brownsberger, a State Senator for the Second Suffolk and Middlesex District of Massachusetts. He had served on an informal conference committee that tried to hammer out the complicated details of the civil SOL bill from August to December of 2012. But once again, by the end of that year, discussions concerning the bill had foundered. In 2013, Sen. Brownsberger once again joined the fight to get the new legislation passed so survivors of childhood sexual abuse would have a way to seek justice from their abuser.

I didn't live in the Senator's district, but he still took the time to email me to keep me up to date with what was going on. He let me know that there was overwhelming sentiment in the legislature to get something done, but that it was going to take some time.

◆ ◆ ◆ ◆ ◆

Another person I met was the president of the Springfield YMCA. He'd heard about me and was interested in talking to me about maybe putting together a program for the Y. It was while I was online looking for ideas about what kinds of programs might be good for the Y that I came across Childhelp.

Childhelp was founded by Sara O'Meara and Yvonne Fedderson, two very inspirational women. It's hard to condense all the good they've done into a few sentences, but their story began in 1959 when they were in Tokyo as part of a government-sponsored goodwill tour. Because of a typhoon, the two had been stuck in their hotel room for days. Now they were restless, and decided to sneak out of the hotel. As they were walking down a side street, they found 11 children huddled together for warmth under a broken awning. They were all orphans with no place to go, so Sara and Yvonne smuggled them into their hotel room, washed them, fed them, tucked them in for the night, and then tried to figure out what to do next.

Childhelp is the long-term result of that first successful attempt to help eleven orphans. It's an amazing organization with many programs, but the program I was interested in was called *Speak Up Be Safe*. In their words,

"Speak Up Be Safe helps children and teens learn the skills to prevent or interrupt cycles of neglect, bullying, and child abuse—physical, emotional, and sexual. The program uses an ecological approach to prevention education by providing materials to engage parents and caregivers, teachers, school administrators, and community stakeholders."

Now that I'd found a program I wanted to use, I asked Tricia Caron (Jordan's high school counselor) if she'd be interested in helping. We'd already done a couple of smaller events together, and she said yes, so I started planning a Childhelp event for the YMCA. April was Child Abuse Prevention Month, so the event was scheduled for April 30, 2013 at the Basketball Hall of Fame. It was organized so that both adults and children would hear about how to recognize, prevent, and react to the reality of child sexual abuse.

I asked Jordan if she wanted to say a few words, thinking that speaking might help her the way it had helped me. There was also the fact that if these kids heard about a real life experience from one of their peers, then maybe the message would sink in deeper than it would by listening to a bunch of us "old" people. Jordan wasn't sure if she was ready and wavered back and forth, but then agreed to speak publicly for the first time about her abuse.

Because the event was being held on a school night, we made the most of every minute. I presented, and was followed by Jeff Londraville M.Ed., the author of *Your Path to Clarity: How to Clear You Mind's Filters and Claim Your Future*, a book that helps teenagers and young adults let go of what's been holding them back so they can take charge of their choices and make decisions about who they want to be, and what they want to do. Next up were Miss Central Massachusetts, Miss Teen Central Massachusetts, and Little Miss Central Massachusetts. Then it was Jordan's turn at the podium. She talked briefly about her abuse, and then read a poem she wrote. People commented to me that when she spoke, it was so quiet you could hear a pin drop. All eyes and ears were on her, and I watched adults, as well as kids, wipe their eyes while she described her abuse.

The event was a total success. In addition to all the people who attended on their own, about 200 kids come to the event on busses. Jordan was relieved it was over, but proud of the fact that she'd found the courage to speak. For weeks after, we heard remarks and got emails about what a good night it had been.

◆ ◆ ◆ ◆ ◆

My sister Sheri called me at work on a Friday afternoon and started yelling at me about Meri getting an $800 Discover bill in the mail, and that I needed to go over there and straighten it out. I politely told her that I no longer handled Meri's financial affairs, and that I had no desire to try and figure out what kind of mess she'd gotten herself into this time. I didn't know if this sister was — or wasn't — up to something, but based on my past experiences with how unpredictable all of my sisters could be, I had no reason to trust any of them.

A few days later while I was visiting my dad, my sister Meri called and left a voice message on our home phone. When I was on my way back home, I called Gary and he played the message so I could hear it. She just kept repeating the same thing over and over, something like, "Kathy, I'm sorry for what I did. I only did it for Roxy. I don't talk to Mom anymore...." It just sounded like a lot of rambling nonsense to me, so I never called back. I didn't want or need any part of their stupid, meaningless games. I had too many other things to do. I guess those sessions with Bart were doing the trick!

◆ ◆ ◆ ◆ ◆

On Wednesday, May 8th, at 10:04 a.m., I emailed my friend Attorney John Stewart to let him know that the Judiciary Committee met the day before to once again discuss the civil SOL bill. Wanting to plan ahead, I asked him if he knew of an attorney who might be willing to take my case in the event that the bill passed.

John responded back in 36 minutes. "Kathy I would gladly accept the honor and privilege of representing you to enforce liability against the perpetrator, even if there is no chance of collection. Let me know how this comes out. I think it would be meaningful to file suit on the first day you could, so others will feel safe to follow suit, or get some courage from your example. This is sad and serious business, but there is some social and individual good that could come out of it. I am here to support you as a friend, and be part of the solution — or at least the fight."

I cried as I read his email and I'm crying now as I reread his response. John B. Stewart is an exceptional man, and I am — to this day — truly grateful that he was on my team.

◆ ◆ ◆ ◆ ◆

I got a phone call from my dad letting me know that my mother had been in contact with him again. She had something else for me and wanted to drop it off at his house. The first time she'd dropped something off, she'd been very clear about him not giving me her cell phone number. But this time, she told him that I could call her if I wanted, so he gave me her number.

I couldn't believe it! I was staring at a means of contacting my mother, the woman I hadn't seen or spoken to for over thirteen years! Why did she want to talk to me now? Did she want to get together and talk? Of course in my mind, I was thinking and planning and actually hoping we might be able to reconnect after all those years and clear the air between us. Maybe we could even have some kind of relationship. Not a close relationship like most mother and daughters would have, but at least something. In my mind, I pictured us grabbing a burger at Red Robin and talking for hours. We would cry and laugh and she would finally understand the whole truth about my childhood. Then she would hold me and everything would be as it should be.

So, on May 13th, at 6:59 p.m., with trembling hands, I picked up the phone and dialed my mother. She told me that there had been some family pictures she'd wanted me to have, but that she couldn't find them. Then she told me my stepfather had finally moved out. And then she said good-bye… and hung up. The call lasted less than a minute. That was it.

Once in a while, out of the blue, Meri would call and update me on family matters. This time she called to tell me that my stepfather had moved out and "gone south." She said our parents had been fighting about me, so it was my fault they'd split up. She also let it slip that she'd told my mother about the time she'd seen my stepfather doing something to me in the laundry room.

Now Meri's last confusing message made sense. She'd told our mom about seeing me and Louis in the basement. Was that the reason they were fighting? I didn't know if that was the case, but if my mother and stepfather were fighting about me, and my sister knew about it, then apparently my mother *was* willing to talk about what happened — just not with me.

Whatever. I just hoped that if I did get my day in court, Meri would be willing to speak on my behalf. But who knows? Our relationship was — still is — difficult. She flip-flops between wanting to be my sister, and taking my parents' side and not having anything to do with me. I think deep down she strives to be a better sister because she still reaches out to me from time to time.

◆　◆　◆　◆　◆

Little by little, John Stewart and I started to build a case against my stepfather. I gave him dates, pictures, and a list of all the relatives who could possibly have known about my abuse. I also gave him my medical records, counseling records, and employment history. I told him everything I could remember, and answered all of his questions. It wasn't like I was able to sit down and tell him everything in an hour though. It was hard diving into the details of all the times my stepfather abused me, but I did it anyway because I was determined to make sure John had anything and everything that could be documented for my case.

Moving into summer, House Bill 1455 had 61 representatives signed on in support of the civil SOL reform. We needed to get at least half of the 140 representatives to sign on, so we all continued to make calls to legislators. I talked to more legislative aides than legislators, but I did get favorable responses. The bill was still in committee getting tweaked, and we were all hopeful and optimistic for a positive outcome. With the Senate, 31 out of 40 had already signed. In the words of my friend Jetta, we were "tantalizingly close."

◆　◆　◆　◆　◆

In July, I decided to call my mother again to ask her if she'd had any luck finding the pictures she'd told my father about. She didn't answer, so I left her a voicemail. I had her email address too though. I'd gotten it from Gina, and after thinking about it for a while, the next day I sent her an email asking her if she'd found the pictures. She sent me a short reply saying that she hadn't found them, and that they were gone.

I was disappointed because I'd been hoping to have some pictures of myself when I was growing up. I sent her another email in August hoping to find out what time I was born, because for some reason it wasn't listed on my birth certificate. After a couple of days, she sent another short reply. She thought I was born at 3:18 p.m., but she wasn't sure, and said the time should be on my birth certificate.

◆　◆　◆　◆　◆

In early October, we received an email from Attorney Carmen Durso's office informing us that the SOL bill was at a critical point. They asked us to call the House Speaker and Senate President, and urge them to get the bill out of Judiciary and onto the floor for a vote.

While I was doing my usual online research, I came across D2L.org, aka, *Darkness to Light*. It's an organization committed to "Protecting children by empowering adults with knowledge about how to prevent child sexual abuse." It's been around since 2000, and has affiliates in all 50 states, as well as 16 international locations. Its focus is on training adults because, in their words, "It is unrealistic to think that a young child can take responsibility for fending off sexual advances by an adult. Adults are responsible for the safety of children. Adults are the ones who need to prevent, recognize and react responsibly to child sexual abuse."

I always learned something of value from the courses I took, and the seminars, workshops, and classes I attended. They offered an online course, so I took it and earned a *Steward of Children* training certificate on Oct 23, 2013. Now, with my certificate of completion issued by D2L.org in hand, I had another resource to share with others.

What I like about websites like this is that anyone can go on their site and take their course. You don't need a degree to take it. You can take it at your own pace, and it doesn't cost so much money that you have to think about it twice (when I took the course it cost $10). And, it's something that anyone can do. It's one of the many sites (you'll find a list of the sites I've found in the back of the book) I've found that's geared towards people who want to pitch in to make their community a better and safer place to live.

◆　◆　◆　◆　◆

I got another voice message from Meri saying, "I know you're talking to Mom. Call me." Once again, I didn't know what Meri was talking about. The only time I'd actually talked to our mom was back in May, and that wasn't exactly a conversation. I'd barely said ten words before she'd hung up on me. When I didn't call Meri back, she called again and left another message. "This is your sister, and I want to talk to you. Please call me back. You want to talk to Mom. I don't think you're funny, and I know everything, so call me back."

I still had no idea what the hell that was all about, but that's how she talked sometimes — what she said didn't make any sense. I called her, and all she wanted to tell me was that Sheri's daughter Ann got married because she was three months pregnant. She never explained what her voice message was about.

◆　◆　◆　◆　◆

My buddy Lou Barry introduced me to a new professor at Western New England University, Sarah L. Stein, PhD. He thought Sarah might be a valuable expert witness for my case. Her credentials were impressive. She had a BA in The Victimology of Pedophilia, a Master's in Forensic Science, and was teaching both Criminal Justice and Forensic Science courses at WNEU. She worked with the Connecticut Police Department evaluating cold cases involving unsolved homicides and missing persons, and assisted families of abducted and murdered children. Sarah was definitely a very interesting and unique person.

Through autumn of 2013, we sent letters to the legislators in Boston urging the passing of the civil SOL bills — House Bill 1455 and Senate Bill 633. Every letter contained a story about some aspect of sexual abuse that happened to the person writing the letter, or to someone close to them. Jordan added a letter of her own, and so did my attorney John Stewart.

2014 – Part One

At the beginning of the New Year, once again, Meri started leaving me voice messages on our home phone. In those messages she often said things that didn't make any sense. She complained that I never called her, but the one thing she said over and over was that the only reason I was spending time with my real father was because of his money. That sounded more like something other people in my idiot family would have said, and I was pretty sure someone else was egging her on with that idea. Maybe the fact that they were always so preoccupied with money had them believing I'd be the same. Whatever. Gary and I didn't waste any of our time looking for handouts. We each worked full-time jobs. We had owned our own mobile homes, had paid for our own wedding, and only had eight years left on our mortgage. What did they think we needed someone else's money for?

The last few times I'd visited my dad on a Sunday morning, he'd fallen asleep while we were having coffee. This morning, he didn't look well. As usual, he was working a lot, and I reminded him that he shouldn't push himself so hard and should enjoy himself more. But he loves his job and doesn't have any plans of slowing down or retiring anytime soon. So as long as he's happy, I'm happy for him.

◆   ◆   ◆   ◆   ◆

The New Year brought good news too. Sen. Brownsberger was appointed Senate Chair of the Joint Committee on the Judiciary, which meant he was in a more influential position when it came to important issues like the SOL bill. He knew all the ins and outs of the bill at this point, so hopefully, with this new position, he would be able to encourage fellow policy makers to vote in favor of the bill.

I was doing more planning with the Springfield YMCA now. Gary thinks I'm spending so much time with them that they should hire me full time. They had definitely been picking my brain for ideas over the past year, so maybe he was right. But right now, I was working on a way to bring Childhelp's *Speak Up Be Safe* program into the Y. I'd been in contact with both Daphne and Andrea at Childhelp, and we were working out the details.

Another project I was working on for them was bringing in comfort dogs to the Y. I received permission from the Greenfield, MA Police Chief to have two St. Bernard dogs make a visit. I believe this kind of program is extremely important because of the calming effect dogs have on people—especially kids. The dogs can help young children feel more secure, and even help them relax. Petting the dogs can take their minds off their troubles—even though it might only be for a short period of time. Comfort dogs have been utilized in children's hospitals, schools, counselor's offices, and even in our own local court system, and have been shown to be effective in getting kids to open up and talk with counselors.

Now that I was getting more involved with the YMCA, I looked at the YWCA to see what kinds of programs they offered. I found a 40 hour Sexual Assault and Domestic Violence Training program and signed up for it. While I was taking it, I finally received approval to teach Childhelp's *Speak Up Be Safe* program at the YMCA.

It was good news, but Gary had concerns about the way things were going with the Y. There had been a bunch of staff changes and cancelled meetings. Plus, it seemed like there was always a new hoop I had to jump through. I wasn't getting paid for any of my time, and he thought I was being used. I didn't know if I felt exactly the same way. For one thing, I was used to working for a good cause without being paid for it. The other thing was that I really believed in the programs I was trying to help them organize. The Y was huge and could reach a lot of people.

◆　◆　◆　◆　◆

There hadn't been any new information coming out of Boston lately, so one day on a lunch break I called Sen. Brownsberger to get an update. He said he'd been doing what he could regarding the SOL. He also asked how old I was, explaining that if an "open window" of time was granted to those of us for whom the criminal SOL had expired, he wanted to make certain I would be covered. He gave me his cell number too, and told me to call anytime. He is a good man.

As time marched on, a few email rumors about the SOL bill started circulating. People were saying it was coming out of committee, and going to be passed by July. In late April 2014, Sen. Brownsberger emailed me to let me know that it appeared all systems were go for moving the bill forward.

It was all very encouraging news, and my dream of seeking justice for what my stepfather did to me was closer than ever to becoming a reality. I'd been talking about it for so many years, and dreaming about it for even longer. Now it was almost real. I might actually get the opportunity to get that son of a bitch on the witness stand.

◆ ◆ ◆ ◆ ◆

After months of hard work, Tricia Caron and I held our first Childhelp class at the YMCA on May 2nd. Unfortunately, the Y wanted us to structure it differently than the way Childhelp had it laid out. Childhelp had it set up so that there were two counselors teaching the class. That way, if one of the kids wanted to talk to someone, they could leave the room with one of the counselors while the other counselor continued with the class. The Y decided to split us up so we could do two classes in half the time. It wasn't perfect, but we agreed. They also offered it as an after school program rather than a class, which meant we had parents coming in to pick up their kids. I only had 2 girls left to finish the class. Tricia only had 6 boys who were able to stay the entire time. We were glad for the kids who were able to finish the class, but it had been a lot of effort for a very small turnout.

◆ ◆ ◆ ◆ ◆

Progress was being made in Boston in late May. The bill was out of the Judiciary Committee and moved on to the Committee on House Steering, Policy and Scheduling. When that happened, the bill number changed. It was now known as H4126.

My hopes were cautiously but steadily rising, so I called John Stewart and we set up a meeting to work on my case. John was even more energized now that he knew the bill was moving forward.

In an email from one of the Boston attorneys, we were asked not to talk publicly about the movement of the bill. So what did I do? I did exactly what they asked—I didn't talk "publicly" about it. Instead, I called each and every member of that committee to ask them to support this bill and to act on it quickly. Then I called my local legislators and updated them on the bill's status. They each pledged their support to do what they could do to move the process along as quickly as possible. I'm not sure if I followed Boston's instructions not to talk "publicly" about what was going on, but I won't apologize for calling all those legislators because I'd worked too hard and waited too long NOT to talk about it.

The State House News Service ran an article on June 4, 2014 detailing the most updated information available. "We think we've crafted a bill that we can put forward that people will feel comfortable with; that gives people who've been abused a chance to face their accusers in a timeline that they're able to. It's complicated," Representative John Lawn of Watertown told the News Service.

The bill would extend — not eliminate — the SOL for civil lawsuits to be filed against the abuser from three years after the victim turns 18, to 35 years, or until the victim turns 53 years old. There were other components to the bill that were important, but the number of years was the only thing I was concerned about right at that moment. My work had always been about making sure that every survivor had the right to pursue their abuser when they were ready, but I wasn't going to make any excuses for the fact that right now, I wanted this bill to pass so I could have *my* day in court.

One of the biggest reasons lawmakers now felt like this new bill had a good chance of passing was due to the Catholic Archdiocese of Boston's "change of attitude" towards the new proposed legislation. The Roman Catholic Church had fought similar legislation in other states, fearful that extending the SOL would expose the church to liabilities they'd need to defend against. But Rep. John Lawn had worked with fellow legislators and several of Massachusetts' Bishops to refine the proposal. With that alliance intact, he was hopeful it would pass this year.

Once that article from the State House News Service appeared, my friends and I exchanged frantic emails of encouragement with each other. Several attorneys emailed me too, all saying basically the same thing — that the article was a good sign, and that we should all stay positive and focused.

While we were all holding our collective breath over this good news, I was beginning to organize another fundraiser. These funds would be used to purchase more of Childhelp's *Speak Up Be Safe* programs so we could educate as many kids as possible. At a cost of five dollars per child, I could literally reach hundreds of kids through the YMCA.

In my opinion, of all the resources I've come across over the years,

Childhelp is still the best. They have the best programs and the best people working for their organization. And now that I'd been working with them for over a year, I was even more impressed and started thinking about visiting their corporate office in Arizona.

◆　◆　◆　◆　◆

My attorney was working on the final drafts of the Complaint, and the Demand for Jury Trial. Since my stepfather lived out of state, John would be filing in Federal Court. Everything was falling into place.

With the House's unanimous support of Bill H4126, we anxiously awaited word from the Senate next. Gary and I had taken the week off, so it was certainly an exciting way to begin our vacation. I bought a few new dresses, had a facial, and got my hair trimmed and colored while I was waiting and hoping to hear good news.

Ray Hershel from Channel 40 News was aware of the growing support, and interviewed me in John Stewart's office. During the interview, I told Ray I'd like to get one of the pens Governor Patrick would be using to sign the bill into law. He thought that was interesting. The interview was broadcast at 5:30 p.m., and as I watched, I wondered if anyone in my idiot family was watching.

I received an email from one of the legislators in Boston informing me it looked like the bill was on its way to the Governor's desk for signing, and sure enough, on June 18, 2014, the House voted 147 yeas to zero nays in favor of passing Bill H4126. The bill sailed through the Senate too.

We'd done it! As a collective group of highly driven individuals, we actually succeeded in creating another new law! We pulled this dirty little secret out of the hidden corners of our society, held it up to the light of day, and faced the challenge of exposing it head on. We convinced an entire state that the right thing to do was to take care of its survivors. Governor Patrick had already stated that if a bill like this made its way to his desk he would sign it. We had been heard, and on June 23rd, the bill would be presented to Governor Deval Patrick for signing!

Not being an overly patient person, I called the Governor's house and left a message on his answering machine. I reminded him that this bill meant so much to so many people, and asked him if he could please make this a public signing so some of us "people" could be there to witness it. And yes, I also told him I'd like one of his pens as a souvenir.

I received a phone call informing me that the signing would take place on Thursday, June 26th, at 2:00 p.m. at the Boston State House in room 157, and that the Governor requested that a limited number of people be allowed to attend. Sen. Brownsberger was going to be there, and requested that I be there too. Then he asked me if I would like anyone else there with me. I told him I would like Lisa Foster and Suzie Burgess to attend with me.

I will be forever grateful to everyone who helped turn my dream into a reality. Gary and I celebrated our good fortune by going to Rogers Ice Cream for large vanilla ice cream cones. But as excited as I was, I was also aware that the real fight was about to begin. Every time I thought about what was going to happen next, my heart would start racing, so I was a nervous wreck for the next few days. My stomach was upset, and my eyes were red and swollen from crying. I didn't sleep well either.

John was awesome though. We talked regularly, and now that the bill was ready to be signed, he had everything set up electronically so all I had to do was text him as soon as Governor Patrick signed the bill. When he got my text, all he had to do was hit the "send" button and my case would be electronically filed in Federal Court.

◆　◆　◆　◆　◆

June 26, 2014 is a day I will never forget. I woke up at 5:30 a.m. knowing this was going to be a special day—a day that would change many lives forever. As I lay there in bed, my mind traveled back through the years and found the little girl that was once me. She was at summer camp sitting on the back stairs of her cabin, alone.

I scrunched down next to her and whispered, "I know, I know.... It'll be alright. But you need to hang in there and be a big strong girl. If you can bear this for now, I promise someday I will make all the bad stuff go away. But you must never give up, not ever, no matter how bad it gets. OK?" I pretend she understands, and we nod, and then hold onto each other. Through our embrace, I feel her thin, trembling body subside into a faint sigh. "I'll always be here right beside you. Always." As I get up to leave, I turn back for one last look and see her on a swing. This time she's smiling. I can honestly say that we have both kept our promise.

This day was for us—all of us survivors. After today, so many survivors—myself included—would have a choice we didn't have before. We could move forward and drag our abusers into court and force them to answer for their hideous crimes. It wouldn't always be easy to do, and sadly, for some people it would still be impossible. I knew firsthand that there would be survivors who would be shunned by their families and friends when they came forward. There was always the risk of being labeled and ignored too, but we still have to be strong and courageous. Today, we might be fighting just to get justice for ourselves, but our fight today could stop or prevent someone else's abuse today, tomorrow, and into the future. We only get one life to call our own, so now is the time to take all of our shame, the stolen years, and the hate, and fight back.

Make the son of a bitch pay!

◆ ◆ ◆ ◆ ◆

I rode with Lisa Foster to Boston for the signing. The entire time we kept saying back and forth to each other, "Can you believe it's finally happening?" We were as giddy as two high school girls on a road trip. We arrived at the State House around 12:30 p.m., went through security, found Press Room 157, and claimed two chairs in the front row. The signing wasn't scheduled until 2:00 p.m. We were early, but neither one of us had been willing to risk being late. Slowly, people started to filter into the room. Suzie joined us, and we walked around the room meeting and talking with as many people as possible.

At 2:10 p.m., Governor Deval Patrick entered the room. We all stood up and applauded. Secretly, he was my new Super Hero. He spoke for a few minutes about the importance of passing this law, then picked up the first of 31 pens and started to sign. I was literally on the edge of my seat just a few feet away from history being made. As he signed, he spoke to all of us. "This is not about me. It's about all of you. This is your day."

As soon as the Governor laid down the last pen (probably even before the ink had a chance to dry!), I texted John that he could hit *send*.

Governor Patrick was in a good mood, and the atmosphere in the room was jovial. The news media was there documenting the event, and the Governor was happy to pose for pictures. One photo that appeared in the newspaper was of the Governor shaking my hand while handing me one of the pens. I was extremely honored to be a part of this ceremony, and it definitely goes down as one of the most important highlights of my life.

After the signing and the pictures, I asked Governor Patrick if he would sign a picture I had that had been taken of us at our first meeting back in August 2009 at the Chicopee Public Library. He wrote, "With thanks for your service — and high hopes." He is really a nice guy, and I

Kathy with Former Governor Deval Patrick

will forever be indebted to him. If he were ever to run for President, he'd have my vote.

I made my way around the room thanking everybody for their hard work—especially Sen. William Brownsberger and Rep. John Lawn. One of the original sponsors of the bill, Rep. Ron Mariano, was in the room too, so I went over to thank him because without his help and support this day might never have happened. While we were talking, he told me he'd heard one of my speeches in Boston way back in 2006, and that he'd never forgotten my story. I was stunned. That was eight years ago, and he was telling me that something I said had made an impression on him. Never underestimate the importance of speaking up and being honest. Never.

After the signing, one of the local TV stations wanted to interview me, but I was scheduled to meet with John in Springfield, so we set up the interview on the steps of the Federal Court House just around the corner and up the street from John's office. Now that the new law extending the civil SOL had passed, I was moving forward with my lawsuit against my stepfather. We believed this was the first suit of its kind to be filed in Massachusetts, so the media was interested in watching it unfold. Because my stepfather lived out of state, my case would be handled in Federal Court. This was good for us because there wasn't a back-log of cases in the Federal Court like there was in the District Court. According to John, this should make for a relatively speedy trial.

Congratulatory emails flooded my inbox with messages of thanks from nurses, attorneys, teachers, and survivors of every kind. This outpouring showed me that people were hearing about the new SOL. But there were also heartbreaking emails from survivors reaching out for help. They didn't know what to do or where to turn. I forwarded everyone who asked as much information as I could.

For us to move forward with my case, we needed to serve papers on my stepfather. Needless to say, his family immediately threw up roadblocks to try and hide him, but word leaked out that he was staying with his brother — my Uncle Moe — in South Carolina. So John forwarded the paperwork to a process server (an ex-police chief) in South Carolina. When Uncle Moe answered the door, he convinced the server that his brother did not live at that address. So the papers were not served that first day, but at least the family knew I meant business, and that we were actively trying to track down my abusive stepfather.

❖　❖　❖　❖　❖

For the most part, my day-to-day life continued on as usual. I went to work every day, and at the end of the day, Gary and I enjoyed our warm summer evenings floating around our pool. I mailed out thank you cards to every legislator in Boston who had supported the new SOL law. The next time I spoke at the Police Academy, I was able to discuss the success we'd had with passing the new law, and what that law meant to survivors.

At my yearly check-up, I told my doctor that I'd been dealing with headaches and battling nausea. She asked me what was going on in my life, and when I told her about everything I was dealing with, she prescribed an anti-anxiety medication.

Friday, July 25th, at 3:32 p.m., I received a call at work from my sister Sheri. She said, "Good Luck. You're not going to win in court." And then hung up.

I called John right away, and we both figured that my stepfather had been served. The enemy was now aware that we were on the hunt and had him in our sights. Let him squirm. The very next day I received an email from the process service stating that my stepfather had been served the day before. *Good,* I thought. *He probably still thinks of me as that "little girl" he was able to squash into silence. Not going to happen this time. Game on.*

Part Four

2014 – Part Two

I spoke with Ryan Wood, co-owner of Samuel's Tavern in Springfield, about the fundraiser I was organizing. He offered us a room. All we had to do was to pay for the food! We decided on Saturday, August 23rd for the event and called it, "Childhelp Charity Night Fundraiser & SOL Victory Party." There would be several guest speakers, food, a cash bar, and a silent auction. One of the people who had agreed to speak was Sen. Brownsberger.

We were able to book photographer Mark Agostino to capture the event, and Channel 22 News would be there for interviews. I specifically wanted to get as much air time as possible for Sen. Brownsberger since he had worked so tirelessly on the behalf of all of us survivors.

One of the most memorable parts of the evening for me was that for the first time ever while I was speaking, I was able to publically say the name of my abuser … "Louis Buoniconti from Springfield." It felt really good to say that out loud.

After expenses, we cleared almost $2200.00 for Childhelp, which translated into teaching 430 kids about sexual abuse prevention.

◆ ◆ ◆ ◆ ◆

Lou Barry and I made plans to meet at Dunkin Donuts on August 29th. When I walked in, Lou was already seated with two women I didn't know, and there was a bunch of roses in the center of the table. *This is odd,* I thought.

Lou said, "I lied to you. I got you here to tell you something. I nominated you for the Pynchon Award for 2014. 25 people were nominated, and you won by a unanimous vote. Not only that, this year, you are the only recipient of the award!"

The two women with Lou were Barbara Perry and Teresa Utt, trustees for the *Order of William Pynchon*. They were very gracious, and explained to me that once a person was nominated, extensive research was conducted. They knew all about me, and said some very flattering things about my advocacy work and how honored they were to meet me. Was this really happening? It was Friday, and I was wearing jeans and probably sneakers and these women were telling me I'd won a major award? Right away I realized what an honor this was, and even though I wasn't dressed like it, they made me feel like a princess.

According to David R. Cecci, President and Club Historian of the Advertising Club of Western Massachusetts, "The Order of William Pynchon was established in 1915 by the Advertising Club of Western Massachusetts (then known as the Publicity Club) for the purpose of giving public recognition to those citizens of the region who have rendered distinguished civic service. The award bears the name of Springfield's founder, whose life and achievements typify the ideals of promoting citizenship and the building of a better community; qualities the award is intended to recognize and encourage." I was to be the 200th person to be inducted into the Order of William Pynchon at the 99th Pynchon Awards dinner, scheduled for Thursday, November 20, 2014.

◆　◆　◆　◆　◆

After my stepfather was served, he had a set number of days to respond. He didn't. So John filed a Notice of Default meaning we could win this case by default. That wasn't what I needed. I needed him in front of a judge and jury.

On September 2nd, Louis sent John a certified letter giving him the address where he was staying. This was two weeks after John had filed the Notice of Default. Three days later, Louis filed a Motion to Set Aside Default, and a Motion for Extension of Time to File Answer to the Plaintiff's Complaint. He must have thought he could win, but right now, the ball was in our court. John advised me of my options. We could ignore his motions and hope his motion was denied and then I would win by default, or we could agree to the extension and battle it out in court. I chose to fight in court, and on September 6th, John filed a Plaintiff's Assent to Defendant's Motion to Vacate Default. Louis was going to represent himself, so we gave him the extension he sought to get his affairs in order.

Before I got too bogged down with the lawsuit, I wanted to visit Childhelp so I could finally meet the wonderful people I'd been communicating with for all these years. I really wanted to meet Childhelp's founders, Sara O'Meara and Yvonne Fedderson, too, so I started planning a warm and sunny Arizona vacation for Gary and me in January of 2015.

At a press conference on September 12th, Pynchon trustee Alta Stark announced that I was the single recipient of this year's Pynchon Award. It was kind of embarrassing hearing about myself in a room full of people with TV cameras rolling and newspaper photographers snapping pictures, but if it helped to raise awareness of childhood sexual abuse, and hopefully inspire others to take action, then it's all good. I only took a half-day off from work though, so when the press conference was over, I headed to work.

◆　◆　◆　◆　◆

Lately, I'd been thinking a lot more about a dream I had. It was a home called *Kathy's House*, and it would be a safe place for sexual abuse victims to go and get the support they needed. In my mind, I pictured an older multi-family dwelling in a residential neighborhood in a nearby town that could be refurbished into offices and living quarters. It would have a counselor or two on staff, easy and quick access to a physician, and an attorney — if needed.

I thought about Lou Barry and Sarah Stein being there to help too. They both had an interest in investigative work, and with Lou's police background, and Sarah's experience working cold cases, they formed a private investigation company called *Justice4Survivors* that handled cold cases like missing persons and homicides. And because of the successful passage of the SOL bill, they would be able to offer their expertise to victims of childhood sexual abuse.

We looked into other possibilities for *Kathy's House* too, like what it would take to get a therapy dog for the house. At first it was just Gary and I talking out the idea while we looked at properties online. But I started telling other people about it too, and as soon as my friends heard about it, they started volunteering to make quilts, blankets, and stuffed animals to help give the place a warm cozy safe atmosphere.

I also mentioned my idea for Kathy's House to my contact at the YMCA. The Y came back asking to see the business plan I'd put together, and wanted to set up a meeting to hammer out the details of how to make it happen. Again, Gary was skeptical. I was providing the Y with a lot of information without getting anything solid back.

◆   ◆   ◆   ◆   ◆

John emailed me to let me know Louis was countersuing me for Defamation of Character and Injury to Reputation. I actually laughed out loud.

◆   ◆   ◆   ◆   ◆

On September 24th, I received a call from Mary Knight, a member of the Zonta Club of Quaboag Valley. One of my first speaking engagements was at a Zonta function, and I have volunteered and kept in touch with the Zontians ever since. They are extraordinary women doing good work for women all over the world. Mary had called to inform me that I'd been selected as the recipient of the 2014 Founder's Day Award! It's an award that's given annually to a woman who exemplifies the objectives of Zonta International. My work in preventing child sexual abuse is in direct correlation with Zonta's mission to raise awareness of, and increase actions to end violence, against women and girls. The awards dinner was scheduled to take place on November 10th.

◆   ◆   ◆   ◆   ◆

I had another meeting with the Y. They'd read my business plan for Kathy's House and loved the idea. They said there were grant monies out there for things like this, but they also went out of their way to assure me that the Y was a reputable organization with enough resources at their disposal to make my dream a reality too. I was overjoyed.

◆   ◆   ◆   ◆   ◆

With John's approval, Lou Barry and Sarah Stein of *Justice4Survivors* started to contact and question possible witnesses for our trial. They contacted my niece Roxy who rudely replied, "I'm all set. Stop harassing me please."

Next on the list was my sister Meri. Lou called her, but her boyfriend answered and asked Lou what he wanted with Meri. When Lou told him, the boyfriend became obnoxious and hung up. We all knew there would be challenges though, and Lou wasn't going to give up that easy. A few days later, he drove to Meri's apartment and knocked on her door. The boyfriend answered and told Lou that Meri didn't live there. More roadblocks to stall me, and protect a child molester.

Sarah Stein contacted my friend Gina, and was able to interview her over the phone. Gina told me it went really well. She got to tell Sarah about a letter she had that had been written between certain family members years ago when she was still married to my cousin. It talked about the abuse I suffered as a child. I knew Lou would be happy to hear about that.

When my Uncle Guilio had left that message on Gina's answering machine a few years ago, I hadn't trusted his motives. After all, he was part of that family. But now Guilio was talking with Lou. It turned out that Guilio had liver disease, was not doing well, and wanted to get stuff off his chest.

October was a busy, sometimes frustrating month. The YMCA canceled our next meeting, but hadn't contacted me about rescheduling. Lou and Sarah kept trying to reach Meri to get her statement without any success. When we were finally able to connect with her, Lou, Sarah, and I made arrangements to take her out to dinner, and hopefully, get a statement from her about the time she walked into the laundry room in the basement and saw my stepfather behind me with my skirt pulled up.

Meri and I had talked about her helping me before, and she'd said she'd like to help me. If that was true, then now was her chance. But sitting in the restaurant with us, she said she didn't remember anything, and just wasn't cooperative. The family must have gotten to her and told her to keep quiet. I should have known better than to hope. It was disappointing for sure, but she was just too far gone to be of any help either as a witness, or a sister.

On a better note, I'd written a letter to the old next door neighbor my Aunt Judi had told me about — the one who might have known about what was happening to me. She'd moved out of state, but I was able to get her new address. I had her phone number too, and after a week went by, I called her. She didn't answer, but I left her a voice message and she called me back. She easily recalled the incident I was calling about. After all, it's not every day that a friend tells you her husband is having sex with her daughter... so it kind of stuck in her memory.

She said my mother showed up at her door one day all distraught. When she calmed down enough to talk, my mother said she'd gone down to the basement to do laundry and caught her husband and daughter having sex. When I heard the story, I immediately remembered the incident. My mother had walked in on one of the times my stepfather was raping me. Of course my stepfather had denied everything. He said I'd fainted and he was just helping me. My mother looked at me and I just remember being terrified by the look on her face. I denied there was anything going on. He was standing right there. I was too scared to say anything else.

They had a huge fight, and my mother stormed out of the house. Based on what this woman was telling me now, my mother had gone next door to her house and spent the night there. The next day, my mother told the neighbor she'd called an attorney, but that the attorney had told her there was nothing she could do because we'd both denied there was anything going on. The neighbor also let me know that my mother had called a few times within the past few weeks, but she hadn't called her back, or talked to her.

When we hung up, I wondered why my mother was trying to contact her now. In a way, it was nice to hear she'd at least tried to help, even if it was in her own feeble way. But if she knew, then why force me to spend time with him? How could she know and still do that? I was just a kid!

When I told John about the phone call, he wondered why the neighbor hadn't called the police or DSS. That's probably the hardest question survivors have to struggle with. Why didn't someone say something? I can say that it was a different time back then because it was. People didn't want to get involved. It's not a very satisfying answer though. At least this woman had stepped up now, and we could count on her testimony if needed.

◆　◆　◆　◆　◆

The week leading up to the Zonta Founder's Day Award ceremony was hectic, but exciting. Gary, Jordan, and I were all speaking, so we all worked on our speeches the week before. It was a wonderful night. Besides having Gary and Jordan by my side, my father was there with his friend. So were my brother Scott, aunts and uncles from my dad's side of the family, and many of my friends.

The night's program started with a brief history of when the first Zonta Club was formed in Buffalo, NY. It was a time in history when women began attending college, earned the right to vote, and ultimately began entering the workforce. It was a time of courage, vision, and change. The speaker said that the Zontians believed I shared that same courage and commitment towards serving and helping others, and that's why they were honoring me with this award. There were a few more speakers, and then the most delicious dinner was served.

After dinner, past president Mary Knight said a few words and presented me with the award, and a $500.00 check made out to Childhelp. She then read two proclamations congratulating me on being the 2014 recipient of the Founder's Day Award — one from Rep. Thomas Petrolati, and one from Rep. Todd M. Smola.

When it was my turn to speak, I thanked everybody in the room for being a part of my life, and went on to explain what I do and why I do it. Gary, my soul mate, spoke next and his words were unbelievably touching. So much so, that even he choked up a few times. But he got the words out which meant so much to me. Jordan spoke about how we met and what we mean to each other. Lou Barry said nice things about the work I did with him and his cadets. Other people spoke too, and I was humbled by each of them. It was a wonderful night spent with the best of people, and I was overwhelmed by all the love and support I felt just being with them.

◆　◆　◆　◆　◆

The Y started talking about creating a job for me, and asked me for my resume. They were still on board with my idea for *Kathy's House* too, so I gave it to them and hoped for the best.

◆　◆　◆　◆　◆

John and I worked on putting together a Plaintiff's Automatic Discovery, which is a list of "Identities of Persons with Knowledge" pertaining to my case. My list consisted of 22 individuals. Of course this list included family members, but also doctors, counselors, therapists, and any documents which could support my claim — like medical records, photos, etc.

◆　◆　◆　◆　◆

The William Pynchon Award ceremony was coming up next. Past recipients have included a chief justice of the Massachusetts Supreme Judicial Court, a rubber-chicken wielding school teacher, a bishop, a poet, a general, various politicians, WWI flying aces, a survivor of the attack on Pearl Harbor, a firefighter, a physician, a librarian, and the inventor of the semi-automatic rifle which helped the Allies win WWII — to name just a few. The evening started with a private invitation-only champagne reception from 5:15 p.m. to 5:45 p.m. During the reception, the media took pictures and conducted interviews. After the reception, guests mingled for about half an hour.

This ceremony was different because the speeches made by the people

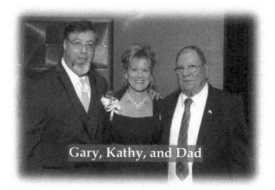

Gary, Kathy, and Dad

closest to me had all been taped ahead of time. It was odd listening to the nice things they each said about me—almost like it was my funeral. I always just thought of myself as someone who was doing what needed to be done, never ever thinking or worrying that there might be people watching me or keeping score.

It was really incredible getting these awards, and having all these great things coming my way, but I knew this really wasn't about me. It was about all the kids and people hurting that needed our attention. I felt the love in the room and was very grateful for every person there, but there is a lot of pain behind an award like this too. People don't win awards like this for making a great apple pie.

My husband has a favorite quote from Jedi Master Yoda. "Try not. Do. Or do not. There is no try." That pretty much sums up my advocacy work.

A few days later, our daily mail included a citation from Governor Patrick for being awarded the William Pynchon Award, in appreciation for my advocacy work throughout the state.

◆　◆　◆　◆　◆

Four weeks after meeting with the YMCA, I called to find out the status of the position they had talked to me about, and of course, to ask about *Kathy's House*. They told me things were on hold until well after the first of the year, but explained what the position would entail and what my responsibilities would be. It sounded like I would pretty much be on my own, and that got me thinking back to my 501(c)(3) and how bogged down in meetings and paperwork I'd been. I didn't have any desire or ambition to be placed in another administrative position like that, so I had a lot to think about.

2015

The New Year started off with me finalizing my plans to visit Childhelp in Phoenix, in January. Technically, it was a vacation for both Gary and me, but I had a lot planned for that week. I couldn't wait to meet Yvonne Fedderson and Sara O'Meara, the two founders of this incredible organization. Daphne was helping me work out the details of my itinerary, and the more I worked with Childhelp, the more I was in awe of what they've accomplished over the years. Every staff person I dealt with was warm and friendly, and an absolute professional in every sense of the word.

As a bonus, I was able to schedule a meeting for the morning after we arrived in Phoenix with a woman I'd first heard about in the news. She was pursuing legal action against her abuser in a very public case, and I'd been so impressed with her that I reached out to her. We became Facebook friends, and over time, we exchanged emails, and then phone calls. Her story is one of courage and tenacity, and when I let her know I was going to be in Phoenix, we arranged to meet.

I wish I could tell you who this amazing woman is, but I was instructed by her attorneys not to include her name, or the details of her on-going case in my book. Again, it was a very public case, and it wasn't like I wanted to write about her story in my book anyway. It made me sad to take her identity out of this book though. Every survivor is proof to victims that there is always a chance for something better. This woman was brave and courageous to speak up. And, like me, she was in the process of seeking justice for what had been done to her. I did what her attorneys asked, but it's still hard to understand what harm mentioning her name would have caused.

◆　◆　◆　◆　◆

John Stewart informed me that Katherine Robertson had become the new Magistrate Judge for the Federal Court. Her background in civil cases was extensive, and he felt certain things would be moving along quickly now that a judge had been assigned to the case.

My personal journal entry for January 15th still had me waiting on a reply from the YMCA: *I don't know, their laid back attitude is the complete opposite of how I work, and I don't feel comfortable about moving forward at all. I love what I do, so why would I want to change that? If Kathy's House is going to happen, I'm going to have to find a different avenue.*

My sister Meri left me a voice message to call her. I never knew what to expect when we talked, but I called. This time, I found out that both Roxy and Roxy's four-year-old daughter were living at our mother's house. She complained that our mother and sisters never called to wish her a happy birthday, and then she went on about her father (Louis) calling to wish her a happy birthday, but then said that in her eyes, "he's just a pig." I listened, but all I could think about was the fact that Lou, Sarah, and I had taken her out to dinner hoping to get her to sign an affidavit about what she'd seen in the laundry room. But that's how it was with her. She could change her mind quicker than anything, and she really couldn't be depended on anyway. After hearing what she said about Louis, I wasn't in the mood to hear anymore family drama, so we said our goodbyes.

◆　◆　◆　◆　◆

Gary and I flew to Denver, and then from Denver to Phoenix, where the temperature was a comfortable 77 degrees. We had a beautiful view of the mountains from our hotel room, and arrived just in time to watch the Patriots beat the Colts 45-7.

I got an email from Andrea at Childhelp confirming that I was going to be picked up the following morning at 9:00 a.m. After that, Gary and I lounged by the pool and hot tub. There was just something special about being in an outdoor pool in January when the people back home were chipping ice and shoveling snow. The sun felt brighter, the pool water seemed to be more sparkly, and the palm trees, well, the palm trees just completed the perfect picture.

When I arrived at Childhelp the next morning, I finally got to meet Marlene. She was the receptionist, and the first person I spoke with whenever I called. Then Daphne, my main contact at Childhelp, took me around and introduced me to some of the staff and people I'd been working long-distance with over the last two years.

I was scheduled to be a guest speaker at their staff meeting, and when Daphne took me to the room where the meeting would take place, I finally got to meet Yvonne and Sara, the two

Yvonne Fedderson and Sara O'Meara with Kathy

extraordinary founders of Childhelp. They were both warm and compassionate, and as we hugged, I admit I became a little emotional. I mean… I was meeting my idols.

The meeting agenda allowed me to speak for ten minutes. I gave them a brief overview of my life, of my advocacy work, about the work I did to help get the law that extended the civil SOL for seeking justice against abusers passed, and how I became involved with Childhelp. To my surprise, Daphne presented me with a gift of a glass angel. I was truly touched. I was also amazed that they had chosen to give me an angel. My Aunt Judi and I both had a thing for angels. It made me feel like she was right there with me.

Next, we viewed a PowerPoint presentation of their most recent fund raising event which pulled in over a million dollars for Childhelp. The founders of this national non-profit organization have been nominated for the Nobel Peace Prize multiple times, and I can see why. They were extremely professional and caring individuals who continued to pour their hearts and souls into helping our most vulnerable children. It takes a special kind of person to carry this kind of responsibility day after day, year after year.

On Thursday, Daphne picked me up at 9:00 a.m. and we headed to the Phoenix Children's Hospital Conference Center where there was a conference on Sex Trafficking Prevention taking place. With all the hoopla and money being spent in the weeks leading up to the Super Bowl, different organizations were setting up workshops to discuss and educate people on the problem of young kids being forced into sexual slavery. This type of trade skyrockets during this time of year, so establishments like hotels and restaurants send their employees to the conference to heighten their awareness, and to learn how to respond if they see signs of this kind of sex trafficking.

Then Daphne took me on a one hour tour of the Childhelp Children's Center of Arizona. It is an advocacy center like no other, with a one-stop multidisciplinary approach designed to reduce the trauma child abuse victims have to face during the interview and examination process. Cheerful colors, teddy bears, and child-friendly paintings line the walls. This center, along with several more throughout the country, provides medical treatment, mental health therapy, investigative resources, and victim support services to address the safety and well-being of children referred to the center. In this location, I saw counselors, a police K-9 unit, a forensic lab, and rooms full of donated children's clothing, toiletries, games, and stuffed animals — all for kids in crisis. All of it free to the child.

By the time our vacation was over, I felt like a walking testimonial for Childhelp. Everything I'd seen and learned about the organization was proof that I had chosen my idols wisely. The depth of every person at Childhelp's honest and sincere desire to help children shined through everything I saw. They are all truly wonderful and inspiring people.

◆　◆　◆　◆　◆

By January 25th, I still hadn't heard from the YMCA, so I emailed them a very long, very detailed explanation of why I would not be taking the position they were offering me. One of the reasons for my decision was that there were locations I would be expected to visit that I didn't feel safe or comfortable driving into. I'd been in those areas before, but always with at least one other person. In this new career I'd be on my own. Springfield is the third largest city in the state of Massachusetts, and in the top five when it comes to crime.

I talked with Tricia during a lunch break one day and expressed how overwhelmed, vulnerable, depressed, and uneasy about this lawsuit I felt. I had no intention of NOT going through with it, but still, it was taking its toll. On top of everything else, Gary and I had been working on this book for over three years now, and it was exhausting having to go through so much of my past again. I know I tend to take on too much, and maybe someday I'll cut back, but there's still so much to do. Gary calls me his workhorse — his Shetland pony actually — because I'm small but sturdy. And even though I know there's still a lot of shit I have to go through, I'll keep pushing on. I just hope it doesn't kill me. If it did though, that would certainly be an interesting ending for this book!

Two days after I emailed the YMCA turning down their job offer, I received a two sentence reply basically thanking me and wishing me luck. That was it. No phone call, nothing. That might be the way people do business now, but the Y had been very gung-ho about creating a position for me when I was getting all the publicity with my awards. Maybe Gary had been right and they hadn't really cared about anything beyond what they wanted.

February was snow, snow, and more snow, and I avoided the treadmill at all costs. The days were short, the nights were long, it was cold, and I was in a depressing winter weather funk.

Lou and Sarah finally got in touch with my mother for an interview, and possibly a statement for my lawsuit, and made arrangements to meet her at her house. It was a workday for me, and I was nervous. My hands were sweaty, I was cold, and my stomach was upset. What a mess I must have been. They were scheduled to meet her at 3:00 p.m., and the day turned into one of the longest days of my life. The clock across from my desk barely seemed to move at all. I was really hoping my mother would help my case now since she didn't do much for me growing up. It would have been the perfect opportunity for her to right a wrong and become the mother I always hoped she would someday become.

Once again, she disappointed me. When she opened the door for Lou and Sarah, she didn't invite them in. The entire conversation took place on the stairs in the February cold. According to Lou and Sarah's report, my mother indicated she didn't want to help me. She said that while she does not condone certain things, breaking up a family is not something one does. She went on to say that she has learned to survive, and that she has moved on with her life. She refused to answer any more questions and refused to take Sarah's business card when it was offered.

Lou and Sarah knew the importance of an eye witness account though, and didn't want to give up on Meri even though she was "unreliable." So they called her again, and this time she agreed to talk with them. When they met with her, right away she apologized for her previous behavior and said she wanted to tell the truth about what she'd seen. Meri told them she entered the laundry room in the basement and observed her sister Kathy standing, but bent over with her skirt lifted up, and her father directly behind her moving against her like they "were screwing." When he realized she was there, her father looked at her and yelled, "Get the fuck out!"

◆　◆　◆　◆　◆

John Stewart called to tell me that our first initial pre-trial conference would take place on April 16th at 1:00 p.m. in front of Judge Robertson. Part of this conference required John and I to make a Demand for Settlement, so John needed me to write a letter to Louis demanding that he agree to the entry of judgment on all claims in my favor in the amount of $500,000.00. John made sure the letter said what it needed to say, but it was still weird writing it. The last time I'd seen or heard from Louis had been at my Aunt Judi's funeral fifteen years ago.

◆　◆　◆　◆　◆

I really loved my job, but like a lot of workplaces ours started to crack down on cell phone usage, and employees using company computers for personal use. There was also one co-worker who went out of her way to make my work life miserable. She got away with bullying and harassing me despite my complaints, and now I was feeling the weight of that last straw. So, after nearly 14 years, Gary suggested I give my two week notice so I could fully concentrate on my upcoming trial.

He had a good point. I was stressed. I looked and felt fragile, haggard, and depressed, and I still wasn't sleeping well. I knew this condition was only temporary, and that one day soon I'd be done writing this book. My court case would be over one day soon too, and then I'd be done reliving those horrid events over and over again. All of that was in the future though, and I needed to think about what was going on now. So on the morning of April 7th, I asked to speak with my boss privately and gave him my notice. It was hard to walk away from a group of people who were like family—in a good way. So many of them had supported me professionally, as well as personally, in all my endeavors, and I knew I would miss them. Fortunately, I left on good terms, and there were absolutely no hard feelings on either side.

◆　◆　◆　◆　◆

On April 16, 2015, a beautiful sunny Thursday, Gary and I met John in his office at noon. We reviewed what the pre-trial conference was about, and what we hoped to get out of it. Then we walked over to the Federal Courthouse. When we got there, we were greeted by our friends Gina, Tim, Jamie (Gina's daughter), and Valerie Utton. We are blessed with good friends. When I looked over at the defendant's side there was just Louis and his daughter.

Court was called into session at 1:13:04 p.m. Because of Louis's faulty hearing aid, the judge allowed Keri to sit next to him and explain something if he couldn't hear properly. The judge went on to explain that we needed to schedule a time frame during which the parties would exchange information. Right away Louis disagreed with what the judge said based on his opinion that things had dragged on long enough already, and that he would like a fair and speedy trial. When the judge pointed out to him that this was not a criminal case, he responded with, "Oh, okay."

The judge reminded Louis of why it had taken so long to get to this point too — because there were problems with getting information to him. (He kept insisting to the judge that his mail wasn't getting delivered, but we all knew he'd worked for the U.S. Postal Service for well over 30 years. How could that happen?!) He finally agreed the problem could be due to the fact that he had changed residences. Then he complained to the judge that my attorney wouldn't take his phone calls.

Both parties wanted to set a trial date for as soon as possible. Louis mentioned receiving information from John stating that we intended to take this to a full trial and said, "If you want a speedy thing, we can end this right now if you give me a half-a-million dollars. I mean, come on." Then he laughed. Was he under the delusion he was going to make money off this case?

In order to make sure the defendant received all documents in a timely manner, the judge requested that both parties to exchange all information and documents via email. All parties agreed.

Since Louis had made repeated remarks about not being able to hire an attorney, the judge told him that the court has often had people defend themselves, and although it wasn't an easy thing to do, the court would work to make sure that both sides got a fair shake in that regard. After five minutes of listening to how ignorant Louis and Keri sounded, I started to relax and felt more and more confident about a positive outcome for our side.

John discussed taking the defendant's deposition along with the possibility of one or two other depositions, and the judge set the deadline for completion of non-expert discovery for June 15th. John informed the judge he would have no difficulty producing the expert reports and supporting materials by that date. The judge had to explain "fact discovery" to Louis, and how requests for information and documents from Mr. Stewart would need to be fulfilled by June 15th as well.

The judge informed Louis that John intended to bring in expert witnesses, and that John would make those documents available to him by June 15th. The judge stated that both parties had until July 15th to respond to the information and documents that had been sent to them by the June 15th deadline.

All parties agreed to a status conference on July 16th at 2:00 p.m., at which time a trial date would be set. The judge then went on to say that she would issue what's called a Scheduling Order. The order basically says what dates have been agreed on, what has to happen by the deadlines, and what's going to happen next. Court adjourned at 1:32:04 p.m., and from beginning to end had taken a total of 19 minutes.

Louis tried to file a motion to have this case closed to the public. His reasons? He was innocent of all the charges, and if this case was open to the public, his daughter and granddaughter would lose their jobs at the post office. His other daughter who worked at a hospital would lose her job too. So he requested, "At The Mercy of the Court, I'm asking for the sake of MY Daughters AND Granddaughter that ALL Court proceedings be PRIVATE."

Yeah... that didn't happen.

◆　◆　◆　◆　◆

I was still trying to adjust to life at home. I'd cleaned the house from top to bottom and was now trying to find other projects to tackle. I liked to mow the lawn, so I took that chore over. Gary told me to watch out for the grounding wire for the pool filter. You guessed it. I ran over it. It made an awful noise, and I'm sure our neighbors heard Gary yelling from the house when he heard it.

My next project was the stove pipe on our wood stove in the living room. It had some scratches on it so I found some black spray paint in the basement and touched it up. Unfortunately it was the wrong kind of paint. Apparently there's a special paint for hot surfaces like stove pipes. Gee, all kinds of new things to learn. The wood stove company only charged me $200.00 for that lesson.

My *next* project was to clean up the front of our vinyl-sided home. We use this fantastic product to clean it. All you have to do is spray it on and leave it. When it rains, the entire surface is cleaned. We've used it for years. What I didn't know was that it should never be used on a windy day — like the day I used it—when I accidently half-killed three shrubs in the front of our house. All the tops turned brown and dried up. I'm hoping they'll come back, but for now, they look pretty pathetic, and Gary has politely asked me not to take on any more new projects around the house. He would prefer that I just relax and take it easy.

John sent out release forms to my past doctors and counselors to obtain copies of my medical reports. I started to sand my kitchen cabinets so I could re-paint them. Gotta keep my mind and body busy! I hope Gary likes light blue.

After talking it over with Gary, I decided it would be good for me to get back into counseling with Bart Nierenberg. He's been so helpful in the past, and we have such a good rapport, that I felt like I could benefit from a few of his professional "guidance and direction sessions" as Gary calls them.

While visiting Psych Care Associates in Ludlow to get a copy of my counseling records for John, I talked to one of the staff members about my idea for a sexual abuse survivors support group. She thought it was a good idea, and said she'd talk to the doctor about it. That very same night, she called me at home to tell me Dr. Mohammed Qayyum thought it was a worthwhile project, and offered me free use of his conference room once a month.

I was elated. Right away I got in touch with The Register and asked them to mention the support group in one of their upcoming issues. We needed to inform people in and around Ludlow of what was coming in September. I was picturing guest speakers, lots of interaction... another project for Kathy. And once again, I was reminded of the fact that you won't know if you don't ask. People really do want to help. Sometimes they just need someone to let them know how.

The Gandara Center in Holyoke contacted me about holding a panel discussion for their staff. The center offers counseling and therapeutic services for residential mental health, substance abuse, and preventative services for children, adults, and families across the Pioneer Valley. I'd been a part of a panel discussion for them before, along with Jordan, and Michael Fitzgerald.

I'd first met Michael when I was speaking to one of Lou Barry's criminal justice classes. After the class, he came up to me and introduced himself. We didn't reconnect for quite a while after that, but when we did, Michael told me how much my talk had meant to him. He'd been sexually abused too, and once he'd seen and heard me, he realized he wasn't alone and was able to start working through what had been done to him. Now Michael is an advocate for educating children. In his words, "They are the most likely victims because they don't know what they don't know."

The panel discussion would start with all three of us telling our stories of sexual abuse to an audience of staff members. That would be followed by questions and answers. Because this residential facility had a "captive" audience, a panel discussion like this would be a good opportunity for their staff to be able to ask us as many personal, professional, and need-to-know questions as they could come up with. It would definitely help them with the work they do.

◆　◆　◆　◆　◆

Louis filed a motion asking to have Keri sitting next to him when he was being deposed. I pointed out to John that this sister was known for being disruptive and emotionally unstable. I was certain she would cause a scene, and because she wasn't a party to this case, did she really need to be there?

John filed our concerns, but the judge ruled that she could sit next to her father for the same reason she was allowed to sit next to him in court— his hearing aids didn't work very well. Because my sister had her own health issues, the judge moved the location of the deposition to the Federal Courthouse so that if anything happened, prompt action could be taken. She wouldn't be allowed to speak to me directly. She could only speak to John. She wasn't allowed to answer Louis's questions either. She couldn't coach him, or otherwise interfere with the deposition. I was pleased with that. John was given seven hours to depose Louis, and together, we put together a list of 53 questions.

◆　◆　◆　◆　◆

One Sunday morning while I was visiting my father, I could see that he was losing weight and just didn't look healthy. He finally told me that his most recent medical tests had not been good, and that he was scheduled for a biopsy the next day. I was upset that he hadn't told me what was going on and tried to get him to understand that it was okay to tell me about stuff like this, but he's a "tough guy" who doesn't like to complain or make a fuss, and just wants to keep his personal information to himself.

I called him the following morning to find out what time his biopsy was scheduled for. When he didn't answer his phone, I called the hospital and was told he was scheduled for 7:30 a.m. I got to the hospital at 7:10 a.m., and both he and his friend were surprised to see me. After they'd taken him in, she said he hadn't told me about everything that was going on because I already had a full plate. She also let me know he was already scheduled for surgery, and asked me not to post anything on Facebook because he hadn't told anyone else what was going on. I understood and promised I wouldn't share what she'd told me.

He was released later that afternoon and called me that night to apologize for not telling me. I tried to get it through to him that we're family, and that it was important for him to keep me in the loop. He promised to try and do a better job of communicating in the future.

The Deposition

Louis's deposition took place on June 4th. There was a stenographer there to record everything that was said, but it was also videotaped, and Louis had to take an oath before the deposition began. It was a stressful day, but it pretty much went the way we thought it would. The whole transcript makes for interesting reading right from the start. It was almost like Louis was trying to play a game of strategy. Unfortunately for him, it wasn't a game he played very well.

> *Attorney Stewart:* Good morning Sir. Can you please state your name for the record?
> *Defendant:* Louis Buoniconti.
>
> *Attorney Stewart:* What is your date of birth?
> *Defendant:* (He states his D.O.B.)
>
> *Attorney Stewart:* What are the last four digits of your Social Security number?
> *Defendant:* I don't believe I have to give you that. Do I?
>
> *Attorney Stewart:* I'm asking for the last four digits, not the whole thing.
> *Defendant:* Where does it say I have to give you my Social Security number, Sir?
>
> *Attorney Stewart:* I'm asking you for the last four digits for identification purposes. There are probably other people named Louis Buoniconti. I want to make sure I have the right one here.
> *Defendant:* All right. (He answers.)

Many of his answers were vague. He couldn't recall certain events in his family's lives, so a lot of his answers were "I don't know" responses. After several of these responses, John asked him:

Attorney Stewart: Do you have any medical conditions that affect your ability to remember things?
Defendant: Not as far as I know, other than old age.

These are just a few of the questions John asked along with the answers Louis provided:

Attorney Stewart: Did you ever tell Kathy Picard that she was your special girl?
Defendant: No.

Attorney Stewart: Did you ever discipline your daughter Kathy?
Defendant: Yes.

Attorney Stewart: Did you do it with a belt?
Defendant: Yes.

Attorney Stewart: Did you understand that... you were to bring the things that are listed in the Schedule of Documents and Things to this deposition today?
Defendant: Yeah.

Attorney Stewart: Have you brought anything with you?
Defendant: I got nothing.

Attorney Stewart: What does --------- Buoniconti (my mother) know that's relevant to this case?
Defendant: Nothing as far as I know about the case.

Attorney Stewart: Were there any court proceedings concerning Roxy?
Defendant: Yeah.

Attorney Stewart: Would you tell me what you remember about that?
Defendant: I hit her and she had me arrested.

Attorney Stewart: When was that?
Defendant: When she graduated from high school.

Attorney Stewart: Why did you hit her?
Defendant: Because she skipped school and didn't get home until 9:00 at night.

Attorney Stewart: So you had to go to court to answer for hitting her?
Defendant: Yes. I pled guilty.

Attorney Stewart: Did you have a lawyer?
Defendant: No. Oh, yes I did. I'm sorry. A court appointed lawyer.

Attorney Stewart: Do you remember the name of that lawyer?
Defendant: No. He's in Holyoke some place.

Attorney Stewart: Are you knowledgeable about what the age of consent is in Massachusetts?
Defendant: I am sure it's probably seventeen, eighteen. I don't know.

Attorney Stewart: So if an adult had sexual relations with a person under, younger than the age of consent, that would be not permitted, correct?
Defendant: I don't know.

Attorney Stewart: You don't know?
Defendant: I would assume it would be. I don't know. I'm not a lawyer.

Attorney Stewart: I understand. And you think you need to be a lawyer to understand having sex with a child is illegal?

Defendant: Yeah.

Attorney Stewart: When an adult has sex with a child, that can have very harmful consequences on the child. Do you agree with that?
Defendant: Could be, I don't know. I'm not a doctor.

Attorney Stewart: Do you accept that a person who is molested as a child is going to have serious psychological damage?
Defendant: I don't know. I'm not a doctor. I keep telling you.

Attorney Stewart: Is an adult having sex with a child a betrayal of trust?
Defendant: I don't know what you call it. I guess.

Attorney Stewart: Well, how about if a family member has access to a child and the family member has sex with the child, would that be a betrayal of trust?
Defendant: Well, the word betrayal don't fit the occasion, for one. It was a — it's wrong.

Attorney Stewart: Is it your position in this lawsuit that Kathy Picard's allegations are false?
Defendant: Yes.

Attorney Stewart: And have you brought documents with you today which you believe are relevant to proving those allegations to be false?
Defendant: No.

Attorney Stewart: Are you knowledgeable about why she brought this case against you?
Defendant: No.

Attorney Stewart: Have you ever been diagnosed with any conditions that are associated with excessive drinking?
Defendant: No.

Attorney Stewart: How much alcohol do you drink currently?
Defendant: I don't keep count.

Attorney Stewart: When you buy alcohol how much do you buy?
Defendant: I buy a case.

Attorney Stewart: How often do you buy a case?
Defendant: Whenever I need it.

Attorney Stewart: Now, in the years between when Kathy Picard was age seven to seventeen, are you with me so far on my question?
Defendant: Yeah.

Attorney Stewart: Well, in those years, did you have a normal sex life with your wife?
Defendant: Yes.

Attorney Stewart: Would you agree with me that if you had a normal sex life with your wife, that you would less likely be molesting children?
Defendant: I'm not answering that question. I plead the fifth. How's that?

From these few questions, you can see that Louis didn't prepare himself, or take this deposition seriously. The transcript goes on for 134 pages! Believe me, there was more we could have included, but I think what's here paints a fairly accurate picture of Louis. Of course he denied everything when it came to me.

When I got home, I was mentally and physically exhausted, and frustrated because I couldn't challenge all the lies he'd spewed out under oath. It had been sickening to look at him and remember all the things he made me do, and I couldn't help but wonder if there had been more victims after me. I was drained and I just wanted to not think or feel anything. Gratefully, by 8:30 p.m., I was fast asleep.

Friends kept calling and emailing to see how the deposition went. I know they just wanted me to know they were there for me, and I was so grateful for their love and support, but I was still feeling tired and bummed out and didn't feel like talking about it. Reliving my childhood was making me both sad and pissed off, and then I'd feel guilty because I felt like I needed to stop feeling sorry for myself. I was so looking forward to a normal life someday!

◆　◆　◆　◆　◆

My father's surgery lasted four hours. When it was over, the doctor walked in the room and gave us a "thumbs up." When I arrived at the hospital early the next morning, he was awake and seemed pretty good considering he'd just had major surgery. They'd removed his IV, and he was eating a big breakfast. The nurses had him up and walking twice that day, and he was able to sit up in a chair.

The next morning I was at his bedside by 7:00 a.m., but he was out of it from the medication. I stayed for a little while, and then decided to come back later in the day. At 1:30 p.m. I got a call from my brother telling me that as soon as the nurses removed his drain, he went to the bathroom, got dressed, and informed the nurses he was going home.

The biggest reason I left my job was to focus and concentrate on my lawsuit. But now that my father was willing to let me help him out—a little—it was nice to have the time to take him to and from his doctor's appointments, go out for lunch, and just hang out. It felt good to know that I could be there when he needed me. It made me feel like I was making a difference in his recovery too. But he was still determined to prove that he didn't need anyone's help, and at the end of barely two weeks, he decided he was well enough to go back to work.

Like I've said, he's tough. It's times like this that I'd like to conk him on the head with a coconut though. And then there are the times when he's thoughtful and sweet—like when he thanked me for helping him while he was recovering. He even said that he wished he could have been a part of my life when I was much younger. That was nice to hear, and it really touched me. I'd waited so many years to have a real relationship with my real father. Right now, the situation sucked, but I was still glad that he knew I was there for him.

◆　◆　◆　◆　◆

That entire summer I didn't feel like myself. I kept getting dizzy. I was used to having a bout of vertigo every few years, but normally, it went away after a few days. This wasn't going away, but I just attributed all my ills to the stress of my lawsuit, being out of work, and not taking good enough care of myself. What really helped me relax was floating in the pool with Gary at the end of our day. We would talk and just let all the stress drain away. It was the best kind of therapy.

I went for a physical, and all the test results came back negative, except for my thyroid. The dosage needed to be adjusted, and that could have been why I'd been feeling "off" lately. I continued to see Bart for counseling on a regular basis, and that helped too. I just needed to keep it together for a little while longer.

The trial date was set for November 2, 2015 from 9:00 a.m. to 1:00 p.m. John told me that the trial would take about three days. The next time we were in court for one of the pre-trial conferences, Louis and Keri showed the judge a pile of unopened mail and claimed it was delivered to them after the agreed upon date. The judge explained to them that it was their responsibility to read their mail. Also, the same information had been sent through email. So there was no way they could blame anyone other than themselves.

Both parties were required to exchange pieces of evidence that would be used in court, but Louis kept making requests for copies of my personal tax filings and assets, which were denied on the grounds that they had nothing to do with the case at hand.

◆　◆　◆　◆　◆

My dizziness wasn't going away, so my doctor set me up for an MRI on August 20. The reading would take a few days, and they said they would call me when they got the results back. Four long torturous days later, and still no phone call. I couldn't take it anymore so I called my doctor's office. I was told they needed to see me right away, and instantly I thought, *Oh, this can't be a good thing.* So the very next morning Gary and I were nervously waiting in the doctor's office.

Brain tumor! Are you kidding me? Can you believe this shit?! As if I didn't have enough stuff to deal with, I had to hear that I had a brain tumor? Yup. It was located above my right eye socket and it was approximately the size of a golf ball. I teared up as the doctor spoke. Really? Are the gods so determined to mess with me that now they have to throw this into the mix? I can't have a tumor... I'm still helping my dad, my trial is set for November, and Gary needs my help finishing this book. I don't have time for this!

This type of tumor is called a meningioma, and in all likelihood it's benign. The doctor said they see this type often, especially in women. Still, I had this thing in my melon, and it was creeping me out. It was Tuesday, and they already had me scheduled for another MRI on Friday, but this time it was with contrast. The dye would allow the neurologist to see the tumor in much greater detail.

After the results of the second MRI were ready, Gary, my friend Gina, and I met with the neurologist. She explained that the tumor was located on the liner of my brain—which was a good thing because it was in a spot that wouldn't affect any nerves or blood vessels that would interfere with speech, motor skills, eye sight, or memory. The bad news was that it had grown since the MRI I'd had in 2010. The tumor had been there then too, but it had been smaller, and nobody picked it up. So this tumor was growing. Again, not something anyone wants to hear—ever. And even though we wanted to, we couldn't ignore it. We had to deal with it.

The doctor told me that based on the location of the tumor, in all likelihood, it wasn't the cause of my symptoms. She suggested they might be due to the onset of menopause, and that it might be a good idea to have a sleep test too. I didn't have time for the sleep test though. In addition to everything else I was doing, I was working on putting together the sexual abuse support group in town.

She was a truly terrific doctor though. She answered all of Gina's questions, along with the few Gary and I had. She spent over an hour with us, and we all felt better about the situation after our visit, but Gary and I definitely had some serious thinking to do. I wanted to get a second opinion too—maybe even a third.

◆ ◆ ◆ ◆ ◆

Louis entered a motion with the Court to delay the trial for one year. Keri had suffered a stroke, and they were trying to use it as an excuse for delaying the case. I, on the other hand, had a brain tumor and didn't want this case dragged out for another year. I'd waited too long for this, and since Keri was not a party to the proceedings, she had no right to request this. So John notarized some paper work, made some magic happen, and the Court sided with us. This case would not be delayed, and would proceed as scheduled.

I like to keep my friends informed about everything, so of course I had to talk about my tumor. And the doctor was right. I was amazed how many of my friends knew someone who'd had the same thing or had experienced something similar. My neighbor across the street had a similar tumor. They removed it, it grew back, and they removed it again. Now they keep a very close eye on her. Another one of my elderly neighbors has a brain tumor, but because of her age, they won't operate. She goes for MRIs on a regular basis so they can monitor her condition. She's had it for years. So it's nice to know this might not kill me before the trial is over.

We talked with my second-opinion neurosurgeon, and he told me I had three choices. I could leave it alone, but in 20 years it could cause serious problems. I could go through radiation to kill it. Or I could have it surgically removed. Yikes!

John and I kept plugging away. We had to put together a list of names and addresses for the witnesses who were going to testify at trial, along with the purpose of their testimonies. Both Tricia Caron and Bart Nierenberg agreed to be expert witnesses testifying on my behalf. We also put together a list of proposed exhibits that would be offered at the trial. Because it was going to be a jury trial, we also started creating a list of questions to ask potential jurors.

Meanwhile, I was working on scheduling the details of the third and fourth opinions on my brain tumor. I hadn't decided which way I was leaning yet, but I knew it was safe to wait until after the trial to decide. Gary wanted it removed so we could be done with it. He's such a guy. I'd rather agonize over it and talk it to death. Hey, it's my head.

Three people showed up for our first support group session. It's not the quantity, but the quality that counts — except for when it comes to getting reimbursed by your insurance company. For that we needed a minimum of six people per session. I'm sure attendance will increase once word gets out. If it doesn't, that means it's not needed, and that would be a very good thing.

On September 18th, we went for my third opinion with the head of neurosurgery at Baystate, Dr. Thomas Kaye. This was by far the best visit we had. Gary, Gina, and I spent 1½ hours with Dr. Kaye. He was very thorough, and took time to answer all of our questions. He showed us a model of the human brain and explained all about my MRIs. He had a great sense of humor and was very down to earth — good qualities to have when you're a neurosurgeon. He went on to say this type of surgery is routine and not complicated at all. It was a three hour surgery with two weeks of recovery time.

He said, "Kathy will call me when she's ready. I'm a father and a grandfather, and there are many women in my life. When she's ready she'll know. No one can make this decision for her. So Gary, try not to make up her mind for her. Let her decide what to do when she's ready."

I felt very comfortable with Dr. Kaye, and if I decided to have surgery, I wanted him to do it.

◆　◆　◆　◆　◆

Sheri called and left a message on our home answering machine. "Kathy, if you're going to have me as a witness, I will not be going up on the stand as I will not be here. I hope you have a good life, and it will be on your head that I will not be here. I hope you have a good life." Then she hung up. I had absolutely no idea what the hell she meant, or what she was talking about.

◆　◆　◆　◆　◆

Pat Whitney is a neighbor and a dear friend. We met up one day and I told her about my tumor and how I was thinking of going with Dr. Kaye for the surgery. Pat is a semi-retired nurse who still works per diem whenever she's needed. She told me to relax, and offered to handle everything. Pat said she'd pick the anesthesiologist and make sure everything went smoothly. I've known Pat for years and she's a wonderful person. She's volunteered her valuable time at two of my child safety events, and most recently with a charity event for Zonta. She assured me I would literally be in good hands with Dr. Kaye.

I called Baystate to schedule my surgery, and that night at 7:30 p.m., I received a phone call from Dr. Kaye. He asked how I was feeling. I told him I was nervous, but that I wanted the surgery done after the trial. We settled on November 10th, at 7:30 a.m., when I could be his first patient of the day. He was a really kind soft-spoken nice guy, and he was going to make me all better.

Lisa Foster drove me to Boston for my fourth and final opinion. I was happy with the decision I'd made, but I already had the appointment scheduled and wanted to hear this Boston doctor's advice too. He pretty much said what I expected him to say. The tumor should be removed because if it wasn't, it would very likely cause me problems 15 to 20 years from now.

Pat assured me, once again, that everything was set and I was good to go for the surgery. Knowing this did provide a sense of comfort, but my nerves were still off the chart.

◆　◆　◆　◆　◆

John has been a huge blessing in my life. We talked and emailed about my case often. As the trial date got closer, he made sure I was kept up to date with everything that was going on — what motions were being filed by us or them, what they meant, and how they affected my case. We talked about what to expect during the trial, how to act, about certain statements the defendant was likely to make, etc. It was just like you see on TV. The only difference was that this was real life.

The final pre-trial conference took place at the end of October. It was attended by the judge, a court officer, myself, my attorney John, Gary, Keri, and Louis. Louis tried to complain to the judge about the fact that the trial was being covered by the media, saying that he didn't feel as though he would get a fair trial because of it. The judge explained that she couldn't control the media. The trial was open to the public, and that was part and parcel of the whole democratic system.

At the end of the conference, we stood as the judge left the courtroom, and as Louis walked past us to leave the courtroom, I heard Gary say, "Hey Louis. I'm not a shy seven-year-old girl, why don't you take a swing at me. Come on, you're a big tough guy… hit me. Come on, I'm not some scared little girl. You think you're so tough, come on—"

Then the court officer moved in front of Gary to avoid any physical confrontation, but it wasn't necessary. Louis shrank back like some little wuss. The court officer kept repeating to Gary, "Sir, I can't have you act this way. If you do, you won't be allowed in court. Sir, do you understand me? You cannot act this way when court is in session."

Calmly, Gary replied, "Yes, I understand."

Gary got the result he desired, but John wasn't too happy with his outburst and told him so. I was kinda proud of him for it. He was able to do something I wasn't. I always knew Gary was there for me. And in just a few short days, I was going to have my shot at Louis too.

Part Five

Valerie's Trial Notes

It may seem odd that this book's editor would write the first part of the chapter about the trial, but it just seemed right that you should know what it was like for us in the courtroom.

The trial was held in the new Federal Court building in Springfield. The first time I'd been in this building was for one of Kathy's pre-trial conferences. That day was also the first time I ever saw Louis Buoniconti. I didn't know it was him at the time. I'd just passed by him on my way to the courtroom. Nor did I know that the woman walking next to him was his daughter Keri, the oldest of Kathy's twin sisters.

What was my first impression of Louis? He was old. He didn't look like an especially friendly guy, but it wasn't like I'd been in a position to stop and openly stare at him to size him up, or maybe get a glimpse into his character. The reality was that I didn't need or want to either. I might not have known who he was at first sight, but I already knew what kind of person he was. He was the kind a person who could consciously choose to rape and assault a child, repeatedly, over the course of a decade.

On the first day of the trial, I sat behind Kathy and her attorney, John Stewart. The benches on her side of the courtroom were almost full. The benches on Louis's side were not.

Other than Kathy's friend Gina, I didn't recognize any of the people I was sitting with, but it was safe to assume that everybody on this side of the room was on Kathy's side both literally and figuratively. For a while, I was sitting next to a woman who had a frown on her face. Her expression wasn't out of place though. This was serious business. At the end of the day, I was surprised to learn that she was Kathy's mother. Perhaps it was good that I hadn't known who she was in advance. Mom had definitely played a part in what Louis had done to Kathy. She'd further expanded her complicity by refusing to talk to Lou and Sarah when they'd gone to her house to try and get her to give a statement. And yet she'd come here today and chosen to sit on Kathy's side of the court. Too little too late? It was the only day she attended though.

A total of eight jurors were selected on that first day. The selection had taken place in another room, so we didn't get to hear what questions people were asked during the selection process. As they were selected, each person came in and took a seat in the jury box. The first juror was a young man who'd brought a book to read. There was a young woman who fidgeted a lot. There was only one person of color. Once the eight seats were filled, I could see that their ages varied, as did the way they dressed. I wondered if any of them had been sexually abused and/or assaulted. Was that one of the questions they were asked before being chosen?

The second day was the first full day of the trial. When I arrived, Kathy and Gary were standing in the hall outside the courtroom surrounded by a group of friends and supporters. Kathy looked like her usual friendly self, but confessed to being really nervous. When we all went into the courtroom, Kathy and John Stewart took their seats on the opposite side of the room, now sitting right next to the jury. Kathy was nicely dressed, and sitting tall and straight in her chair. Louis and Keri were not. Louis was wearing jeans and white sneakers.

Attorney Stewart's opening statement was to the point. He gave the jury a brief history of Kathy's abuse and explained the claims she was making against Louis. They were:

- Battery: Unconsented sexual touching
- False Imprisonment: Holding someone in a confined space by physical and/or emotional force
- Outrageous Conduct: Conduct that isn't tolerable in a civilized community
- Invasion of Privacy: An intrusion upon a person's reasonable expectation to be left alone

Louis started his opening statement by making sure everyone understood that he was not a lawyer. He said he couldn't get a lawyer. He said he never touched Kathy, and that he never broke into the bathroom. His statement was a bit all over the place with him trying to talk about things a "good" father might do, but the context of what he said was consistent: bear with me, I'm not a lawyer, I'm going to do my best to prove my innocence.

There's no doubt that I'm biased. Kathy, Gary, and I have been working on this book for over three years now. I've had to ask questions to clarify content. I've had to read sections over and over. Now I was watching this man stand in front of the jury and lie without blinking an eye. The one thing he never said in his opening statement was that Kathy was lying. He said that her attorney had painted an ugly picture of him, and that he never touched her; but he never said she was lying, that she wasn't telling the truth, or that the claims against him were false.

The first witness Attorney Stewart called to the stand was Kathy's Uncle Guilio (Louis's brother). He testified that for several months Louis had allowed him to sleep on the couch in the basement. During that time, he'd witnessed Louis going into Kathy's bedroom late at night. When Louis was in Kathy's bedroom, Guilio said he heard heavy breathing and crying. He testified that it happened more than once, and that Louis stayed in the room for between 15 and 20 minutes.

It was compelling testimony, but not very nice to hear because her uncle had been there and hadn't done anything to stop Louis. Over the course of Louis's cross-examination though, it became clear that Louis made Guilio nervous. It was clear that Louis was trying to discredit Guilio too, but his efforts did a better job at showing the animosity between them. At one point, Louis asked Guilio if he was staying at a hotel. Guilio didn't want to answer and explained to the judge that he felt like Louis was trying to find out where he was staying, adding that Louis was a "time bomb." Kathy had said that everybody was afraid of Louis, but this was years later. Louis was an old man now, and his younger brother — who was twice the size of Louis — was clearly still nervous about what Louis might do to him for finally speaking up.

When Louis was done, John asked Guilio a few more questions, and then Louis stood to re-cross his brother. Louis asked his brother if he'd been subpoenaed, or if he'd come here to testify voluntarily. Guilio said that he'd talked to his pastor who had helped him make the decision to "come clean," and that he had not been subpoenaed.

The next witness was Tricia Caron, one of John's expert witnesses. Her testimony was what you might expect. Once her extensive credentials were established, she answered John's questions about the effects of sexual abuse.

When John was done, the judge asked Louis if he had any questions for Ms. Caron. He said yes, and asked her, "With the right treatment, can't victims lead a successful life?" His next question to her was, "What would you recommend for these people that have been the victim, to help them?" He asked a few more questions too, but with each one he was just digging the hole deeper. If, as he claimed, he'd never touched Kathy, why would he ask those questions? Why would the answers matter? Did he think that if there was a way for a victim of sexual abuse to recover then sexual abuse was okay?

Kathy was called to the stand next. This was the hardest part of the trial for me—for many of us I think. John started with all the basic questions about who she was and where she lived. And then he asked, "Are you ready?" When Kathy nodded, he continued. "Let's talk about what happened before you turned eight." Then it began.

John started asking Kathy the questions that would allow her to start giving the details of her years of repeated sexual abuse. But these weren't the details Kathy had shared publicly over the years. They weren't just the details that were included in this book. Today, her answers exposed the true horrors of sexual abuse. At one point, her voice started quavering. I knew she was beginning to struggle, and all I could do was look at the floor. I couldn't look anywhere else because I was blown away by how much worse it had been beyond what I'd already known. Her voice trailed off for a moment and then I heard the kind of sobs no human being should ever make. I could feel my own tears, and it was as if my own heart was being pulled right out of my chest thinking of her as a young child being forced to do those things.

I didn't look around to see what anybody else thought or felt. I wish I'd looked at the jury, or at Louis, or at Keri, to see if they'd reacted to what they were hearing, but I didn't. And in that moment I knew I wasn't as brave as Kathy was. In one way, she was here to seek justice, but in another, she was also advocating for other survivors who might be terrified of seeking justice because of what they'd have to go through on the stand. They might have to answer questions like this too, and she was setting an example for them. If she could do it... then they could too.

If you've never met Kathy, then you wouldn't know she's quite petite. She's 5' 3" tall. She's thin too. Obviously there's no "size" requirement for being a victim of sexual abuse, but I think it's very impressive when someone's strength and courage is so much larger than they are. We look at soldiers and believe they're both brave and strong... and they are. But answering John's questions so honestly and openly was one of the bravest and most courageous acts I've ever witnessed.

The last questions John asked were about a picture of Kathy when she was young.

Q: When was this picture taken?
A: I was a flower girl at a wedding.

Q: What do you tell people in your seminars when you show them this picture of you?
A: That I was just an innocent young girl, and I was sexually abused.

After a brief recess, it was time for Louis to cross-examine Kathy. His questions were strange. It was like he was trying to trap her into saying something that would discredit her. This is how it went when he was questioning her about the time her sister Meri had caught him raping her in the laundry room:

Q: You claim that your sisters both had seen us together in the laundry room?
A: Yes.

Q: And neither one told your mother?
A: They could have told her upstairs. I don't know. You told them to get the F upstairs. I don't know if they told her upstairs.

Q: Did your mother ever question you on it?
A: Yes, she did.

Q: And what did you say?
A: I said nothing happened, lying again for you.

Q: Thank you.

Thank you? I heard him say it, and I have the transcript right in front of me that proves he said it, but it's still hard to believe he actually said "thank you." In all honesty, I doubt he realized what he was saying, but the truth has a funny way of popping up sometimes. I could only hope the jury understood what he'd just said too.

At 1:00 p.m., after one of John's objections, the judge adjourned court for the day. When court reconvened the next morning, it was decided that the second expert witness, Bart Nierenberg, would testify out of order because of his schedule. Bart's professional assessment was that Kathy presented issues and concerns that were consistent with having been sexually abused. After Bart's testimony, Kathy once again took the stand so Louis could continue with his cross-examination of her.

Today it was a little bit different though. Kathy had had time to talk and digest what had happened the day before. Her Uncle Guilio's testimony had been good. Louis's cross of her yesterday had been unsettling, but today was a new day, and Kathy held her own. She even got to throw in one or two good verbal punches. She got to look him in the eye and say that he raped her. In fact, she got to say it twice. The judge cautioned her to stay on track, and cautioned both of them at one point. Kathy did great though, and by the end of the cross, it was evident that the only person Louis had tripped up was himself.

John was done presenting Kathy's side of the case, and now it was time for Louis to call his first witness. He called Keri to the stand. There were no surprises in her testimony. No, they weren't allowed to take baths once they were old enough to take showers. Yes, he'd hit them all with a belt. No, he'd never tried to get her (Keri) to drink beer. No, he'd never touched her. And no, she hadn't ever seen him touch Kathy.

Kathy's niece Roxy took the stand next. Louis's questions to her seemed to be designed to prove three things: that he was a really good grandfather, that he'd never touched his granddaughter (or his granddaughter's daughter), and that Kathy was a liar and trouble maker. That was the end of day two.

Day three started with Sheri, Keri's twin, testifying. It was her first day in court, so she hadn't heard her twin testifying. Like her twin, Sheri wasn't exactly "friendly," and looked very uncomfortable. She gave similar answers, but there were a few different answers too. One was that the downstairs bedroom had been built for Kathy. Keri had testified that it had been built for them.

After that, Louis was allowed to testify for himself, under oath, reading his statement from the witness stand. His statement didn't add much to what had already been said. He talked about the house they'd all lived in while Kathy was growing up. He said that the reason he hit his daughters was because his father had hit him. He reminded everyone that they had been poor — too poor to share his beer with his kids (yes, he said that). He talked about his work as a postman and about his daughter's work at the post office too, but that was about it. The only new thing we found out as he testified was that his counterclaim against Kathy had been dismissed by the court.

When Louis was done reading his statement, John was allowed to cross-examine him. The cross could only be described as annoying because it seemed as though Louis suddenly couldn't hear anything. John had to repeat many of his questions. But these questions were many of the same questions Louis had been asked at his deposition. So every time Louis gave a different answer, John opened the deposition to the appropriate page and had Louis read what he'd already said before — under oath.

Louis was first with closing arguments, during which he said something really strange. He said that from what he knew about sexual abusers, most abusers had a mental illness or had been sexually abused themselves, and that was what made them abusers. He said that they were very abusive people in general too. In the very next sentence, he said that he'd never been diagnosed with any mental illness or mental disorder. Was that supposed to be evidence that he couldn't have sexually abused Kathy?

John's closing argument was what you'd expect — a review of the reasons why we were all here. But he also made sure the jury understood that the reason it had taken Kathy so long to file suit against Louis was because she didn't have a legal means of pursuing justice until June 26, 2014, when the civil statute of limitations was legally extended to 35 years.

That was it. The trial part was over. Next, the judge gave instructions to the jury, and at noon on the third day of the trial, the jury was sent out to deliberate.

It was very strange to think that someone like Kathy would have to "prove" what Louis had done to her when she was a child, but she'd had to. She'd bared her soul in front of friends, strangers, foes, a judge, and a jury, and she'd done it with as much grace as I've ever seen anyone do anything.

One of the most bizarre parts of the trial for me was Louis. Listening to him had me wondering if he really believed what he'd done was okay. He certainly made it sound like he believed Kathy should have just "gotten over it." After all, according to the testimony some of his witnesses had offered, two of his female relatives had both been raped — and they'd gotten over it. According to him in his closing statement, he'd been beaten by his father, but had loved his father anyway.

Ignorance of the truth is no defense for a full-grown human being though. Even if someone could get past the ridiculous supposition that he might not have known that what he did wasn't okay, no normal adult looks at a child and thinks, "Man, I've got to figure out how to tap that." In no shape, fashion, or form, regardless of the circumstance or situation, is it ever okay to harm, molest, or sexually abuse a child.

Now, with the assistance of the law, and eight of her peers, we all sat and waited to find out if Kathy had done enough to make sure that truth came through loud and clear.

Gary's Trial Notes

Day 1

John Stewart, Kathy, and I are walking to the new federal courthouse on State Street in Springfield, MA on a beautiful fall morning with bright sunlight and a blue sky. The walk is exhilarating, but draining at the same time. When I think of everything it took to get here to this point, I'm amazed.

The building is glass and concrete which allows the light to infiltrate the dark places and illuminate the truth. Inside, the floors are not scuffed yet, and shine brightly with fresh polish. There is no history here; no old stories to tell. The courtroom itself does not look "New England." It's too modern with its blonde laminate walls and benches, sloped ceiling, and television monitors. The carpet is blue. It's quiet inside too.

The judge is late for the first day of the trial, and enters at 9:20 a.m. Today they will pick eight jurors. This is real. It's finally happening, and I feel tense. They will select the jurors from a pool of 70. Every seat is taken, and more people are coming in. This is what we've been working towards — this is the culmination of an entire life. Lives will be altered in this room, and a girl will finally tell her story.

At 12:07 p.m., the eighth and final juror takes her seat. They have already been sworn in, and as I look at each one of them, I wonder who they are and what their backgrounds are. But mostly, I wish they could see the Kathy I know. I hope they'll see through the lies they're going to hear and realize what she's had to overcome to get to this courthouse on this day.

At 12:11 p.m., both parties re-enter the courtroom followed by the judge. All the other prospective jurors are thanked and dismissed. You could hear a pin drop and feel the excitement growing.

The defendant is tall with a beer belly. He's out of place in this courtroom with his sweater, jeans, and white sneakers. He looks like he should be shopping at a lumber yard instead of defending himself against abuse charges brought against him by his adoptive daughter. As soon as the courtroom hears his ignorant white-trash talk, he will become his own worst enemy.

I'm sitting approximately twenty feet from the defendant and his daughter, and it's a good thing my wife is depending on me for moral support because I have visions of running to Louis's table and grabbing him by the throat. All I needed was five seconds. In five seconds, I believe I could have ripped his throat out with my hands. In my mind, I went over and over how I would do it. To this day, when I think about it I can feel my heart race and my palms get sweaty.

The weeks leading up to the trial have been a drain on Kathy and me. I go to work, we eat and do a few chores, but that's about it. At night we sit on the couch and face each other and talk for hours. She is nervous and needs to talk it out. I understand. It's all she can think about—it's all consuming.

I need to stay focused at work. I'm the only person in my department and I need to produce every day. We wake up tired because we haven't slept well in months. But she needs this lawsuit for closure. She needs to look that monster in the eyes and call him a rapist. Which she does. Twice.

Hopefully, when this is over, she can find peace and comfort enough to last a lifetime. She deserves it.

A short break is taken and then the jurors get their instructions. Opening statements will begin the next morning followed by the first witness. Court is dismissed at 12:55 p.m.

Day 2

The jurors enter the courtroom at 9:11 a.m., followed a couple of minutes later by the judge. Attorney John Stewart makes his opening statement at 9:14 a.m.

Day 3

Our attorney feels we're ahead on points. The support from friends is overwhelming and helpful, and it feels like we're not alone. Kathy will be cross-examined by Louis again today, but she is confident and more focused than I've seen her in a while. We talked last night and she realizes she needs to unload on him today because she will never get another chance. The truth is most definitely on her side, and that comes across to everyone sitting in the courtroom. I can't believe I can control myself, but I do because I need to be here for her. When Kathy gives detailed answers to the defendant's questions, he interrupts her several times to say, "Just answer the question please." To which the judge intercedes, "That's exactly what she is doing."

When Kathy's half-sisters and niece are called up to the stand, I'm outraged at their lies, but we'd expected that because lies were all they had.

Day 4

The last day... both John and Louis address the jury with their closing arguments. The end is near. I get my wife back after this day. She did it. The story she'd tried to tell her Grammy when she was a little girl, and was able to tell her Aunt Judi when she was older, had now been told in its entirety. Her sisters and mother, aunts and uncles, and many cousins and their wives had turned their backs on her, believing that labeling her a trouble maker and a liar would stop her. It didn't.

Kathy had her day in court. Our supporters told us about jurors wiping away tears during her testimony. I hadn't seen that because my eyes had been on Kathy. I'd watched her speak the painful truth of what Louis had done to her, and felt joy for her when she was finally able to look him in the eye and let go of words she'd been holding onto for far too long.

The judge dismisses the jury for deliberation, and now Kathy's truth is in the hands of eight beautiful strangers. In essence, we'd already won.

Life with My Idiot Family

Kathy's Trial Notes

I tried to stay calm, but bumper-to-bumper traffic due to bridge repair work was threatening to make me late for my first day in court. I pride myself on being punctual, so I'd made sure we'd left the house extra early that morning. We hadn't planned on this though, and while Gary tried to stay calm, I lashed out. How could this be happening to me on one of the most important days of my life?! We'd left early and everything! Was this some kind of sign? Was this an omen of how the day was going to go? Would they wait for me to start the trial? Would the judge be mad at me if I was late? They were all crazy questions, but better out than in. And when it was all said and done, we made it to John's office with ten minutes to spare.

When I'm nervous, I talk a lot, and that's how it was on our ten minute walk from John's office to the federal courthouse. It was a beautiful sunny morning, but I started talking about the rain that was expected in the afternoon, and how I hoped it wouldn't rain because I hadn't brought an umbrella. John must have sensed how wound up I was and took over the conversation. He reminded me—for what was probably the thousandth time—how the trial would unfold. As he talked, my mind wandered.

Entering the building, I felt a strange combination of anxiety and excitement. I was so looking forward to seeing Louis in court because I was making him do this. I was sure he didn't want to be here, but my actions had forced him to be here to answer for his past and pay for all the things he'd forced me to do.

My stomach was full of knots, but they were nothing compared to the anger I felt at seeing Louis and Keri sitting there in the courtroom. Outwardly I was calm, but inside I was holding down an overwhelming desire to scream.

The first day was for jury selection, and I was anxious to get this out of the way. John and I took our seats at our table, and I made sure to sit straight and tall in my chair. I could hear people coming into the courtroom behind me, but I didn't look. These people were here because of me too — even the potential jurors — and I struggled to feel worthy of their presence.

My Courthouse Support Team

Gary, my rock, was behind me, and with that knowledge, I focused on my attorney, my note pad, and the two small pictures I'd brought with me. The first was of me with my Aunt Judi. The second was of me when I was a young innocent flower girl.

Jury selection took place in a back room. The judge asked each prospective juror a series of questions, and both parties got to decide whether to keep or dismiss that individual. About three hours later, we had our eight jurors. When we were back in the courtroom, out of the corner of my eye, I could see my sister Keri staring over at me, but I refused to give her the satisfaction of turning towards her. She was less than nothing to me.

After the jury was selected, the judge issued a short recess. Gary and I, along with all my friends and supporters, were gathered outside the courtroom mingling. When I saw my mother approaching, I was beyond shocked. I hadn't seen her in fifteen years, and wow, did she look old.

"Hi Kathy," she said. "It seems we've all gotten a lot older looking over the years."

I was so stunned all I could do was nod.

"People know what happened to you," she said. "You just need to ask the right people."

And I'm thinking, *Well, then why don't YOU help me and do the right thing for once in your life and tell these people what you know!*

Instead, she told me she wouldn't be coming back and to take care of myself. While she was talking, Gary had come over and was now standing by my side. Looking at me, and then at Gary, she said, "I married the wrong brother."

Then she turned and walked away. I haven't seen or heard from her since, and have let go of the few remaining bits of hope I had about her and I ever being able to have any kind of relationship. She'd had one last chance to be the mother I needed, and once again, decided to walk away.

As soon as she was gone, the friends who had been gathered around me and heard our exchange wanted to know what that was all about. None of them knew she was my mother, and the truth was that I was just as perplexed by what she'd said as they were.

That night, Gary and I had discussed the day's activities over and over, but we were both so spent, we went to bed early. It was another restless night though, and the next morning I started wondering if I was ever going to have a restful night's sleep again.

At 9:12 a.m., the jury filed into the courtroom and took their seats. The judge had a few words with them and I braced myself. *Oh my God! This is finally happening. This is for real. This is what I and my fellow advocates and survivors have been fighting for, for so many years: the opportunity to sit in a courtroom, bare our souls to the world, and face the monsters who'd stolen part of our lives.* I was so excited, I was tingling. I was also hoping that the son of a bitch sitting to my far right was scared stupid.

The judge looked at my attorney. "Mr. Stewart, I'm going to ask you to begin by making your opening statement."

Please, please, please be strong, I beg of myself. *My husband and friends are here with me. Louis can't touch me anymore. I am safe and always will be. Please God, just this once, help me get through this.*

"Thank you, Your Honor," John began. "If it pleases the Court, Ladies and Gentlemen of the jury...." And with those words, my wonderful attorney John Stewart was off and running, just like you see in the movies.

While John outlined my life for the jury, I found myself beginning to relax — a little — and thought about what was happening around me. For so many years, it had been as if my family had been on a mission to convince the world that I wasn't a good person. But I *was* a good person, and I decided a long time ago that we all deserve to be happy, and that meant I deserved to be happy just like everybody else. I even felt kind of proud of the way I'd handled myself through all the dark times. I always strived to take the high road and be the better person I knew I could be. I'd met all sorts of people throughout this entire process of healing too — good people who serve and help others. I learned how to trust from those people, and learned how to be a friend and even how to accept help when it was offered. I'm proud of who I've become, but prouder still of all the friends who've stood by me, and will always stand to do the right thing. It was a powerful feeling to know that the people seated behind me had my back, and I was determined not to let them down. And, as John wrapped up his opening statement, I sat up a little taller, and a little more confident in who I was and what we had all accomplished.

John's opening statement was ten pages long. Louis's opening statement (which he delivered because he was representing himself) was three pages — even though he was facing what had to be the biggest threat he'd encountered in his entire life.

My Uncle Guilio was the first witness John called. Uncle Guilio had lived fast and hard in his younger days. I don't remember him having a soft or tender side, but listening to him on the witness stand made me proud to call him my uncle. He'd been larger than life when I was a young girl. Like it has with many of us through the years though, both age and time had brought him to the place where he "wanted to come clean" and make God and his pastor proud that he'd told his story to help me. He was actually pretty ill, but he'd still flown up from down south to take the witness stand in my defense.

He told the jury about the months he'd been staying at Louis's house and sleeping on the couch in the basement. That was when my bedroom was in the basement, and he testified that he saw Louis enter my bedroom late at night, and that he heard heavy breathing and crying coming from the room. He said it happened several times that he could remember. When John was done questioning him, it was Louis's turn to cross-examine. It was difficult for Guilio to stand against his big brother. They fought and bickered, and even though the judge had to intervene multiple times, Uncle Guilio stuck to his story and I will be forever grateful to him.

Next on the stand was my friend Tricia Caron. Tricia is a licensed independent clinical social worker (LISCW), with over 25 years of experience. She was professional and never faltered or stuttered once while she testified about the trauma of childhood sexual abuse. She was another person in my life who did the right thing and stood up for me, and I was so proud of her, I could have burst.

The first question Louis asked Tricia was, "Ms. Caron, with the right treatment, can't victims lead a successful life?"

I'm sorry… did he just ask that?! Was that a slip of the tongue? Because to me it sounded like, in his mind, he did molest me, but what was the big deal because my life was good now?!

He asked Tricia a total of five questions. That was it. Fine by me. In my mind, I could almost visualize the hole he was digging getting deeper.

"Your Honor, I call Kathy Picard," my attorney called out.

Me. It was my turn. Me. Now everyone gathered here would be looking at me. They would hear filth, but they would hear the truth. My entire life had led me to this day. Now was my chance. I'd waited 35 years for this exact moment, and actually felt pretty good.

On the stand, I was relaxed and focused (partly because it was John asking me the questions), but it still felt sort of weird… I mean… just look at what I was going through. John used his questions to hit all the highlights of my life, most of which have already been mentioned in this book, but there were a few additions: like knowing that the man I believed was my father was not circumcised and that he always wore Fruit of the Loom underwear. What little girl would know that about her father unless she had firsthand knowledge? I described how he'd showed me how to peel back the foreskin on his penis while he referred to it as his "lollipop." It made me sick to my stomach to talk about how bad he smelled. Louis was not a clean person.

When Louis cross-examined me, his questioning was all over the place, and it didn't seem like there was any kind of a connecting thread, except for one. He was clearly trying to portray me as a slut. I remember how jealous he was of my boyfriends, and it was showing through his questioning. He was fixated on who I was dating and what we did together. He was really getting worked up about it too, and the judge had to stop him a few times, instructing him to discontinue that line of questioning.

At 1:06 p.m., the judge decided we were done for the day, and that Louis could continue his cross-examination when we reconvened the next day. I was glad for the break because it gave John and me some extra time to discuss our strategy for the next day.

The next morning, Bart Nierenberg, LICSW, was allowed to testify before me because of a scheduling issue. Bart has a master's degree in clinical social work and over 30 years of experience in his field. He's also been my counselor for about eight years. Bart discussed his work experience and how it related to my case, and as was the case with Tricia, the court considered him an expert witness. He said I exhibited many symptoms of someone who suffered severe trauma as a child.

When it was Louis's turn to cross-examine Bart, he didn't waste any time trying to pin down the exact dates of my visits. Instead, he proceeded to ask him bizarre questions that had nothing to do with my case. Bart did a terrific job, and I was so thankful he took time out of his schedule for me. He's an extremely caring and compassionate counselor, and I consider myself very lucky to have found him.

Judge: "Mrs. Picard, would you resume the stand. Let me remind you that you're still under oath. Thank you very much."

One of the things Gary and I had talked about the night before was that I really, really wanted to call Louis a rapist. It wasn't long after he resumed his questioning of me that I got to do it too — twice! What a feeling that was!

He had me read a few old Father's Day cards where I'd written that he was the best father ever. I told him they were lies to cover up for him. He seemed to be a little bit more on the ball today which was good because I was in the mood to give it right back to him. For a while, he focused on my first job at Friendly's and how he or my mother would drop me off and pick me up from work. He was probably trying to make himself look like a good father. But after I started dating one of my co-workers, I didn't need him to drive me to and from work anymore, and that had really pissed him off.

He kept trying to ask questions about my sex life, but neither John's objections nor the judge let him get away with it. The judge even sent the jury out of the room at one point to make it clear what he could and couldn't ask. And even when he did ask the questions, they didn't make a lot of sense. At one point, he kept trying to get me to admit that Gary's brother was living with us. Obviously it wasn't true.

Louis was all over the place with his questions now. He asked me how many jobs I'd held since graduating from high school. What did that have to do with anything? How ridiculous. I don't know how he came up with all the strange stories he was trying to use to make some kind of point, but I easily handled all his attacks, and he looked like a fool.

Louis was upset that his name was in the local newspaper too, and tried to make it sound like I'd done it intentionally.

Q: Did you feel satisfied on what you put in the paper?
A: If it helps other people, yes.

Q: About your stepfather?
A: The only time I mentioned your name was recently. Your name

was never mentioned in the paper. But, for what you did, by raping me at twelve years old, it was wrong."

Q: That wasn't asked for. I said ... Did you feel satisfied about putting my name in the paper?

A: If it gets out there... it's not like I'm going to jump up and ... I'm embarrassed about what you did to me.

Q: I've done nothing to you.

A: You did.

Q: Answer the question, please, no more. And you wanted to destroy my reputation, correct?

A: I didn't want to—

Q: Yes or no Ms. Picard.

It went back and forth like this until the judge finally interrupted. "Just move on to the next question, Mr. Buoniconti."

Then he started asking me questions about my niece Roxy. I explained that since she was being raised in the abusive house I grew up in, I was concerned for her safety. So yes, I had called DSS a few times to see if they could check up on her, but nothing ever came out of it, and I never got an answer back that satisfied me.

He kept asking irrelevant questions, and the judge repeatedly cut in to say things like: "I'm going to put a stop to this because I don't think it's really relevant to the relationship." Louis claimed his questions would "enlighten" the judge and jury's opinion of me, but the judge would have none of that.

I would answer certain questions in a detailed manner, and Louis would blurt out: "Just answer the question, please." The judge finally interceded with: "Mr. Buoniconti, she is answering the question. That is an answer to your question."

After I stepped down from the witness stand, John rested our case, and it was Louis's turn to call his first witness. He wasn't ready. He'd left his notes at home. Nevertheless, the judge told him we would proceed, so he could either call one of his daughters as a witness, or he could give a narrative of his side of the story. He and the judge went back and forth like this for an embarrassingly long time. Finally, when he realized he couldn't talk himself out of proceeding, he called Keri to the stand.

Louis asked her questions. Some she answered truthfully, but there were definitely lies too. Then John cross-examined Keri. I could tell you about the lies she told in response to his questions, but that's on her – not me. She's the one who has to live with the lies she told under oath. I admit I was tempted to add the details of the realities John exposed in this book, but why give her the satisfaction of any kind of reaction to her story?

Next, Louis called my niece Roxy to the stand. The questions he asked her were all designed to make us believe he was a wonderful grandfather who doted on his grandchildren. It was hard to listen to her lies too. I tried for years to help her, and to be a good aunt. She even spent Thanksgiving and Christmas at our home one year. I really thought we were connecting, but when she realized she couldn't manipulate me or Gary, she suddenly had no use for us.

Court was dismissed at 12:12 p.m., with the judge making it very clear the jury would get the case tomorrow. Thank God there was only one more day to put up with this. It was just so embarrassing to even be in the same room with them.

On the final morning of the trial, Louis called the other twin sister, Sheri, to the witness stand. She lied too, but she also contradicted what her twin had said a couple of times.

Then it was Louis's turn to take the stand. He was sworn in like we all were, and he began to give his side of the story. He spent a lot of time talking about the layout of the house I grew up in, and how there was always somebody else at home, so how could any of those events have taken place? He talked about me as a young girl, and said that I was constantly lying. But here's the thing about that. People are not born with the ability to lie. That is a learned behavior and Louis put a lot of time into making sure I knew exactly what to lie about. If I didn't lie, then my family would suffer, and it would be all my fault. So yes, there were times when I lied. I was too scared to do anything else.

Louis admitted that he hit his daughters with a leather belt hard enough to make us cry. He tried to use the excuse that his dad hit him. Not much of an excuse. He really tried to drive home the point that we were poor and had no extra money too. But that's like saying everybody who's poor has an excuse to be a child molester. What he did to me had nothing to do with being poor. And the truth was that even though we were "poor," there was always beer in the refrigerator for him and his buddies, and cigarettes for him and my mom. And the clothes shopping! My mother was always shopping for herself.

Louis's big chance to defend himself and clear his reputation filled about six pages of the 397 page trial transcript. And then it was time for John to cross-examine him.

Q: You agree it is always wrong for an adult to have sex with a child, correct?

A: I didn't understand your question.

John and Louis went at it like this for a bit, with Louis acting like he suddenly couldn't hear or understand what John was saying, but Louis finally agreed that an adult having sex with a child was wrong. When John asked Louis if an adult having sex with a child would be harmful to the child, Louis's answer was, "I'm not a psychiatrist.... I guess it could be after the testimony I heard."

As the cross-examination continued, there were more, "I don't understand your question," "Is it what?" and "I couldn't understand that word, Your Honor." It just went on and on as if he were some poor frail innocent old man wrongly accused. There were so many "I don't remember what I said" responses that I wanted to walk up to the witness stand and slap him in the face.

Without an attorney to help him, it seemed like Louis was losing his grip on things. He must have thought acting that way would garner him some sympathy, but in reality, he was helping us. There was a whole group of questions John asked Louis that basically came right out of the deposition. Each time Louis tried to avoid giving a straight answer to John's question, John just opened the deposition to the appropriate page and asked Louis to read his response. During the deposition, Louis had been a smart ass, and now he was paying for it.

Why didn't Louis have an attorney to help him? John brought that question up too because there were certainly other times in his life when Louis had hired an attorney. He said he couldn't afford one, and there was probably some truth to that. It would have probably been very expensive to hire someone who was willing to lose a case like this.

When John was done cross-examining Louis, the evidence part of the trial was officially over, and all that remained now were closing arguments.

In preparation, the judge instructed the jury to put aside their notebooks because their verdict would be based on the evidence they'd heard, and not on the closing arguments. The judge explained that this was one more chance for each side to lay out the inferences they wanted the jury to draw from the evidence, to suggest what conclusions the jury should draw, and that: "This is their opportunity to come before you the last time and argue to you about what they think the evidence shows."

Louis went first, and this is how he began: "I am being sued by Ms. Picard, which she claims she would take the money and build a safe house for sexual abuse victims and other purposes, have other buildings available to them here. If not in this town, in another town. Because I am unable to make a testament before the court on my opening statement, I wasn't completely prepared to have most of my facts. As you could see, I'm still stumbling."

Louis had more than a year to prepare for this trial. I'm not going into detail about what he said. However, John objected twice to something Louis said, and both objections were sustained by the judge.

John's closing statement was very cohesive and to the point. The following is a collection of excerpts taken from the statement.

"This is the case of stolen innocence... What you saw in this courtroom this week took a lot of courage, took a lot of guts... Kathy Picard was badly hurt by this man... This was a source of great shame to her, great humiliation... She continues to have problems... Used to pull out her eyebrows and eyelashes... Trauma survivor... PTSD... Depressed... Many fears of being watched... The need to lock her doors... Feels betrayed by her mother... Crying attacks... Anxiety... Low self-esteem.

"The affects of this abuse had a dramatic effect on her life... She has conditions that run around in her head when she's trying to sit down or trying to go to sleep... Can't get rid of memories... She has tried therapy... Has improved some... But what she has found helps her the most is her volunteer work... She speaks at colleges about safety and education of young children.

"Advocacy for the statute of limitations reform... June 26, 2014, that was when the statute of limitations was changed and allowed her to bring this case in this court. She filed the case that day... She can come before a jury and ask for justice... And have a judgment made about the value of her claim against her stepfather for these terrible things that happened in childhood.

"November 5th, 2015 is going to be a very important day for Kathy Picard and for justice in this Commonwealth… Judging was there an invasion of privacy… Was there an outrageous event… Was it an intrusion on her solitude… You will be deciding all these things.

"I submit for your consideration that Kathy Picard has proven to you that there was a sexual offense… The judge will instruct you that if the elements of the claims are fairly met, you will find in favor of the plaintiff… emotional distress, false imprisonment, coming into a confined area, and not letting someone out. There's one amount of damages for all four of these claims.

"What is the price of taking someone's childhood away from them? What is the price of taking someone's security away, of damaging someone so that they have intrusive thoughts? A lot of people have problems, but not like these problems… These are well beyond what a lot of people have for bad things that happen.

"In this society, folks, we place value on things that matter to us… I'm asking you to make an award of damages that is complete, that gives Kathy Picard full compensation for the years when she was actually being molested, when she was actually feeling physical pain, when she was having those awful things done to her. When she was having to deal with those disgusting smells and tastes that no child should ever have to deal with… That's an awful thing to have to deal with for the rest of someone's life… I thank you very much for your attention and for your verdict."

The judge then gave a long speech to the jury with instructions on how to proceed to a verdict. Then she released them to begin their deliberations.

At 3:40 p.m. we were called back to the courtroom and the judge informed us that the jury had a question for us. She read the slip of paper out loud: "We are having trouble awarding damages. Can you give us guidance on scope?"

We all knew what that meant, and everyone on my side of the courtroom was buzzing with excitement! We won! The jury found for the plaintiff! I could hear everyone behind me whispering excitedly, all of us trying to contain ourselves. After the jury had been brought into the room, the judge explained that she couldn't decide monetary damages, that it was their responsibility to make that decision, and then sent them back to continue with their deliberation. If they awarded us $1.00 I would have been thrilled. It wasn't the money. It was the victory that meant the world to me.

As soon as the court recessed, John pulled Gary and me into one of the side conference rooms. We were all smiling, but he cautioned us to be cool, and briefly explained how this was going to go down.

When court reconvened a little after 4 p.m., we took our seats feeling giddy and vindicated. The blank look on Louis's face could have meant anything. It could have meant that he didn't understand what was happening. But it was probably caused by the realization that he hadn't been able to lie or bully his way out of the situation, and now he was totally screwed.

Judge: "I understand the jury has a verdict, is that correct?"

Foreman: "That's correct."

The court clerk collected the jury slips, from the foreman.

Clerk: "As to question number one: *Has Plaintiff Kathy Picard proven by a preponderance of the evidence that the Defendant Louis Buoniconti committed a battery on her?* Answer: *Yes.*

"As to question number two: *Has Plaintiff proven a preponderance of the evidence that the defendant intentionally or recklessly inflicted emotional distress on her?* Answer: *Yes.*

"As to question number three: *Has Plaintiff proven by a preponderance of the evidence that the defendant invaded her privacy?* Answer: *Yes.*

"As to question four: *Has Plaintiff proven by preponderance of the evidence that the defendant falsely imprisoned her?*" Answer: *Yes.*

"As to question five: *What amount of money will fairly and reasonably compensate Plaintiff for her damages?*" Answer: **$250,000.00**."

Court was recessed at 4:22 p.m.

John Stewart, Kathy and Gary
after the win!

Epilogue

The day of my surgery, Gary and I were at the hospital at 5:30 a.m. Gina showed up just as they were taking me in to prep me for surgery. Pat had told the nurses all about me, so I'm sure they were expecting a big cry baby. But they were all professional, and very friendly, and did the best they could to try and make me feel at ease — despite the fact that my melon was about to be cut and pulled open. I was so nervous I couldn't stop talking. When it was time, I slipped on the famous hospital johnny, watched them prepare the IV, and then asked if they could please use a small needle. A few minutes later, I said goodbye to Gary and Gina and they wheeled me away. I sure hoped I was going to wake up from this!

Gary and Gina came to see me after the surgery, but I was still out of it from the anesthesia. They tried waking me, but I didn't respond. Gina had to leave for work, but Gary stayed with me. While he was sitting next to my bed, he noticed a marker board across the room with the line, "I like to be called…." He filled in the blank with "Princess." My father and brother stopped in but I was still zonked out. Jordan came to see me too, and used my cell phone to call all our friends to tell them I was recovering. She was a big help because Gary doesn't have a cell phone, and really doesn't know how to use one anyway.

A lot of people stopped by to visit, but I was still medicated and not really responding. We found out from Dr. Kaye the next morning that I'd been given extra anesthesia to keep me out so I couldn't cough or sneeze as the pressure could affect my wound.

The next morning, Gary arrived at 6:00 a.m. and I was finally awake. We shared breakfast together and then Dr. Kaye came in for a visit. The surgery was a success. The tumor had been sent out for testing, and I was the proud owner of a dog-bone shaped titanium plate with six screws keeping my skull together, along with nineteen stitches. What fun! Now I get to tell people I'm a bit screwy!

After Gary left, the nurses said they'd read on the marker board that I liked to be called "Princess," and figured I'd either be a bitch or a sweetheart. I explained that my husband wrote Princess because that's what my late aunt used to call me. The nurses later told me they wished they had more patients like me.

I'll never forget going into the bathroom and seeing what I looked like in the mirror. My right eye was swollen shut, my face was swollen, the right side of my head was shaved, and I had this HUGE red, bloody scar on my head that went from the back of my right ear over the top of my head stopping right about at my hair line. I looked and felt hideous.

For the four days I was in the hospital, Gary arrived in my room at 6:00 a.m., and stayed until 8:00 a.m. when he had to go to work. He spent the evenings there too—after he'd gone home and let Abbey out. I didn't eat or sleep much. I was afraid to move my head, and my jaw was very sore so chewing was painful. Gary seemed to enjoy the hospital food though.

The day I went home, Pat stopped by to see how I was progressing. She stopped by many times, and I was grateful for her visits. Nothing like a "professional" stopping by and saying things like, "You look good Kathy—considering you just had major surgery," and "That's to be expected," and let's not forget, "It's going to take time, but you're going to be fine. You'll see."

I went for my follow-up visit on November 25th. When I walked into his office, Dr. Kaye gave me a hug and said, "I hear you've been singing my praises." It was true. I'd contacted the hospital and told them what a terrific doctor he was, and how great the staff was too. I was very pleased to have put my life in his hands.

I still felt dizzy and still battled headaches, but Dr. Kaye said that is to be expected. He said the same thing about my blurry vision, and the tingling in my hands and feet. Eventually, all those problems would go away, as would my swollen face, sore jaw, and all the other post-surgery aches and pains I was experiencing. In fact, he said I was healing nicely. I believed him, but it was still hard to look in the mirror.

He showed Gary and me pressure points on my hand that could be squeezed to help alleviate the pain in my head. As for my jaw pain, he showed Gary which muscles on the side of my head to massage while I slowly opened and closed my mouth.

November 26, 2015 was Thanksgiving, and Gary and I had so much to be thankful for. A few days before Christmas, my dad called to let me know that he'd been given a clean bill of health from his doctor too!

After Christmas, Gary talked to my former boss about me going back to work, but he said that they didn't have anything for me. So I decided that for the time being, I was retired. It meant that I got to spend more time with my father, and he seemed to like having me around.

◆ ◆ ◆ ◆ ◆

Everything's settled down now, and I'm completely recovered from the surgery except for the slight dent on the right side of my head. My hair has grown out, and my scar has completely healed. I picked up a few new recipes, kept the wood stove going all winter, and, even though Gary didn't want me shoveling for fear of falling and hitting my head, I just took it easy when I shoveled. This past summer, I got much better at mowing the lawn.

Jordan finished her first year at college and made the Dean's List. The support group I started still meets once a month, and we've finally finished this book! The pool is open and we are truly enjoying floating around in it while talking about what to do next. Whatever that is, I hope it's "normal!" Well, maybe not too normal.

◆ ◆ ◆ ◆ ◆

Years ago, after Gary and I had been together for a while, I'd told him that I thought my life's story would make a good book. We both think it would be a great movie too. It has everything in it—including a surprise appearance by a brain tumor. The best part of this movie would be the ending because it would prove that even though we can't always choose what happens to us, we can usually choose what to do about it. Gratefully, the ending of my movie will be… "And they lived happily ever after."

Now that you're holding this book, you're sharing in that dream. I know life can be scary and frightening at times. But it can also be filled with excitement, surprises, and love. I've met many caring and wonderful people over the years. Each one of them has enriched my life, and that's what has helped me to complete this journey. I could not have done this on my own. My hope is that you find help and inspiration in these pages. After all, I wrote this book for you.

End Notes

Kathy's Author Notes

To say I'm thrilled that this book is finally completed is an understatement! I'm not sure I knew I was going to write a book way back in the 1990s when I started collecting and documenting everything, but I'm glad I kept such good records. I'm not sure what to do with all of it now that we're done either, but it sure made the writing easier.

When I tried to start writing my story, I didn't have any luck finding someone who was willing, or able, to help, and Gary and I realized we were going to have to write it ourselves. Besides, how many books about one's personal life involving sexual abuse have been written with the help of their spouse? None that I have read.

Writing this book with my wonderful caring loving husband sure did have its ups and downs though. There were many emotional nights, especially in the beginning, when I had to explain to Gary the abuse I went through as a young girl. I relived what my stepfather did to me in the words I shared with my husband. He felt my hurt, embarrassment, and loneliness. When we started writing about my older years, he understood that standing up to that monster, and my idiot family, had made me the strong forceful woman I am today.

Going through the memories of what I went through made me even more determined to stand up not just for myself, but for others too. I was going after what I knew all victims want—justice! Without Gary's help and understanding, writing this book would not have been possible. There were many times when we got so angry at each other that we just about stopped writing this book, but we never quit. It was too important. Gary, I promise you, our lives will get back to normal after this book! I love you for making my dream of getting my story into print come true.

Of course having an editor/coach like Valerie helping us was the icing on the cake. She kept the work on the book flowing by asking us questions and editing along the way so my life would make sense to you. It took us over five years to write, and without Valerie's help over the past three of those years, we'd probably still be writing!

I have met so many caring, loving, and understanding people in my lifetime! I have received so much support from so many too. Without that help, this book may not have been possible. Today, my father's side of my family, and my friends, are the family I didn't have when I was growing up. Thank you all for helping me share my story!

With Special Thanks and
Acknowledgments from Kathy to:

My supportive husband, Gary. My story would not be in print without your help, your understanding, your support, and your hard work! You truly are my soulmate. I love you!

My dad Ron, brother Scott, aunts, uncles, and cousins.

Our editor, Valerie Utton, for your professional editing and understanding of what we wanted to accomplish with my story.

My wonderful attorney, John B. Stewart of Murphy & Manitas, LLP, in Springfield, Massachusetts. Without your help, I wouldn't have won my case! Your compassion, understanding, and skill helped me get justice!

My investigators and friends, Lou Barry and Sarah Stein. I am sincerely grateful for all your work and support.

The Politicians—and their staff—for all their help through all the years of working to get the SOL bills passed: Former Senators Gale Candaras and Scott Brown, Senator William Brownsberger, Representatives John Lawn, Thomas Petrolati, Angelo Puppolo, and Ronald Mariano, and Speaker of the Massachusetts House of Representatives Robert DeLeo.

All the Representatives and Senators who voted in favor of extending the Civil and Criminal time frames for survivors to pursue justice.

Former Massachusetts Governor Deval Patrick for the pen that was used to sign the civil SOL bill into law. It is one of my most cherished mementoes!

Former Lieutenant Governor Kerry Healey who signed the criminal bill to extend the SOL time frame in 2006.

Bart Nierenberg and Tricia Caron, the counselors who have helped me over the years.

The organizations that spend every day dedicated to the prevention of child abuse: Childhelp, The National Center for Missing & Exploited Children, the Massachusetts Medical Society, and the Enough Abuse Campaign.

The members of Zonta of Quaboag Valley, and The William Pynchon Committee.

Schaler Photography for the wedding picture we used in the book.

Pamela Shrimpton and Janet Gary for their help with proofreading.

All the friends and survivors I've had the privilege to meet, get to know, work with, share stories with, etc.

All the people who've been a friendly and supportive part of my life: Suzie, Neil, Mark and Adam Burgess, Gina and Jamie Buoniconti and Tim, Maureen, Ashley, Morgan, and Don Ingram, Jordan Chmura, Michael Fitzgerald, Michael Stevens, Mitch, Tracy Goodfield, Kaye Lani, Kristine Pospolita, Rosanne and her family and friends, Lisa Foster, Sandra Belcastro, Emily Thurlow, Barbara, Sari Starr, Priscilla, Gretchen, Father Scahill and Patty Baran, Benjamin Lublin, Lise-Lotte Lublin, Olivia Jasriel, Jose and Maria, John and Marylou Bowen, Carolyn de Chavigny, Rebecca Street, Marilyn Van Debur, Charlie Ramos, Darlotte Justice, Christine Lozier, Bruce Teague, Chip Harrington, David O'Regan, Doug Wilson, Eva Montibello, Grace Dias, Heather Crow Connor, Jeff and Christy Londraville, Jessica Nicely, Jill Starishevsky, Kerry-Beth, Jill Cricones, Jo Lee Descoteaux and Marc, Judy Norton, Bill and Liz Corbett, Nancy Goode Talalas, Audrey Murph, Donna Jenson, Julie Gamache, Kathleen Burke Regan, Kathryn Robb, Kevin Cullen, Ray Hershel, Sy Becker, Jim Madigan, Laurie Myers, Laurie Duchesne-Jankiewicz, Maggie Sullivan, Marci Hamilton, Lou Brault Jr., Lou DellaCroce, Marie and Sue Laflamme, Ed Pidgeon, Jeff Cloud, Garry White, The Evans Family, The Bish Family, Lynn Kelleher, Julie Quink, Bev, Sheryl, Debbie Vanaria, Beth Donahue, Ward Schline, Pat and Michael Whitney, Michelle Flanagan Black, Vivian Farmery, Renee Serra Chisholm, C. David Moody, William Lynch, Savannah Sander, Svava Brooks, Joe DiPietro, Chris Gavagan, Bill Blodgett, Blanche Jackson-Hill, Joan Paris, Shawn Gundersen, Anne Barrett Doyle, Sam Krupczak, Jon Liebermann, Mitchell Garabedian, Ana Ferris, Ed Opperman, Susan Wells, Joanie Winberg, Jetta Bernier, Atty Carmen Durso, Mike Tremble, Dave Vermette, Tom King, Prestley Blake, Jen Falcone… and everybody else who helped!

Gary's Author Notes

Kathy and I went back and forth for years about writing her life's story. When we finally agreed it was time to do it, we went about the process of finding someone to actually do the writing. The first person to agree was an author of children's books, but she changed her mind before the first word was ever written. The second writer was an acquaintance of Kathy's, but the collaboration fizzled out quickly. The third writer was a student at Smith College who was way too busy to do a thorough enough job.

One afternoon (and I remember this like it was yesterday) I was sitting on my spot on the couch when Kathy came into the living room with tears in her eyes and asked me if I would write her story. I didn't want to say yes because I knew how painful so much of her life had been, and I didn't want to be the one to make her relive her past in order to write the book. But she had nowhere else to turn, so I reluctantly agreed.

The good news was that through the years, Kathy had kept everything, and we had boxes and boxes of pictures, e-mails, newspaper articles, cards, and letters. So in one sense, her life was already documented. We just had to put it in order and write it. We started by organizing everything according to dates. For example, everything that happened in 2006 went into a box labeled 2006. If Kathy couldn't verify or recall something without any doubt, then we didn't put it in the book. The bad news was that the story was about a black-hearted family full of lies, threats, violence, and child rape.

There were times when I had to put the writing aside for weeks and months because it took such an emotional toll on us. Kathy's my best friend, and I didn't want to disappoint her by quitting, but there were times when I wanted to. I couldn't believe some of the evil things she told me, and some of it just gave me the creeps. It wasn't a happy story, so it was stressful writing it. There were times when we fought over it and swore at each other over it, and times when I didn't want anything more to do with it, but we always got past them. We'd started the book together, and we were both committed to seeing it done—even though it's been like a dark cloud hanging over our heads for over five years.

But every dark cloud has a silver lining, and our silver lining was all the people we met while she plugged away at her advocacy work. Those people are just as responsible for the completion of this book as Kathy and I. We were determined not to let them down either.

Then, one day, Kathy had the extreme good fortune to mention to Bill Corbett that we were writing a book. He suggested we contact his editor, Valerie Utton. Kathy and I fell in love with Valerie the first time we met her. She has been our steady inspiration, our coach, and our friend for about three years now. If not for Valerie, this book would not exist. We owe her an enormous debt of gratitude. When I started this project I was not a writer, but with Valerie's guidance, I am now.

I don't know if a story like this can qualify as a great piece of literature. What it is, is the accurate true life story of a young girl who grew up to accomplish great things. I am so proud to be sharing my life with her, and to call her my wife and best friend... Kathy.

With Special Thanks from Gary

We've all had positive influences in our lives, but some people just stand out more than others and we remember them for our whole lives. For me, a select few were teachers, and it just seems right to mention them here because in some way, they each impacted me with a belief in myself and my ability to accomplish something good in my life. I consider this book one of those "good" things, and would like to extend my thanks to these teachers for being so good at their job:

Cynthia (Kostek) Nawrocki, a sweet and caring teacher at the Szetela School.

Judith (Segzdowicz) Chelte, one of my English teachers at Chicopee Comprehensive High School in the 1970's. I was always inspired to try my best in her class.

Alex Wagman, my creative writing teacher at Holyoke Community College, for her enthusiasm and ability to draw from us that which had been buried.

Michael C. Foran, one of my English teachers at Holyoke Community College. Without Mike, this book simply wouldn't be. He picked apart my writing and challenged me to do my best. I couldn't wait to get my writing assignments back from him so I could read his notes in the margins.

And, a heartfelt thanks to:

Daniel Montuori, who showed real interest in the beginning stages of this book. His ideas and encouragement motivated me to keep at it.

Valerie Utton, our editor and dear friend for life.

To my wife and soul mate Kathy Jean.... You mean the world to me!

Life with My Idiot Family

Resources

Childhelp National Child Abuse Hotline

If you suspect a child is being abused, you should call your local child protective services agency, or the agency in the county or state in which the abuse occurred. To find the appropriate agency number, or to speak with a crisis counselor, contact **Childhelp National Child Abuse Hotline 1-800-4-A-CHILD (800-422-4453).** Childhelp is dedicated to the prevention of child abuse throughout the United States, its territories, and Canada. The hotline is staffed 24 hours a day, 7 days a week, with professional crisis counselors who (through interpreters when needed) can provide assistance in over 170 languages. The hotline offers crisis intervention, information, literature, and referrals to thousands of emergency, social service, and support resources. All calls are confidential. **www.childhelp.org**

RAINN (Rape, Abuse & Incest National Network)

RAINN is the nation's largest anti-sexual violence organization. RAINN created and operates the **National Sexual Assault Hotline: 1-800-656-HOPE (800-656-4673), www.rainn.org and www.rainn.org/es**. They are in partnership with more than 1,000 local sexual assault service providers across the country.

When you call 800-656-HOPE (4673), you will be routed to a local RAINN affiliate organization based on the first six digits of your phone number. Cell phone callers have the option to enter the ZIP code of their current location to more accurately locate the nearest sexual assault service provider. RAINN operates the DoD Safe Helpline for the Department of Defense, and carries out programs to prevent sexual violence, help victims, and ensure that perpetrators are brought to justice. **www.rainn.org**

Educational Resources

<u>Childhelp Speak Up Be Safe Prevention Education Curriculum</u> is a research-based developmentally appropriate curriculum for Pre-Kindergarten through 12th grade. This program helps children and teens learn the skills to prevent or interrupt cycles of neglect, bullying, and child abuse — physical, emotional, and sexual.

The program uses an ecological approach to prevention education by providing materials to engage parents and caregivers, teachers, school administrators, and community stakeholders. In addition to increasing children's ability to recognize unsafe situations and abusive behaviors, and to build resistance skills, lessons focus on helping children build a responsive safety network with peers and adults who the child identifies as safe. **www.childhelp.org**

<u>Darkness to Light's Stewards of Children</u> training for adults empowers people to prevent child sexual abuse. Their programs raise awareness of the prevalence and consequences of child sexual abuse by educating adults about the steps they can take to prevent, recognize, and react responsibly to the reality of child sexual abuse. The training also educates on what to do if you know of children being abused. **www.d2l.org**

<u>Educate4Change:</u> Svava Brooks is a survivor of child sexual abuse, and the co-founder of nationwide child sexual abuse prevention and education. She is also a certified instructor and facilitator for Darkness to Light's Stewards of Children, as well as a certified crisis intervention specialist, a certified parent educator, and an abuse survivor coach. Svava has dedicated her life to ending the cycle of child sexual abuse through education, awareness, and by helping survivors heal and thrive. **www.educate4change.com**

<u>PAVE (Promoting Awareness/Victim Empowerment):</u> PAVE works to shatter the silence, prevent sexual violence, and help survivors heal. PAVE is a national nonprofit that works to engage people, in a positive way, to end sexual and dating violence. PAVE maintains over 50 chapters and affiliates across the country, and has trained over 50,000 college students, 5,000 high school students, and over 2,500 professionals — including military service members. To learn more, visit **www.pavingtheway.net**

Support for Men

1in6

The mission of 1in6 is to help men who have had unwanted or abusive sexual experiences in childhood live healthier happier lives. They also provide information and support to family members, friends, and partners. **www.1in6.org**

Male Survivor

This organization has been a leader in the fight to improve the resources and support available to male survivors of all forms of sexual abuse in the US, and around the globe. Their informational programs and services help us understand males who have been sexually abused, and most important, promote actions we all can take to confront and fight the realities, and destroy the myths of male sexual abuse. **www.malesurvivor.org**

Clergy Abuse Resource

SNAP (Survivors Network of those Abused by Priests)

SNAP, Survivors Network of those Abused by Priests, is a self-help group that supports people who have been victimized by clergy, helping them pick up the pieces of their lives, heal, and move forward. SNAP also cooperates with the news media by providing reliable information when possible, as a way to help the recovery process and prevent future abuse. **www.snapnetwork.org**

Missing Children/Child Abduction

National Center for Missing & Exploited Children

Established in 1984, the National Center for Missing & Exploited Children® is a leading nonprofit organization in the U.S. working with law enforcement, families, and professionals to help find missing children, reduce child sexual exploitation, and prevent child victimization. **National toll-free hotline, 1-800-THE-LOST (800-843-5678). www.missingkids.com**

General Resources

<u>Justice4Survivors</u> is a subsidy of the CRUC LLC, concentrating on the investigation of past sexual assaults for civil litigation. They can be reached at: **L.barry@comcast.net**

<u>**Massachusetts Citizens for Children (MassKids)**</u> is the oldest state-based child advocacy organization in the country. Its mission is to improve the lives of the state's most vulnerable children through advocacy by concerned citizens. Since 1986, MassKids has served as the Massachusetts Chapter of **Prevent Child Abuse America**. MassKids currently works to prevent child abuse through the work of the **Shaken Baby Syndrome Prevention Center,** and the soon to be launched **Choose Your Partner Carefully** project. It also leads the **Enough Abuse Campaign**.
Phone: 617-742-8555 and 866-216-1072   **www.masskids.org/index.php**

SOL Reform

This website provides current and helpful information about the Statute of Limitations for child sex abuse in the United States, by state. The information on the website is curated by Professor Marci Hamilton **www.sol-reform.com.**

The National Child Traumatic Stress Network (NCTSN)

The NCTSN works to accomplish its mission of serving the nation's traumatized children and their families, and to raise the standard of care and improve access to services for traumatized children, their families, and communities throughout the United States. **www.nctsn.org**

Winged Hope Family Advocacy Foundation

Winged Hope was established in January 2013 by Jessica Nicely. As a child abuse survivor, and a child abuse prevention advocate for 18 years, Jessica was feeling frustrated about the number of cases of child abuse going un-prosecuted. After learning about the effectiveness of child and family advocacy centers, Jessica established **Winged Hope Family Advocacy Foundation**. Winged Hope's programs focus on child abuse and domestic violence awareness, prevention and treatment. The foundation helps both new and existing advocacy centers around Arizona. **www.wingedhope.org.**

Book Resources

My Body Belongs to Me by Jill Starishevsky. This straightforward, gentle book offers a tool parents, teachers, and counselors can use to help children, from 3-10 years old feel, be, and stay safe.

Letter to a Monster by Caroline de Chavigny. This book is a compilation of letters written by survivors, directed toward their abusers. *Letter to a Monster* is a compilation of survivors' journeys, from beginning to end, and the end result is much the same theme: Just as Superman always wins, Survivors WILL prevail!

Letters of Apology: How to Stop Waiting for Permission to Be the Wonderful Person You Are by Valerie A. Utton. This book is a collection of anonymously written letters of apology combined with insights into how to get over needing, wanting, and waiting for the apology you're never going to get.

You Can Help by Rebecca Street. This book educates people who want to help survivors of sexual abuse and sexual assault recover from trauma.

Personal Body Safety for Kids by Nancy Goode Talalas. This is an educational children's book to teach your child personal body safety in a positive and empowering way.

Some Secrets Should Never Be Kept by Jayneen Sanders, is an illustrated children's picture book that sensitively broaches the subject of keeping children safe from inappropriate touch.